Library Looking-Glass

A  BOOK

David Cecil

Library Looking-Glass
A Personal Anthology

Harper & Row, Publishers
New York, Hagerstown, San Francisco, London

FIRST U.S. EDITION

ISBN: 0-06-010696-4

LIBRARY OF CONGRESS CATALOG CARD NUMBER: 76-23516

To the memory of

ROBERT SALISBURY

my dear brother

who, delightfully and when I was still a boy,
introduced me to the writings of
Keats and Shelley and Walter Pater and Max Beerbohm
– and many others

Contents

Contents

Foreword

Is writing in printed books a bad practice? I suppose so, if the book is itself a precious object, elegantly bound and on fine expensive paper. Otherwise there is surely much to be said for it. It helps to make a book seem more one's own; and, unless what is written insults its author, it is a compliment to him. It treats him as a living man, with whom one wants, as it were, to converse.

Anyway I have done it for longer than I can remember. In particular when anything in the text has especially struck me, I have noted on the end-paper the number of the page where this has occurred. Sometimes my note simply indicated admiration; but more often admiration of a special and personal kind. The passage referred to was beautiful or comical or well-written in ways that had a peculiar appeal to my own taste, or it stated a view which I found especially illuminating; or it stimulated in me a fruitful train of thought. This volume is a selection of passages referred to in these end-papers and which belong to this personal category; to them I have generally added a comment suggesting why they have evoked my special interest. This accounts for the book's sub-title. It is a personal anthology. It could even be described as a sort of self-portrait; myself, as mirrored in the looking-glass of my reading.

The fact that it is personal has conditioned my choice of contents. The reader will notice that at least three quarters of these are about the arts, and especially the art of writing. This is because I have spent my working life partly as a teacher of literature and partly as an author. But indeed I cannot recall a time when stories and rhymes and pictures and tunes were not for me the chief source of interest and pleasure in life.

I stress the word pleasure. Pleasure has played a large part in my life; pleasure, solitary or sociable, carnal or spiritual; pleasure in the beauties of art and nature, in the enthralling variety of the human scene; and pleasure in jokes. Nothing has been included here, however interesting its subject matter, which does not also give me pleasure.

There are also a number of pieces in the book about places which have special associations for me: old English country houses, because I grew up among them; Oxford and Dorset, because I have lived my mature life in one or the other; Venice, because I spent many months there – enchanted months, they were! – during the impressionable years of youth. Sometimes I have come across a poem or a prose piece that recalls other impressionable phases of my past, especially of my childhood. These are in the book.

One word more: the reader will note that, with two or three exceptions, every piece in this book is by an English author. This is not a symptom of literary xenophobia. On the contrary I read and admire and enjoy a great deal of foreign literature. But I read it all, except French, in translation; and even my French is not so good as to enable me to discern its finer subtleties of language. Since the art of writing is the art of using words, I prefer to confine my anthology mainly to the work of authors whose sense of words I feel myself qualified to appreciate.

At this point a doubt assails me. No doubt a personal anthology of this kind is interesting to oneself: but is it likely to interest anyone else? I can only reply to this that most of the book is written, not by me, but by very good authors, whose work should appeal to any reader of taste. Secondly I would plead that I myself have enjoyed personal anthologies by other writers; by W. H. Auden, by Aldous Huxley, by Maurice Baring. I therefore hope it is possible that other readers may enjoy mine.

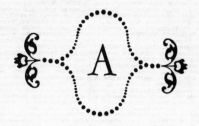

ART

(1)

Egypt's might is tumbled down,
　　Down a-down the deeps of thought;
Greece is fallen and Troy town,
Glorious Rome hath lost her crown,
　　Venice's pride is nought.

But the dreams their children dreamed
　　Fleeting, unsubstantial, vain,
Shadowy as the shadows seemed,
Airy nothing, as they deemed,
　　These remain.

Mary Coleridge

Of course this last is not strictly true. Man's imaginative achieve-
ments, though more durable than his material ones, are in the end
equally subject to the onslaught of devouring time. Homer's *Tale
of Troy* may last a few thousand years longer than Troy itself; but
no more. Shakespeare's powerful rhyme will fade into oblivion
at last, even if it has outlived marble and the gilded monuments
of princes.

　　Why then is Mary Coleridge's little poem mysteriously moving,
and to a degree unjustified by its actual literary distinction?
Because what it says, though on the surface false, voices a deep
truth. It is inspired by the realization that the imagination belongs
to man's immortal part. The soul, temporarily imprisoned in her
corruptible and fleshy integument, is homesick for the perfect and
timeless world whence she sprang; and for her solace makes use

of her imagination to create images of the condition of her life there. These images are what we call works of art. What Walter de la Mare says of music is true of all art:

> When music sounds, all that I was I am
> Ere to this haunt of brooding dust I came;

A landscape painting stirred Wordsworth to realize the same truth:

> Praised be the Art whose subtle power could stay
> Yon cloud, and fix it in that glorious shape;
> Nor would permit the thin smoke to escape,
> Nor those bright sunbeams to forsake the day;
> Which stopped that band of travellers on their way,
> Ere they were lost within the shady wood;
> And showed the Bark upon the glassy flood
> For ever anchored in her sheltering bay.
> Soul-soothing Art! whom Morning, Noontide, Even,
> Do serve with all their changeful pageantry;
> Thou, with ambition modest yet sublime,
> Here, for the sight of mortal man, hast given
> To one brief moment caught from fleeting time
> The appropriate calm of blest eternity.

The artist then is right to glory in his achievement as in some sense a triumph over time. He must realize indeed that it is futile to desire literary immortality: sooner or later his work is bound to be forgotten. Yet in its very conception, and while it lasts, it is evidence that there exists a divine eternal element in man's nature. Marcel in Proust's novel perceived this when reflecting on the death of Bergotte the writer:

> The circumstances of his death were as follows. An attack of uraemia, by no means serious, had led to his being ordered to rest. But one of the critics having written somewhere that in Vermeer's *Street in Delft* (lent by the Gallery at The Hague for an exhibition of Dutch painting), a picture which he adored and imagined that he knew by heart, a little patch of yellow wall (which he could not remember) was so well painted that it was,

if one looked at it by itself, like some priceless specimen of Chinese art, of a beauty that was sufficient in itself, Bergotte ate a few potatoes, left the house, and went to the exhibition. At the first few steps that he had to climb he was overcome by giddiness. He passed in front of several pictures and was struck by the stiffness and futility of so artificial a school, nothing of which equalled the fresh air and sunshine of a Venetian palazzo, or of an ordinary house by the sea. At last he came to the Vermeer which he remembered as more striking, more different from anything else that he knew, but in which thanks to the critic's article, he remarked for the first time some small figures in blue, that the ground was pink, and finally the precious substance of the tiny patch of yellow wall. His giddiness increased; he fixed his eyes, like a child upon a yellow butterfly which it is trying to catch, upon the precious little patch of wall. 'That is how I ought to have written,' he said. 'My last books are too dry, I ought to have gone over them with several coats of paint, made my language exquisite in itself, like this little patch of yellow wall.' Meanwhile he was not unconscious of the gravity of his condition. In a celestial balance there appeared to him, upon one of its scales, his own life, while the other contained the little patch of wall so beautifully painted in yellow. He felt that he had rashly surrendered the former for the latter. 'All the same,' he said to himself, 'I have no wish to provide the "feature" of this exhibition for the evening papers.'

He repeated to himself: 'Little patch of yellow wall, with a sloping roof, little patch of yellow wall.' While doing so he sank down upon a circular divan; and then at once he ceased to think that his life was in jeopardy and, reverting to his natural optimism, told himself: 'It is just an ordinary indigestion from those potatoes; they weren't properly cooked; it is nothing.' A fresh attack beat him down; he rolled from the divan to the floor, as visitors and attendants came hurrying to his assistance. He was dead. Permanently dead? Who shall say? Certainly our experiments in spiritualism prove no more than the dogmas of religion that the soul survives death. All that we can say is that everything is arranged in this life as though we entered it carrying the burden of obligations contracted in a former life; there is no reason inherent in the conditions of life on this earth that can make us consider ourselves obliged to do good, to be fastidious, to be polite even, nor make the talented artist consider himself obliged to begin over again a score of times a piece of work the admiration aroused by which will matter little to his body devoured by worms, like the patch of yellow wall painted with so much knowledge and skill by an artist who must for ever remain unknown and is barely identified under the name Vermeer. All these obligations which have not their sanction in our present life seem to belong to a different world, founded upon kindness, scrupulosity, self-sacrifice, a world entirely different from this, which we leave in order to be born into this world, before perhaps returning to the other to live once again beneath the sway of those unknown laws which we have obeyed because we bore their precepts in our hearts, knowing not whose hand had traced them there – those laws to which every profound work of the intellect brings us nearer and which are invisible only – and still! – to fools. So that the idea that Bergotte was not wholly and permanently dead is by no means improbable.

They buried him, but all through the night of mourning, in the lighted windows, his books arranged three by three kept watch like angels with outspread wings and seemed, for him who was no more, the symbol of his resurrection.

Marcel Proust, La Prisonnière
translated by C. K. Scott-Moncrieff

Recognizing this and realizing that almost certainly his own work will be soon forgotten, the artist will still dedicate himself to his art. As Bridges put it with classic lucidity and concentration:

I Love all beauteous things,
I seek and adore them;
God hath no better praise,
And man in his hasty days
Is honoured for them.

I too will something make
And joy in the making;
Altho' to-morrow it seem
Like the empty words of a dream
Remembered on waking.

ART

(11)

Henry James reflects on Ruskin's *Mornings in Florence*:

... Art is the one corner of human life in which we may take our ease. To justify our presence there the only thing that is demanded of us is that we shall have a passion for representation. In other places our passions are conditioned and embarrassed; we are allowed to have only so many as are consistent with those of our neighbours; with their convenience and well-being, with their convictions and prejudices, their rules and regulations. Art means an escape from all this. Wherever her brilliant standard floats the need for apologies and exonerations is over; there it is enough simply that we please or that we are pleased. There the tree is judged only by its fruits. If these are sweet, one is welcome to pluck them.

One may read a great many pages of Mr. Ruskin without getting a hint of this delightful truth; a hint of the not unimportant fact that art, after all, is made for us, and not we for art. This idea of the value of a work of art being the amount of illusion it yields is conspicuous by its absence. And as for Mr. Ruskin's world of art being a place where we may take life easily, woe to the luckless mortal who enters it with any such disposition. Instead of a garden of delight, he finds a sort of assize-court, in perpetual session. Instead of a place in which human responsibilities are lightened and suspended, he finds a region governed by a kind of Draconic legislation. His responsibilities, indeed, are tenfold increased; the gulf between truth and error is for ever yawning at his feet; the pains and penalties of this same error are advertised, in apocalyptic terminology, upon a thousand sign-posts; and the poor wanderer soon begins to look back with infinite longing to the lost paradise of the artless. There can be no greater want of tact in dealing with those things with which men attempt to ornament life than to be perpetually talking about 'error'. A truce to all rigidities is the law of the place; the only thing that is absolute there is sensible charm. The grim old bearer of the scales excuses herself; she feels that this is not her province. Differences here

are not iniquity and righteousness; they are simply variations
of temperament and of point of view. We are not under theo-
logical government. . . .

Portraits of Places

Henry James is here talking about Ruskin's strict peremptory
directions as to what and what not to admire in Florence. But
what he says applies to many other critics speaking about
many other works of art and literature; to Professor 'X' pontifi-
cating on 'The Novel' or Mr 'Y' of the Sunday press laying down
the law about what poets today should or should not write about.

AUTUMN

Go not yet away, bright soul of the sad year

Thomas Nashe

Autumn is not a more beautiful season than Spring or Summer or
Winter. But for myself at any rate, autumnal is a more beautiful
word than summery or wintry or springlike. This is partly because
it has a more rich and resonant sound; the strong 'au' of the first
syllable, the pause made by the two consonants 'mn' at the end
of the second syllable. It is still more because of the associations
given it by the poets. Autumn has been especially inspiring to
poets because it appeals at the same time to the sense of beauty and
the sense of transience; the glowing splendour of autumn pre-
figures and precedes the death of the year.

Keats's ode to Autumn is the most famous of autumn poems –
too famous, I think, to be quoted here. Here are a handful of
passages and lines less well known but also deserving of fame. In
this piece a country squire meditates on a walk:

It was a fair and mild autumnal sky,
And earth's ripe treasures met th' admiring eye,
As a rich beauty, when her bloom is lost,
Appears with more magnificence and cost:
The wet and heavy grass, where feet had stray'd
Not yet erect, the wanderer's way betray'd;
Showers of the night had swell'd the deep'ning rill,
The morning breeze had urged the quick'ning mill;

Assembled rooks had wing'd their sea-ward flight,
By the same passage to return at night,
While proudly o'er them hung the steady kite,
Then turn'd him back, and left the noisy throng,
Nor deign'd to know them as he sail'd along.
Long yellow leaves, from oziers, strew'd around,
Choked the small stream, and hush'd the feeble sound;
While the dead foliage dropt from loftier trees
Our squire beheld not with his wonted ease,
But to his own reflections made reply,
And said aloud: 'Yes! doubtless we must die.'

George Crabbe, Tales of the Hall

. . . Now Autumn's fire burns slowly along the woods,

William Allingham

Now thin mists temper the slow-ripening beams
Of the September sun; his golden gleams
On gaudy flowers shine, that prank the rows
Of high-grown hollyhocks, and all tall shows
That Autumn flaunteth in his bushy bowers;
Where tomtits, hanging from the drooping heads
Of giant sunflowers, peck the nutty seeds;
And in the feather aster bees on wing
Seize and set free the honied flowers,
Till thousand stars leap with their visiting:
While ever across the path mazily flit,
Unpiloted in the sun,
The dreamy butterflies
With dazzling colours powdered and soft glooms,
White, black and crimson stripes, and peacock eyes
Or on chance flowers sit,
With idle effort plundering one by one
The nectaries of deepest-throated blooms.

With gentle flaws the western breeze
Into the garden saileth,
Scarce here and there stirring the single trees,
For his sharpness he vaileth:

So long a comrade of the bearded corn,
Now from the stubbles whence the shocks are borne,
O'er dewy lawns he turns to stray;
As mindful of the kisses and soft play
Wherewith he enamoured the light-hearted May,
Ere he deserted her;
Lover of fragrance, and too late repents;
Nor more of heavy hyacinth now may drink,
Nor spicy pink,
Nor summer's rose, nor garnered lavender,
But the few lingering scents
Of streakèd pea, and gilly-flower, and stocks
Of courtly purple, and aromatic phlox.

And at all times to hear are drowsy tones
Of dizzy flies, and humming drones,
With sudden flap of pigeon wings in the sky,
Or the wild cry
Of thirsty rooks, that scour ascare
The distant blue, to watering as they fare
With creaking pinions, or – on business bent,
If aught their ancient polity displease, –
Come gathering to their colony, and there
Settling in ragged parliament,
Some stormy council hold in the high trees.

Robert Bridges, 'The Garden in September'

The green elm with the one great bough of gold
Lets leaves into the grass slip, one by one, –
The short hill grass, the mushrooms small, milk-white,
Harebell and scabious and tormentil,
That blackberry and gorse, in dew and sun,
Bow down to; and the wind travels too light
To shake the fallen birch leaves from the fern;
The gossamers wander at their own will.
At heavier steps than birds' the squirrels scold.
The rich scene has grown fresh again and new
As Spring and to the touch is not more cool
Than it is warm to the gaze; and now I might

As happy be as earth is beautiful,
Were I some other or with earth could turn
In alternation of violet and rose,
Harebell and snowdrop, at their season due,
And gorse that has no time not to be gay.
But if this be not happiness, – who knows?
Some day I shall think this a happy day,
And this mood by the name of melancholy
Shall no more blackened and obscurèd be.

Edward Thomas

Calm is the morn without a sound
  Calm as to suit a calmer grief
  And only thro' the faded leaf
The chestnut pattering to the ground:

Calm and deep peace on this high wold,
  And on these dews that drench the furze,
  And all the silver gossamers
That twinkle into green and gold:

Calm and still light on yon great plain
  That sweeps with all its autumn bowers,
  And crowded farms and lessening towers,
To mingle with the bounding main:

Tennyson, 'In Memoriam'

A spirit haunts the year's last hours
Dwelling amid these yellowing bowers:
  To himself he talks;
For at eventide, listening earnestly,
At his work you may hear him sob and sigh
  In the walks;
  Earthward he boweth the heavy stalks
Of the mouldering flowers:
  Heavily hangs the broad sunflower
    Over its grave i' the earth so chilly;
  Heavily hangs the hollyhock,
    Heavily hangs the tiger-lily.

The air is damp, and hush'd and close
As a sick man's room when he taketh repose
  An hour before death;
My very heart faints and my whole soul grieves
At the moist rich smell of the rotting leaves,
  And the breath
  Of the fading edges of box beneath,
And the year's last rose.
  Heavily hangs the broad sunflower
    Over its grave i' the earth so chilly;
  Heavily hangs the hollyhock,
    Heavily hangs the tiger-lily.

Tennyson

Tennyson was born to be the poet of Autumn; for his delight in beauty and his sad awareness of her transience were both peculiarly acute. Indeed, the awareness enhanced the delight to create a complex mood half sweet, half sad, to which he intensely responded. Tennyson's exquisite sensibility was not without a touch of exquisite pleasure in the beauty of decay. The pleasure is not less keen because of this: on the contrary it lends it a seductive equivocal charm. He wrote most often about still and early autumnal days: but he can evoke the later wilder autumn just as vividly.

From '*In Memoriam*' again:

Tonight the winds begin to rise
  And roar from yonder dropping day:
  The last red leaf is whirl'd away,
The rooks are blown about the skies:

The forest crack'd, the water curl'd,
  The cattle huddled on the lea;
  And wildly dash'd on tower and tree
The sunbeam strikes along the world:

From '*Maud*':

. . . the flying gold of the ruin'd woodlands . . .

and from '*The Lady of Shalott*':

In the stormy east winds training
The pale yellow woods were waning
The broad stream in his banks complaining,
Heavily the low sky raining . . .

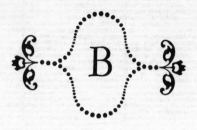

BEAUTY

(1) IMPERSONAL

This divine beauty is evident, fugitive, impalpable, and home-less in a world of material fact; yet it is unmistakeably individual and sufficient unto itself, and although perhaps soon eclipsed, is never really extinguished: for it visits time and belongs to eternity.

George Santayana

Beauty as a critical term has been so overworked and misused that critics hesitate to employ it. None the less it is an indispensable term; for it alone describes something that appeals at once to the imagination and to the senses. It would be incorrect to call a well-cooked steak beautiful; it appeals to the senses but not to the imagination. An unselfish act on the other hand appeals to the imagination but not to the senses; only metaphorically can it be called beautiful. But a rose tree or a melody of Mozart are rightly called beautiful because they appeal to both senses and imagination.

The sense of the beautiful is the source of the highest satisfaction life has to offer. A fragile satisfaction on the face of it; for it fails to work if one is in pain or even in discomfort. Furthermore the satisfaction it brings is ephemeral in the sense that nothing has the power to stir it continuously: the most beautiful tune ceases to rouse a response in the listener if he hears it played over and over again. Yet, in another sense, sensibility to beauty is in-destructible. The ear, even if tired by one tune too often repeated, is always ready to respond freshly to another: and when pain or discomfort is ended, the sense of beauty soon revives. Nor, in my experience, does it weaken with age. The beautiful can stir the spirit when other sources of satisfaction have failed with the years; when friends have died and ambitions have dwindled and interest in the future, personal or public, has faded away.

> Since brass, nor stone, nor earth, nor boundless sea,
> But sad mortality o'ersways their power,
> How with this rage shall beauty hold a plea
> Whose action is no stronger than a flower?

Shakespeare's words are true enough: yet the root of the flower remains in the earth, ready to blossom again next year. Santayana is right: beauty 'visits time and belongs to eternity'.

> There is no excellent beauty that has not some strangeness in the proportion.
>
> *Francis Bacon*

If artistic beauty is meant, this is one of the most penetrating statements ever made. Great works of art are nearly always notable for the fact that they combine in harmony elements that one might expect to find incongruous; Jane Austen's robust and realistic outlook and the delicate elegance of her art, the naive directness with which Hardy tells his stories and the subtle moral and aesthetic sensibility which these stories reveal; Burns's unexpected blend of virile animal vitality and deft light-footed grace.

(II) PERSONAL

> So may thy cheekes red outwear scarlet dye
> And their white, whiteness of the Galaxy,
> So may your mighty, amazing beauty move
> Envy in all women, and in all men, love, . . .
>
> *John Donne, 'Sappho to Philaenis'*

The ancients venerated physical beauty as an expression of divinity. We on the other hand tend to minimize its value on the grounds that it reflects no moral or intellectual credit on its possessor. 'She has nothing but her looks', we say contemptuously of an actress. But surely the ancients were right. Great beauty has something about it divine, mysterious and fatal; and all the more because it is a gift that cannot be acquired by the conscientious or the clever, however much effort they may make. Very beautiful persons are, as it were, the blood-royal of humanity and as such are exempt from the operation of those laws which condition the lives of ordinary homely-faced mortals. It is right, we feel, that after the fall of Troy, beautiful Helen went unpunished, though she was the cause of all its ten long years of suffering.

Many writers have sought to describe great beauty; most have failed. Clearly it is no use enumerating a catalogue of faultless features; large eyes, golden hair, etc: for there is a contradictiousness in the human mind that makes it refuse to visualize them as the author intended. We imagine the person described, if at all, as not especially beautiful. Beauty is most effectively conveyed in terms of the impression it makes. Henry James is a master of this. His beauties are the most convincing in fiction; they are never described in much physical detail.

Mme de Vionnet:

Her bare shoulders and arms were white and beautiful; the materials of her dress, a mixture, as he supposed, of silk and crêpe, were of a silvery grey so artfully composed as to give an impression of warm splendour; and round her neck she wore a collar of large old emeralds, the green note of which was more dimly repeated at other points of her apparel, in embroidery, in enamel, in satin, in substances and textures vaguely rich. Her head, extremely fair and exquisitely festal, was like a happy fancy, a notion of the antique on an old precious medal, some silver coin of the Renaissance; while her slim lightness and brightness, her gaiety, her expression, her decision, contributed to an effect that might have been felt by a poet as half mythological and half conventional. He could have compared her to a goddess still partly engaged in a morning cloud, or to a sea-nymph waist-high in the summer surge.

The Ambassadors

Verena Tarrant:

. . . had curious, radiant, liquid eyes (their smile was a sort of reflection, like the glisten of a gem), and though she was not tall, she appeared to spring up, and carried her head as if it reached rather high . . .

Her splendid hair seemed to shine; her cheek and chin had a curve which struck him by its fineness; her eyes and lips were full of smiles and greetings. She had appeared to him before as a creature of brightness, but now she lighted up the place, she irradiated, she made everything that surrounded her of no consequence; dropping upon the shabby sofa with an effect as charming as if she had been a nymph sinking on a leopard-skin, . . .

The Bostonians

Henry James's most splendid exhibition in this manner is his portrait of the Princess Casamassima:

She might well be a princess – it was impossible to conform more to the finest evocations of that romantic word. She was fair, shining, slender, with an effortless majesty. Her beauty had an air of perfection; it astonished and lifted one up; the sight of it seemed a privilege, a reward . . . Her dark eyes, blue or grey, something that was not brown, were as kind as they were splendid, and there was an extraordinary light nobleness in the way she held her head. That head, where two or three diamond stars glittered in the thick, delicate hair which defined its shape, suggested something antique and celebrated, something he had admired of old – the memory was vague – in a statue, in a picture, in a museum. Purity of line and form, of cheek and chin and lip and brow, a colour that seemed to live and glow, a radiance of grace and eminence and success – these things were seated in triumph in the face of the Princess, and her visitor, as he held himself in his chair, trembling with the revelation, questioned if she were really of the same substance with the humanity he had hitherto known.

The Princess Casamassima

Thackeray's account of Beatrix Esmond coming down the stairs with the candle in her hand is another show-piece that splendidly comes off:

. . . from one of these [doors], a wax candle in her hand, and illuminating her, came Mistress Beatrix – the light falling indeed upon the scarlet riband which she wore, and upon the most brilliant white neck in the world.

. . . She was a brown beauty; that is, her eyes, hair, and eyebrows and eyelashes were dark: her hair curling with rich undulations, and waving over her shoulders; but her complexion was as dazzlingly white as snow in sunshine: except her cheeks, which were a bright red, and her lips, which were of a still deeper crimson. Her mouth and chin, they said, were too large and full, and so they might be for a goddess in marble, but not for a woman whose eyes were fire, whose look was love, whose voice was the sweetest low song, whose shape was perfect symmetry, health, decision, activity, whose foot as it planted itself on the ground was firm but flexible, and whose motion, whether rapid or slow, was always perfect grace – agile as a nymph, lofty as a queen – now melting, now imperious, now sarcastic – there was no single movement of hers but was beautiful.

Henry Esmond

I used to wonder about 'the bright red' of her cheeks. Taken literally, it sounds like the description of an old-fashioned Dutch doll. But further reflection has convinced me it was right. The phrase contributes to intensify the impression of extreme vividness which was the keynote of Beatrix's beauty: among other women she stood out as a magnificent Venetian red does among other colours. Once again, literal exactness is shown not to be necessary to convey physical impression.

The most evocative description of an older woman's beauty that I know is Virginia Woolf's account of Mrs Ramsay in *To the Lighthouse*:

. . . and all at once he realised that it was this: it was this: – she was the most beautiful person he had ever seen.

With stars in her eyes and veils in her hair, with cyclamen and wild violets – what nonsense was he thinking? She was fifty at least; she had eight children. Stepping through fields of flowers and taking to her breast buds that had broken and lambs that had fallen; with the stars in her eyes and the wind in her hair . . .

'But she's no more aware of her beauty than a child.' . . . For always, he thought, there was something incongruous to be worked into the harmony of her face. She clapped a deer-stalker's hat on her head; she ran across the lawn in goloshes to snatch a child from mischief. So that if it were her beauty merely that one thought of, one must remember the quivering thing, the living thing, . . . and work it into the picture; or if one thought of her simply as a woman, one must endow her with some freak of idiosyncrasy; or suppose some latent desire to doff her royalty of form as if her beauty bored her and all that men say of beauty, and she wanted only to be like other people, insignificant.

To the Lighthouse

Here the author gets her impression by mingling fact and imagination, the prosaic and the poetic. Mrs Ramsay claps a deerstalker on her head, dashes across the lawn. At the same time she is a nymph, a Muse, the sight of whom stirs the beholder to dream of her as crowned with violets, bearing in her arms flowers, and of whom it can exquisitely be said that 'The Graces had joined hands in meadows of asphodel to compose that face'.

The poets tackle the task with even less reference to the facts. We may compare the manner in which three of the greatest have spoken of Helen, universally accepted in literature as the most beautiful woman that ever lived. Marlowe says that her face 'launched a thousand ships' and that it was

. . . fairer than the evening air,
clad in the beauty of a thousand stars.

Shakespeare, in *Troilus and Cressida*, calls her 'the mortal Venus, the heart-blood of beauty, love's indivisible soul'. Homer is even less explicit. He simply tells us that when Helen appeared upon the ramparts of Troy, the old men sitting there said that it was not surprising that for ten whole years two nations should have fought for such a woman. None of these three writers mentions a single one of Helen's features. Yet triumphantly they all dazzle us with the glory of her 'mighty amazing beauty'.

There are fewer memorable descriptions in our literature of male beauty. But Marlowe's Leander is a boy as lovely as the David of Donatello.

> Amorous Leander, beautiful and young,
> (Whose tragedy divine Musaeus sung)
> Dwelt at Abydos; since him dwelt there none
> For whom succeeding times make greater moan.
> His dangling tresses, that were never shorn,
> Had they been cut, and unto Colchos borne,
> Would have allur'd the venturous youth of Greece
> To hazard more than for the golden fleece.
> Fair Cynthia wish'd his arms might be her sphere;
> Grief makes her pale, because she moves not there.
> His body was as straight as Circe's wand;
> Jove might have sipt out nectar from his hand.
> Even as delicious meat is to the tast,
> So was his neck in touching, and surpast
> The white of Pelops' shoulder: I could tell ye,
> How smooth his breast was, and how white his belly;
> And whose immortal fingers did imprint
> That heavenly path with many a curious dint,
> That runs along his back; but my rude pen
> Can hardly blazon forth the loves of men,
> Much less of powerful gods; let it suffice
> That my slack Muse sings of Leander's eyes;
> Those orient cheeks and lips, exceeding his
> That leapt into the water for a kiss
> Of his own shadow, and, despising many,
> Died ere he could enjoy the love of any.
> Had wild Hippolytus Leander seen,
> Enamour'd of his beauty had he been:
> His presence made the rudest peasant melt,
> That in the vast uplandish country dwelt;
> The barbarous Thracian soldier, mov'd with nought,
> Was mov'd with him, and for his favour sought.
> Some swore he was a maid in man's attire,
> For in his looks were all that men desire, –
> A pleasant-smiling cheek, a speaking eye,
> A brow for love to banquet royally;

And such as knew he was a man, would say,
'Leander, thou art made for amorous play:
Why art thou not in love, and lov'd of all?
Though thou be fair, yet be not thine own thrall.'

'Hero and Leander'

BEGINNINGS

The best beginnings for a book or a poem are marked by two
characteristics. They immediately interest the reader so that he is
enticed to go on reading and they strike a note which induces in
him the mood which is to characterize the work as a whole.
Milton is a master of beginnings. *Paradise Lost* starts with a state-
ment of the theme of the poem as decisive as that of a fugue by
Bach. *'Lycidas'* and *Comus* each open with a majestic brief prelude
that sets the tone for all that follows:

Of Man's first disobedience, and the fruit
Of that forbidden tree, whose mortal taste
Brought death into the world, and all our woe,
With loss of Eden, till one greater Man
Restore us, and regain the blissful seat,
Sing, Heavenly Muse, that on the secret top
Of Oreb, or of Sinai, didst inspire
That shepherd, who first taught the chosen seed,
In the beginning how the Heavens and Earth
Rose out of Chaos: or, if Sion hill
Delight thee more, and Siloa's brook that flowed
Fast by the oracle of God, I thence
Invoke thy aid to my adventurous song,
That with no middle flight intends to soar
Above the Aonian mount, while it pursues
Things unattempted yet in prose or rhyme.
And chiefly thou, O Spirit, that dost prefer
Before all temples the upright heart and pure,
Instruct me, for thou know'st; thou from the first
Wast present, and, with mighty wings outspread,
Dove-like sat'st brooding on the vast Abyss,

And mad'st it pregnant: what in me is dark
Illumine, what is low raise and support;
That, to the height of this great argument,
I may assert Eternal Providence,
And justify the ways of God to men.

                                        Paradise Lost

Yet once more, O ye laurels, and once more,
Ye myrtles brown, with ivy never sere,
I come to pluck, your berries harsh and crude,
And with forced fingers rude
Shatter your leaves before the mellowing year.
Bitter constraint and sad occasion dear
Compels me to disturb your season due;
For Lycidas is dead, dead ere his prime,
Young Lycidas, and hath not left his peer.
Who would not sigh for Lycidas? he well knew
Himself to sing, and build the lofty rhyme.
He must not float upon his watery bier
Unwept, and welter to the parching wind,
Without the meed of some melodious tear.

                                        'Lycidas'

Before the starry threshold of Jove's court
My mansion is, where those immortal shapes
Of bright aerial spirits live insphered
In regions mild of calm and serene air,
Above the smoke and stir of this dim spot
Which men call Earth, and, with low-thoughted care,
Confined and pestered in this pinfold here,
Strive to keep up a frail and feverish being,
Unmindful of the crown that Virtue gives,
After this mortal change, to her true servants
Amongst the enthroned gods on sainted seats.
Yet some there be that by due steps aspire
To lay their just hands on that golden key
That opes the palace of Eternity.
To such my errand is; and, but for such,
I would not soil these pure ambrosial weeds
With the rank vapours of this sin-worn mould.

                                        Comus

Jane Austen is another master – or should I say mistress – of beginnings. All of her six novels start admirably: they stir curiosity, they create the appropriate comedy mood, and they also communicate painlessly and effortlessly the facts necessary for the reader to know from the outset.

About thirty years ago, Miss Maria Ward, of Huntingdon, with only seven thousand pounds, had the good luck to captivate Sir Thomas Bertram, of Mansfield Park, in the county of Northampton, and to be thereby raised to the rank of a baronet's lady, with all the comforts and consequence of an handsome house and large income. All Huntingdon exclaimed on the greatness of the match, and her uncle, the lawyer, himself allowed her to be at least three thousand pounds short of any equitable claim to it. She had two sisters to be benefited by her elevation; and such of their acquaintances as thought Miss Ward and Miss Frances quite as handsome as Miss Maria, did not scruple to predict their marrying with almost equal advantage. But there certainly are not so many men of large fortune in the world as there are pretty women to deserve them. Miss Ward, at the end of half a dozen years, found herself obliged to be attached to the Rev. Mr. Norris, a friend of her brother-in-law, with scarcely any private fortune, and Miss Frances fared yet worse.

Mansfield Park

Sir Walter Elliot, of Kellynch Hall, in Somersetshire, was a man who, for his own amusement, never took up any book but the Baronetage; there he found occupation for an idle hour, and consolation in a distressed one; there his faculties were roused into admiration and respect by contemplating the limited remnant of the earliest patents; there any unwelcome sensations arising from domestic affairs changed naturally into pity and contempt as he turned over the almost endless creations of the last century; and there, if every other leaf were powerless, he could read his own history with an interest which never failed.

Persuasion

Thomas Hardy's beginnings in their very different way are as good as Jane Austen's. Jane Austen is concerned with the comedy of individual characters: so also are the opening paragraphs of her novels. Thomas Hardy is concerned with man confronting destiny and he embodies destiny as visible nature. His most memorable beginnings therefore are descriptions of scenery, of the setting in which the drama takes place and which is itself a character in that drama. The chapter-long description of Egdon which opens *The Return of the Native* is his most sustained achievement in this kind; that of *The Woodlanders* is equally splendid:

> The rambler, who, for old association's sake, should trace the forsaken coach-road running almost in a meridional line from Bristol to the south shore of England, would find himself during the latter half of his journey in the vicinity of some extensive woodlands, interspersed with apple-orchards. Here the trees, timber or fruit-bearing as the case may be, make the wayside hedges ragged by their drip and shade, their lower limbs stretching in level repose over the road, as though reclining in the insubstantial air. At one place, on the skirts of Blackmoor Vale, where the gold brown of High-Stoy Hill is seen two or three miles ahead, the leaves lie so thick in autumn as to completely bury the track. The spot is lonely, and when the days are darkening the many gay charioteers now perished who have rolled along the way, the blistered soles that have trodden it, and the tears that have wetted it, return upon the mind of the loiterer.

Dickens is another writer who sometimes starts with a description of a scene vividly realistic in itself but also symbolic of the theme of the book. The description of London in the fog which starts *Bleak House* is a marvellously real description of a London fog: it is also a symbol of a fog blinding and paralysing the English legal system which is the villain of the drama.

> London. Michaelmas Term lately over, and the Lord Chancellor sitting in Lincoln's Inn Hall. Implacable November weather. As much mud in the streets, as if the waters had but newly retired from the face of the earth, and it would not be wonderful to meet a Megalosaurus, forty feet long or so, waddling like an elephantine lizard up Holborn Hill. Smoke lowering down from chimney-pots, making a soft black drizzle, with flakes of

soot in it as big as full-grown snow-flakes – gone into mourn-ing, one might imagine, for the death of the sun. Dogs, un-distinguishable in mire. Horses, scarcely better; splashed to their very blinkers. Foot passengers, jostling one another's umbrellas, in a general infection of ill-temper, and losing their foothold at street-corners, where tens of thousands of other foot passengers have been slipping and sliding since the day broke (if this day ever broke), adding new deposits to the crust upon crust of mud, sticking at those points tenaciously to the pave-ment, and accumulating at compound interest.

Fog everywhere. Fog up the river, where it flows among green aits and meadows; fog down the river, where it rolls defiled among the tiers of shipping, and the waterside pollutions of a great (and dirty) city. Fog on the Essex marshes, fog on the Kentish heights. Fog creeping into the cabooses of collier-brigs; fog lying out on the yards, and hovering in the rigging of great ships; fog drooping on the gunwales of barges and small boats. Fog in the eyes and throats of ancient Greenwich pensioners, wheezing by the firesides of their wards; fog in the stem and bowl of the afternoon pipe of the wrathful skipper, down in his close cabin; fog cruelly pinching the toes and fingers of his shivering little 'prentice boy on deck. Chance people on the bridges peeping over the parapets into a nether sky of fog, with fog all around them, as if they were up in a balloon, and hanging in the misty clouds.

Gas looming through the fog in divers places in the streets, much as the sun may, from the spongy fields, be seen to loom by husbandman and ploughboy. Most of the shops lighted two hours before their time – as the gas seems to know, for it has a haggard and unwilling look.

Here are three other model beginnings; the first is majestic, the second elegiac and the third entertaining.

Ye who listen with credulity to the whispers of fancy, and pursue with eagerness the phantoms of hope; who expect that age will perform the promise of youth, and that the deficiences of the present day will be supplied by the morrow; attend to the history of Rasselas prince of Abissinia.

Samuel Johnson, Rasselas

I had not visited Eton for many years, when one day passing from the Fellows' Library into the Gallery I caught sight of the portrait of my school-friend Digby Dolben hanging just without the door among our most distinguished contemporaries. I was wholly arrested, and as I stood gazing on it, my companion asked me if I knew who it was. I was thinking that, beyond a few whom I could name, I must be almost the only person who would know. Far memories of my boyhood were crowding freshly upon me: he was standing again beside me in the eager promise of his youth; I could hear his voice; nothing of him was changed; while I, wrapt from him in a confused mist of time, was wondering what he would think, could he know that at this actual moment he would have been dead thirty years, and that his memory would be thus preserved and honoured in the beloved school, where his delicate spirit had been so strangely troubled.

Robert Bridges, Memoir of Digby Mackworth Dolben

I shall not say why and how I became, at the age of fifteen, the mistress of the Earl of Craven. Whether it was love, or the severity of my father, the depravity of my own heart, or the winning arts of the noble Lord, which induced me to leave my paternal roof and place myself under his protection, does not now much signify: or if it does, I am not in the humour to gratify curiosity in this matter.

The Memoirs of Harriette Wilson

As a boy of ten I thought the most enticing first sentence I had ever read was that which opens *Rookwood* by William Harrison Ainsworth.

Within a sepulchral vault, and at midnight, two persons were seated.

I still think it good, though a trifle comical.

BITTER-SWEET

Close up the casement, draw the blind,
  Shut out the stealing moon,
She wears too much the guise she wore
  Before our lutes were strewn
With years-deep dust, and names we read
  On a white stone were hewn.

Step not out on the dew-dashed lawn
  To view the Lady's Chair,
Immense Orion's glittering form,
  The Less and Greater Bear:
Stay in; to such sights we were drawn
  When faded ones were fair.

Brush not the bough for midnight scents
  That come forth lingeringly
And wake the same sweet sentiments
  They breathed to you and me
When living seemed a laugh, and love
  All it was said to be.

Within the common lamp-lit room
  Prison my eyes and thought;
Let dingy details crudely loom,
  Mechanic speech be wrought:
Too fragrant was Life's early bloom,
  Too tart the fruit it brought!

Thomas Hardy, 'Shut Out That Moon'

Half-hidden in a graveyard,
  In the blackness of a yew,
Where never living creature stirs,
  Nor sunbeam pierces through,

Is a tomb-stone, green and crooked –
  Its faded legend gone –

With one rain-worn cherub's head
  To sing of the unknown.

There, when the dusk is falling,
  Silence broods so deep
It seems that every air that breathes
  Sighs from the fields of sleep.

Day breaks in heedless beauty,
  Kindling each drop of dew,
But unforsaking shadow dwells
  Beneath this lonely yew.

And, all else lost and faded,
  Only this listening head
Keeps with a strange unanswering smile
  Its secret with the dead.

Walter De La Mare

If I might see another Spring
  I'd not plant summer flowers and wait:
I'd have my crocuses at once,
My leafless pink mezereons,
  My chill-veined snowdrops, choicer yet
  My white or azure violet,
Leaf-nested primrose; anything
  To blow at once, not late.

If I might see another Spring,
  I'd listen to the daylight birds
That build their nests and pair and sing,
Nor wait for mateless nightingale;
  I'd listen to the lusty herds,
  The ewes with lambs as white as snow,
I'd find out music in the hail
  And all the winds that blow.

If I might see another Spring –
  Oh stinging comment on my past
That all my past results in 'if' –
  If I might see another Spring

I'd laugh to-day, to-day is brief;
I would not wait for anything:
    I'd use to-day that cannot last,
    Be glad to-day and sing.

Christina Rossetti, 'Another Spring'

Flow down, cold rivulet, to the sea,
    Thy tribute wave deliver:
No more by thee my steps shall be,
    For ever and for ever.

Flow, softly flow, by lawn and lea,
    A rivulet then a river:
No where by thee my steps shall be,
    For ever and for ever.

But here will sigh thine alder tree,
    And here thine aspen shiver;
And here by thee will hum the bee,
    For ever and for ever.

A thousand suns will stream on thee,
    A thousand moons will quiver;
But not by thee my steps shall be,
    For ever and for ever.

Tennyson

The sigh that heaves the grasses
    Whence thou wilt never rise
Is of the air that passes
    And knows not if it sighs.

The diamond tears adorning
    Thy low mound on the lea,
Those are the tears of morning,
    That weeps, but not for thee.

A. E. Housman

Five examples of bitter-sweet, one of the most exquisite flavours
the banquet of literature has to offer. The sweetness strikes one

first, sweetness of sound or image or both. But, infiltrating the sweetness, sounds a different note – sad or ironic or disillusioned – which yet by its very dissonance, contributes to achieve a subtler richer harmony.

These poems are all by Romantic writers. The bitter-sweet is a Romantic mood: for it expresses the typical Romantic mixed emotion which comes from a sense of the contrast between man's rapturous ideal dreams and the hard fact of his experience in this imperfect world. Pre-Romantic writers seldom strike the bitter-sweet note, though myself I hear it at the close of Feste's song in *Twelfth Night*:

> O mistress mine, where are you roaming?
> O stay and hear; your true love's coming,
>   That can sing both high and low:
> Trip no further, pretty sweeting;
> Journeys end in lovers' meeting,
>   Every wise man's son doth know.
>
> What is love? 'tis not hereafter;
> Present mirth has present laughter;
>   What's to come is still unsure:
> In delay there lies no plenty;
> Then come kiss me, sweet-and-twenty:
>   Youth's a stuff will not endure.

Of course, the last line may be taken as no more than a casual light-hearted utterance of conventional 'gather-ye-rosebuds' sentiment. But I doubt it. It rings too poignantly; and this poignancy is emphasized by the mood of the original minor-key tune to which it was set and which Shakespeare must have known.

The bitter-sweet note can be heard in prose too. Charles Lamb strikes it in his essay on 'New Year's Eve':

> . . . Not in childhood alone, but the young man till thirty, never feels practically that he is mortal. He knows it indeed, and, if need were, he could preach a homily on the fragility of life; but he brings it not home to himself, any more than in a hot June we can appropriate to our imagination the freezing days of December. But now, shall I confess a truth? – I feel these audits but too powerfully. I begin to count the probabilities of my

duration, and to grudge at the expenditure of moments and shortest periods, like misers' farthings. In proportion as the years both lessen and shorten, I set more count upon their periods, and would fain lay my ineffectual finger upon the spoke of the great wheel. I am not content to pass away 'like a weaver's shuttle.' Those metaphors solace me not, nor sweeten the unpalatable draught of mortality. I care not to be carried with the tide that smoothly bears human life to eternity; and reluct at the inevitable course of destiny. I am in love with this green earth; the face of town and country; the unspeakable rural solitudes, and the sweet security of streets. I would set up my tabernacle here. I am content to stand still at the age to which I am arrived; I and my friends: to be no younger, no richer, no handsomer. I do not want to be weaned by age; or drop, like mellow fruit, as they say, into the grave. Any alteration, on this earth of mine, in diet or in lodging, puzzles and discomposes me. My household-gods plant a terrible fixed foot, and are not rooted up without blood . . .

Hans Andersen is another bitter-sweet writer; as in the story of 'The Top and the Ball'. Here the contrast is between matter and manner, between the wry little tale and the playful mischievous charm with which it is told.

A Top and a Ball were lying close together in a drawer, among other playthings.

Thus said the Top to the Ball:

'Why should we not become bride and bridegroom, since we are thrown so much together?'

But the Ball, who was made of morocco leather, and fancied herself a very fashionable young lady, would not hear of such a proposal.

The next day, the little boy to whom the playthings belonged came to the drawer; he painted the Top red and yellow, and drove a brass nail through the middle of it; it was glorious after that to see the Top spin round.

'Look at me now!' said he to the Ball: 'what do you say to me now? Why should not we become man and wife? We suit each other so well – you can jump, and I can spin; it would be hard to find a couple happier than we should be.'

'Do you think so?' said the Ball; 'perhaps you do not know that my father and mother were morocco slippers, and that I have cork in my body.'

'Yes, but I am made of mahogany,' returned the Top; 'the Burgomaster manufactured me with his own hands; for he has a lathe of his own, and took great pleasure in turning me.'

'Can I trust you in this?' asked the Ball.

'May I never be whipped again if I lie,' said the Top.

'You don't talk amiss,' replied the Ball; 'but I am not at liberty, I am as good as betrothed to a young Swallow. Whenever I fly up in the air, he puts his head out of his nest and says, "Will you marry me?" I have said "Yes" to him in my heart, and that is almost the same as a betrothal. But one thing I promise you, I will never forget you!'

'That will be of great use!' quoth the Top, and no more was then said on the subject.

Next day the Ball was taken out. The Top saw it fly like a bird into the air – so high that it could be seen no longer; it came back again, but every time it touched the ground, it sprang higher than before. Either lover, or the cork she had in her body, must have been the cause of this.

The ninth time she did not return; the boy sought and sought, but she was gone.

'I know well where she is,' sighed the Top; 'she is in the Swallow's nest, celebrating her wedding.' The more the Top thought of it, the more amiable did the Ball appear to him: that she could not be his only made his love the more vehement. Another had been preferred to him; he could not forget that! And the Top spinned and hummed, but was always thinking of the dear Ball who, in his imagination, grew more beautiful every moment. Thus passed several years – there was a constant love!

The Top was no longer young! however he was one day gilded all over; never before had he looked so handsome. He was now a gilt top, and spun most bravely, humming all the time yes, that was famous! But all at once he sprang too high and was gone! They sought and sought, even in the cellar; he was no where to be found.

Where was he?

He had jumped into a barrel full of all sorts of rubbish,

cabbage-stalks, sweepings, dust, etc., which had fallen in from the gutter.

'Alas! here I lie; my gay gilding will soon be spoiled; and what sort of trumpery can I have fallen in with?' And he peeped at a long cabbage-stalk which lay fearfully near him, and at a strange round thing somewhat like an apple; but it was not an apple, it was an old Ball, which had lain several years in the gutter, and was quite soaked through with water.

'Thank goodness! at last I see an equal, with whom I may speak,' said the Ball, looking fixedly at the gilt Top. 'I am made of real morocco, sewed together by a young lady's hands, and I have cork in my body; but I shall never again be noticed by anyone; I was on the point of marriage with the Swallow, when I fell into the gutter, and there I have lain five years, and am now wet through. Only think, what a wearisome time for a young lady to be in such a situation!'

But the Top answered not a word; he thought on his long-lamented companion, and the more he heard, the more certain he felt that it was she herself.

The servant-maid now came, and was going to turn the barrel over. 'Hurrah!' exclaimed she, 'there is the gilt Top.'

And the Top was brought back to the play-room; it was used and admired as before: but nothing more was heard of the Ball, nor did the Top ever again speak of his love for her; such a feeling must have passed away. How could it be otherwise, when he found that she had lain five years in the gutter, and that she was so much altered he scarcely knew her again when he met her in the barrel among rubbish?

Danish Fairy Tales and Legends

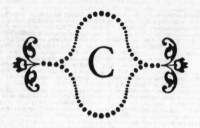

CHANGE OF KEY

A change of key, as lovers of Schubert know, can be the source
of some of the most powerful and moving effects in music. It has
its parallel in poetry: the poem, while maintaining its regular
movement and coherent flow of sense, modulates from one mood
to another. Generally it is from gay to grave, from major key to
minor. In Marvell's poem 'To His Coy Mistress', the change
comes with the words 'But at my back I always hear'.

> Had we but world enough, and time,
> This coyness, lady, were no crime.
> We would sit down, and think which way
> To walk, and pass our long love's day.
> Thou by the Indian Ganges' side
> Should'st rubies find: I by the tide
> Of Humber would complain. I would
> Love you ten years before the Flood:
> And you should if you please refuse
> Till the conversion of the Jews.
> My vegetable love should grow
> Vaster than empires, and more slow.
> An hundred years should go to praise
> Thine eyes, and on thy forehead gaze.
> Two hundred to adore each breast:
> But thirty thousand to the rest.
> An age at least to every part,
> And the last age should show your heart.
> For lady, you deserve this state;
> Nor would I love at lower rate.

But at my back I always hear
Time's wingèd chariot hurrying near:
And yonder all before us lie
Deserts of vast eternity.
Thy beauty shall no more be found;
Nor, in thy marble vault, shall sound
My echoing song; then worms shall try
That long preserv'd virginity:
And your quaint honour turn to dust,
And into ashes all my lust.
The grave's a fine and private place,
But none I think do there embrace.
   Now therefore, while the youthful hue
Sits on thy skin like morning dew,
And while thy willing soul transpires
At every pore with instant fires,
Now let us sport us while we may;
And now, like am'rous birds of prey,
Rather at once our Time devour,
Than languish in his slow-chapt pow'r.
Let us roll all our strength, and all
Our sweetness, up into one ball,
And tear our pleasures with rough strife,
Through the iron gates of life.
Thus, though we cannot make our sun
Stand still, yet we will make him run.

There is a similar modulation at the words 'For that lovely face will fail' in Thomas Carew's parallel poem which expresses similar sentiments in the same metre:

Think not, 'cause men flattering say
You're fresh as April, sweet as May,
Bright as is the morning star,
That you are so; or, though you are,
Be not therefore proud, and deem
All men unworthy your esteem:
For, being so, you lose the pleasure
of being fair, since that rich treasure
of rare beauty and sweet feature
Was bestow'd on you by nature

To be enjoy'd; and 'twere a sin
There to be scarce, where she hath bin
So prodigal of her best graces.
Thus common beauties and mean faces
Shall have more pastime, and enjoy
The sport you lost by being coy.
Did the thing for which I sue
Only concern myself, not you;
Were men so framed as they alone
Reap'd all the pleasure, women none;
Then had you reason to be scant:
But 'twere a madness not to grant
That which affords (if you consent)
To you, the giver, more content
Than me, the beggar. Oh, then be
Kind to yourself, if not to me.
Starve not yourself, because you may
Thereby make me pine away;
Nor let brittle beauty make
You your wiser thoughts forsake;
For that lovely face will fail.
Beauty's sweet, but beauty's frail,
'Tis sooner past, 'tis sooner done,
Than summer's rain, or winter's sun;
Most fleeting, when it is most dear,
'Tis gone, while we but say 'tis here.
These curious locks, so aptly twined,
Whose every hair a soul doth bind,
Will change their auburn hue and grow
White and cold as winter's snow.
That eye, which now is Cupid's nest,
Will prove his grave, and all the rest
Will follow; in the cheek, chin, nose,
Nor lily shall be found, nor rose.
And what will then become of all
Those whom now you servants call?
Like swallows, when your summer's done,
They'll fly, and seek some warmer sun.
Then wisely choose one to your friend
Whose love may, when your beauties end,

Remain still firm: be provident,
And think, before the summer's spent,
Of following winter; like the ant,
In plenty hoard for time of scant.
Cull out, amongst the multitude
Of lovers, that seek to intrude
Into your favour, one that may
Love for an age, not for a day;
One that will quench your youthful fires,
And feed in age your hot desires.
For when the storms of time have moved
Waves on that cheek which was beloved,
When a fair lady's face is pined,
And yellow spread where red once shined;
When beauty, youth, and all sweets leave her,
Love may return, but lover never:
And old folks say there are no pains
Like itch of love in aged veins.
O love me, then, and now begin it,
Let us not lose this present minute;
For time and age will work that wrack
Which time or age shall ne'er call back.
The snake each year fresh skin resumes,
And eagles change their aged plumes;
The faded rose each spring receives
A fresh red tincture on her leaves:
But if your beauties once decay,
You never know a second May.
O then, be wise, and whilst your season
Affords you days for sport, do reason;
Spend not in vain your life's short hour,
But crop in time your beauty's flower,
Which will away, and doth together
Both bud and fade, both blow and wither.

'Persuasions to Love'

Here are two briefer examples of literary change of key. In each the change does not come till the last two lines of the poem: in each it is abrupt, surprising, and ravishing:

Four ducks on a pond,
A grass bank beyond,
A blue sky of spring,
White clouds on the wing;
What a little thing
To remember for years –
To remember with tears!

William Allingham

Sweet Chance, that led my steps abroad,
   Beyond the town, where wild flowers grow –
A rainbow and a cuckoo, Lord,
How rich and great the times are now!
   Know, all ye sheep
   And cows, that keep
On staring that I stand so long
   In grass that's wet from heavy rain –
A rainbow and a cuckoo's song
   May never come together again;
   May never come
   This side the tomb.

W. H. Davies

Every literary effect can be found in the works of Shakespeare.
There is a compelling example of change of key – this time from
tense agitation to piercing pathos – in the ninth line of his hun-
dred and forty-eighth sonnet:

O me, what eyes hath Love put in my head,
Which have no correspondence with true sight!
Or, if they have, where is my judgment fled,
That censures falsely what they see aright?
If that be fair whereon my false eyes dote,
What means the world to say it is not so?
If it be not, then love doth well denote
Love's eye is not so true as all men's: no,
How can it? O, how can Love's eye be true
That is so vex'd with watching and with tears?
No marvel then, though I mistake my view;
The sun itself sees not till heaven clears.

O cunning Love! with tears thou keep'st me blind,
Lest eyes well-seeing thy foul faults should find.

CHARM

. . . Et, son cahier à la main, elle allait de l'un à l'autre, chose légère et charmante. 'Pas de teint, pas de figure, pas de corps, pas de voix', disaient les femmes, et elle emplissait l'espace de mouvement, de couleur et d'harmonie. Fanée, jolie, lasse, infatigable, elle était les délices du voyage. D'humeur inégale et cependant toujours gaie, susceptible, irritable et pourtant accommodante et facile, le langue salée avec le ton le plus poli, vaine, modeste, vraie, fausse, délicieuse, si Rose Thévenin ne faisait pas bien ses affaires, si elle ne devenait point déesse, c'est que les temps étaient mauvais et qu'il n'y avait plus à Paris ni encens ni autels pour les Grâces. . . .

Anatole France, Les dieux ont soif

A charming picture of charm. It occurs in a scene set in the period of the Revolutionary Terror in Paris. I remember reading it in 1943 and thinking it topical. When bombs are falling, people are in no state to build altars to the Graces: no more in war-time London than in revolutionary Paris would Rose Thévenin have been recognized as a goddess. There are periods in the world's history – deplorable ignoble periods – in which the Graces are wasted on a humanity too numbed or too barbarous to appreciate them.

THE CHILD IN THE HOUSE

(1)

The old-fashioned, low wainscoting went round the rooms, and up the staircase with carved balusters and shadowy angles, landing half-way up at a broad window, with a swallow's nest below the sill, and the blossom of an old pear-tree showing across it in late April, against the blue below which the perfumed juice of the find of fallen fruit in autumn was so fresh.

At the next turning came the closet which held on its deep shelves the best china. Little angel faces and reedy flutings stood out round the fireplace of the children's room. And on the top of the house, above the large attic, where the white mice ran in the twilight – an infinite, unexplored wonderland of childish treasures, glass beads, empty scent-bottles still sweet, thrum of coloured silks, among its lumber – a flat space of roof, railed round, gave a view of the neighbouring steeples; for the house, as I said, stood near a great city, which sent up heavenwards, over the twisting weather-vanes, not seldom, its beds of rolling cloud and smoke, touched with storm or sunshine. But the child of whom I am writing did not hate the fog because of the crimson lights which fell from it sometimes upon the chimneys, and the whites which gleamed through its openings, on summer mornings, on turret or pavement. For it is false to suppose that a child's sense of beauty is dependent on any choiceness or special fineness, in the objects which present themselves to it, though this indeed comes to be the rule with most of us in later life; earlier, in some degrees, we see inwardly; and the child finds for itself, and with unstinted delight, a difference for the sense, in those whites and reds through the smoke on very homely buildings, and in the gold of the dandelions at the roadside, just beyond the houses. . . .

So the child of whom I am writing lived on there quietly; things without thus ministering to him, as he sat daily at the window with the birdcage hanging below it, and his mother taught him to read, wondering at the ease with which he learned, and at the quickness of his memory. The perfume of the little flowers of the lime-tree fell through the air upon them like rain; while time seemed to move ever more slowly to the murmur of the bees in it, till it almost stood still on June afternoons. How insignificant, at the moment, seem the influences of the sensible things which are tossed and fall and lie about us, so, or so, in the environment of early childhood. How indelibly, as we afterwards discover, they affect us; with what capricious attractions and associations they figure themselves on the white paper, the smooth wax, of our ingenuous souls, as 'with lead in the rock for ever', giving form and feature, and as it were assigned house-room in our memory, to early experiences of feeling and thought, which abide with us ever afterwards, thus, and not otherwise. The realities and passions, the rumours of the greater world without, steal in upon us, each by its own special little passage-way, through the wall of custom about us; and never afterwards quite detach themselves from this or that accident, or trick, in the mode of their first entrance to us. Our susceptibilities, the discovery of our powers, manifold experiences – our varied experiences of the coming and going of bodily pain, for instance – belongs to this or the other well-remembered place in the material habitation – that little white room with the window across which the heavy blossoms could beat so peevishly in the wind, with just that particular catch or throb, such a sense of teasing in it, on gusty mornings; and the early habitation thus gradually becomes a sort of material shrine or sanctuary of sentiment; a system of visible symbolism inter-weaves itself through all our thoughts and passions; and irresistibly, little shapes, voices, accidents – the angle at which the sun in the morning fell on the pillow – become parts of the great chain wherewith we are bound.

Walter Pater, 'The Child in the House'

(11)

Then I told how good she was to all her grand-children, having us to the great house in the holidays, where I in particular used to spend many hours by myself, in gazing upon the old busts of the Twelve Caesars, that had been Emperors of Rome, till the old marble heads would seem to live again, or I to be turned into marble with them; how I never could be tired with roam-ing about that huge mansion, with its vast empty rooms, with their worn-out hangings, fluttering tapestry, and carved oaken panels, with the gilding almost rubbed out – sometimes in the spacious old-fashioned gardens, which I had almost to myself – unless when now and then a solitary gardening man would cross me; and how the nectarines and peaches hung upon the walls; without my ever offering to pluck them, because they were forbidden fruit, unless now and then; and because I had more pleasure in strolling about among the old melancholy-looking yew trees, or the firs, and picking up the red berries,

and the fir apples, which were good for nothing but to look at –
or in lying about upon the fresh grass with all the fine garden
smells around me – or basking in the orangery, till I could
almost fancy myself ripening too along with the oranges and
the limes in that grateful warmth – or in watching the dace that
darted to and fro in the fish-pond at the bottom of the garden,
with here and there a great sulky pike hanging midway down
the water in silent state, as if it mocked at their impertinent
friskings, – I had more pleasure in these busy-idle diversions
than in all the sweet flavour of peaches, nectarines, oranges, and
suchlike common baits of children . . .

The solitude of childhood is not so much the mother of
thought as it is the feeder of love, and silence, and admiration.

Charles Lamb, The Essays of Elia

COLOUR-SENSE

Glory be to God for dappled things –
   For skies of couple-colour as a brinded cow;
     For rose-moles all in stipple upon trout that swim;
Fresh-firecoal chestnut-falls; finches' wings;
   Landscape plotted and pieced – fold, fallow and plough;
And all trades, their gear and tackle and trim.

All things counter, original, spare, strange;
   Whatever is fickle, freckled (who knows how?)
With swift, slow; sweet, sour; adazzle, dim;
He fathers-forth whose beauty is past change:
     Praise him.

Gerard Manley Hopkins 'Pied Beauty'

Subtle almost beyond thought are these dim colours,
The mixed, the all-including, the pervasive,
Earth's own delightful livery, banqueting
The eye with dimness that includes all brightness;
Complexity which the mind sorts out, as the sunlight
Resolves into many purities the mingled

Dun fleeces of the moorland; the quartz sparkles,
The rosy heath glows, the mineral-like mosses
And the heathbells and the myriad lichens
Start each into the eye a separate splendour:
So in the mind's sun bloom the dim dun-colours.

The dry vermilion glow of familiar redbreast
Is not his real glory: that is the greenish,
Light-toned, light-dissembling, eye-deceiving
Dun of his smooth-sloped back, and on his belly
The whitish dun is laid to deceive the shadow:
In the dear linnet the olive-dun is lovely,
And the primrose-duns in the yellowhammer: but most
    beguiling,
Perhaps because of the perfect shape, is the ash-dun,
That quietest, most urbane, unprofaneable colour
Reserved as her livery of beauty to the hedge-sparrow.
There is a royal azure in her blood,
As her eggs prove, and in her nature gold,
For her children's throats are kingcups; but she veils them,
Mingled and blended, in her rare dun-colour.

For the rose-duns, and the blue-duns, look to the finches:
For the clear clear brown-duns, to the fallow deer
(How the sudden tear smarts in the eye wearied of cities)
And for all these and more to the many toadstools,
Which alone have the violet-dun, livid yet lovely:
But the most delicate duns are seen in the gentle
Monkeys from the great forests, the silvan spirits:
Wonderful! that these, almost our brothers,
Should be dressed so rarely, in sulphurous-dun and greenish;
O that a man had grassy hair like these dryads!
O that I too were attired in such dun-colours.

Ruth Pitter, 'Dun-colour'

Rose-red, peacock blue, emerald green, imperial purple – such
are the bright rich colours and set in plain contrast to one another
that most poets single out for admiration. It is strange and delight-
ful to come upon these poems of Hopkins and Ruth Pitter – each

revealing so exquisite an appreciation of subtle tints and complex blends and delicate contrasts and fine gradations of tone.

COMEDY

Taken as a whole, the universe is absurd. There seems an unalterable contradiction between the human mind and its employments. How can a soul be a merchant? What relation to a mortal being has the price of linseed, the fall of butter, and the tax on hemp? . . . 'All the world's a stage' – 'the shining morning face' – 'the strange oaths' – 'the bubble reputation' – 'the eyes severe and beard of formal cut' etc. Can these things be real, surely they are acting. What relation have they to the truth as we see it in experience? What connection with our certain hopes, our deep desires, our craving and infinite thought? In respect of itself it is a good life, says Touchstone, but in respect of a shepherd's life, it is naught. The soul ties its shoes; the mind washes its hands in a basin. All is incongruous.

Walter Bagehot on Shakespeare and his comedy

Shakespeare's comedy, along with that of Cervantes and a few more, is the profoundest kind of comedy. Comedy finds its origin in the perception of incongruities; most of the great comedy of the world – the comedy of Molière or Jane Austen for example – deals with moral and social incongruity. Man, in the works of these authors, is seen in his aspect as a member of society and judged absurd in so far as he does not conform to social standards of virtue and good sense. Marianne in *Sense and Sensibility* despises prudence and cool reason, she thinks the finest natures act always and only under the impulse of heart and imagination. Her life story demonstrates that the consequences of such a view are disastrous and comic. Alceste in Molière's *Misanthrope* takes the view that conscience requires a man always to speak the complete exact truth however indiscreet and tactless it may be to do so. Molière shows the ridiculous results that follow from pursuing so unbalanced an ideal of social behaviour.

The comedy of Shakespeare and Cervantes pierces deeper. It

shows that human actions can be comic, even if apparently virtuous or sensible; it faces the fundamental incongruity of existence. For good sense itself can be an object of laughter, sanity is sometimes as ridiculous as mania. To the eye of good sense Don Quixote is absurd; for he lives under the preposterous illusion that he is a knight-errant living in a world of romantic adventure. But Sancho, his servant, who is the embodiment of earthier values is also comical; events reveal his views as equally inadequate as a standard by which to measure the mysterious complexities of existence. Moreover, Don Quixote is a nobler figure than Sancho or than any of the ordinary men who perceive his illusions and mock them. Are we then to conclude that he is ridiculous in relation to reality, or that ordinary men are ridiculous in relation to the ideal? As Bagehot says 'There is an unalterable contradiction between the human mind and its employments.' No aspect of human life, no phase of human nature, can be contemplated wholly without irony.

This profounder comedy presents man less in relation to his fellows than to some absolute principle of harmony and perfection: equally with tragedy it is concerned with man confronting the eternal. No doubt tragedy communicates an intenser sense of life's beauty and mystery, and as such is nearer to its heart. But it may not give so balanced or accurate an estimate of it. For Bagehot is right: 'taken as a whole, the universe is absurd'. That is the reason why serious enthusiasts and stern reformers are so often slightly comic figures. No man who looks at life without a smile is seeing it as it really is.

THE CLASS SYSTEM

The Rich arrived in pairs
And also in Rolls Royces;
They talked of their affairs
In loud and strident voices.

(The Husbands and the Wives
Of this select society
Lead independent lives
Of infinite variety.)

The Poor arrived in Fords,
Whose features they resembled;
They laughed to see so many Lords
And Ladies all assembled.

The People in Between
Looked underdone and harassed
And out of place and mean
And horribly embarrassed.

For the hoary social curse
Gets hoarier and hoarier,
And it stinks a trifle worse
Than in the days of Queen Victoria,
When they married and gave in marriage,
They danced at the County Ball,
And some of them kept a carriage.
And the flood destroyed them all.

Hilaire Belloc

This admirable piece is, so far as I know, the only poem inspired
by that formidable, comical and incorrigible phenomenon, the
English class-system.

THE CLASSICS

The study of the Classics . . . teaches us to believe that there is
something really great and excellent in the world, surviving all
the shocks of accident and fluctuations of opinion, and raises
us above that low and servile fear which bows only to present
power and upstart authority . . . we feel the presence of that
power which gives immortality to human thoughts and actions,
and catch the flame of enthusiasm from all nations and ages.

It is hard to find in minds otherwise formed, either a real love
of excellence, or a belief that any excellence exists superior to
their own.

William Hazlitt, The Round Table

As a teacher of English literature I was sometimes asked what was the use of my subject. Hazlitt answered the question here better than I ever did.

There is a provinciality in time as well as in space. To feel ill-at-ease and out of place except in one's own period is to be a provincial in time. But he who has learned to look at life through the eyes in turn of Chaucer, of Donne, of Pope and of Thomas Hardy is freed from this limitation. He has become a cosmopolitan of the ages, and can regard his own period with the detachment which is a necessary foundation of wisdom.

COMMITMENT

I think it better that in times like these
A poet's mouth be silent, for in truth
We have no gift to set a statesman right;
He has had enough of meddling who can please
A young girl in the indolence of her youth,
Or an old man upon a winter's night.

W. B. Yeats, 'On Being Asked for a War Poem'

By all means let a poet, if he wants to, write *engagé* poems, protesting against this or that political evil or social injustice. But let him remember this. The only person who will benefit from them is himself; they will enhance his literary reputation among those who feel as he does. The evil or injustice, however, will remain exactly what it would have been if he had kept his mouth shut.

W. H. Auden, A Certain World

Some people nowadays hold that a writer should be 'committed', that is to say he should concern himself with the important public issues of his time and take a line about them. This is a well-meant but mistaken view. For one thing, writers seldom know enough about public issues for their opinion to be worth much. As Yeats says: 'We have no gift to set a statesman right.'

Further, as Auden points out, the words of writers rarely have any effect. Wilfred Owen said that he was not concerned with poetry, that his purpose in writing his war poems was 'to warn', to put people against war. To judge by the history of Europe since his day, he failed: his poems have not stopped a single shot from being fired. What they have done is to show that Owen was a distinguished inspired poet.

Of course great poets write about important subjects: the greatest poets concern themselves with the most important issues raised by the human condition. But they seldom identify these with topical public events of their time. Chaucer tells us nothing of what he thought about the Peasants' Revolt, nor do we hear Shakespeare's views about the conflicts stirred up by the Reformation which were rending Christendom in his day. We do not even know whether he had any views on the subject. It is true that Milton had strong views about the Civil War and proclaimed them loudly. But not in his poems; he confined them to his pamphlets. Even this seems to have been a waste of time. There is no evidence that these pamphlets did anything to affect the course of history: and they are unread today.

It should be added that 'committed' art is generally bad art. The creative imagination refuses to be made use of in this way. To quote Virginia Woolf on the novels of Meredith:

. . . his teaching is too insistent. He cannot, even to hear the profoundest secret, suppress his own opinions. And there is nothing that characters in fiction resent more. If, they seem to argue, we have been called into existence merely to express Mr. Meredith's views upon the universe, we would rather not exist at all. Thereupon they die. . .

The Common Reader

COMPLAINTS

I have always considered complaints of ill usage contemptible, whether from a seduced disappointed girl or a turned-out Prime Minister.

Lord Melbourne, Letters

Melbourne might well have added to his list an author who complains that he has been unjustly treated in a review. Indeed such an author is foolish as well as contemptible; for by voicing his resentment, he is likely to be pleasing his critic. No reviewer ever wrote a hostile notice without secretly hoping that his victim would read it.

COMPARATIVE

Reach, with your whiter hands, to me
Some crystal of the spring;
And I, about the cup shall see
Fresh lillies flourishing.

     Herrick, 'To the Water Nymphs, drinking at the Fountain'

If Herrick had said 'white' instead of 'whiter' the charm of the first line would be lost. It is the use – now an obsolete use – of the comparative which makes this charm so compelling. It is an ambiguous charm; for, I suppose, that Herrick simply meant that the hands of the water nymphs were whiter than lilies. But the fact that this is only stated implicitly and elliptically suggests that they possess some supreme ultimate radiancy of whiteness, that they are whiter than anything else in the whole world.

CONSERVATION

Degenerate Douglas! oh, the unworthy Lord!
Whom mere despite of heart could so far please,
And love of havoc, (for with such disease
Fame taxes him,) that he could send forth word
To level with the dust a noble horde,
A brotherhood of venerable Trees,
Leaving an ancient dome, and towers like these,
Beggared and outraged! – Many hearts deplored
The fate of those old Trees; and oft with pain
The traveller, at this day, will stop and gaze
On wrongs, which Nature scarcely seems to heed:
For sheltered places, bosoms, nooks, and bays,
And the pure mountains, and the gentle Tweed
And the green silent pastures, yet remain.

                                         Wordsworth

Wordsworth's lines strike home more sharply now than they can have ever done when they were written. For the growth of population and technological invention, with all the retinue of building and cars and litter that they bring with them, have proved more destructive than Degenerate Douglas can ever have been. Also one is no longer sure that green silent pastures have a safe chance of remaining anywhere. In the 1970s the last lines of the poem have become ironic as well as very beautiful.

CONTENT

Ah, sweet Content! where is thy mild abode?
Is it with shepherds and light-hearted swains
Which sing upon the downs and pipe abroad,
Tending their flocks and cattle on the plains?
Ah, sweet Content! where dost thou safely rest?
In heaven, with angels? which the praises sing
Of Him that made, and rules at His behest,
The minds and hearts of every living thing?
Ah, sweet Content! where doth thine harbour hold?
Is it in churches, with religious men
Which please the gods with prayers manifold,
And in their studies meditate it then?
    Whether thou dost in heaven or earth appear,
    Be where thou wilt, thou wilt not harbour here!

Barnabe Barnes

Barnes's terms of reference are a little out of date, so far as this world is concerned. Piping shepherds and studious church-goers form a very small part of the population of twentieth-century England. For this very reason, Barnes's enquiry is even more pertinent now than when it was written. 'Ah, sweet Content! where is thy mild abode?'

Where indeed we may well ask, nowadays? I do not suppose that, in fact, many people in the past were contented. But they thought they ought to be. Our age is different in that it does not any longer consider content a virtue. The reason is that in the past the world was thought of as essentially unchanging: and a wise man therefore learned to accept many of life's evils as inevitable and so sought to make the best of things as they were. Now however, the extraordinary and increasing alterations in our way of living brought by technology have taught us to regard the world as always in a state of change. From this, people have begun to argue that it is possible and right to assist in this process in such a way as to change it for the better. It follows that to accept things as they are, is to be treacherous to the cause of life.

This reasoning does not stand up to examination. History shows that inevitable changes in the past have not always been for the better: also that the world we know is still full of inevitable evils and likely to remain so. Surely then it is foolish to refuse to cultivate a contented spirit on the off chance that by so doing we may be happier in some uncertain and indefinite future.

CONTRASTS

So when the sun's broad beam has tir'd the sight,
All mild ascends the Moon's more sober light
Serene in Virgin Modesty she shines,
And unobserved the glaring orb declines.

Pope, 'Of the Characters of Women: an Epistle to a Lady'

How beautiful this is! and I have felt like it sometimes, turning from Kipling to Bridges or listening to Faures's music after Richard Strauss's. The beauty that steals its way gradually and insensibly into our hearts is not 'better' than that which sweeps us at once and irresistibly away. But it makes a refreshing change and in the end the spell it casts may prove equally powerful and often more enduring.

CRITICISM

A genuine criticism should, as I take it, reflect the colours, the light and shade, the soul and body of a work . . . what the essence of the work is, what passion has been touched, or how skilfully, what tone and movement the author's mind imparts to his subject or receives from it . . .

William Hazlitt, 'On Criticism' – Table Talk

. . . The function of the aesthetic critic is to distinguish, to analyse, and separate from its adjuncts, the virtue by which a picture, a landscape, a fair personality in the life or in a book, produces this special impression of beauty or pleasure, to indicate what the source of that impression is, and under what conditions it is experienced . . . He will remember always that beauty exists in many forms. To him all periods, types, schools of taste, are in themselves equal. In all ages there have been some excellent workmen, and some excellent work done.

Walter Pater, The Renaissance

Two admirable comments on the function of criticism. They make clear that its aim should be to interpret the work they are writing about and to help readers to appreciate it, by defining and analysing those qualities that make it precious and by indicating the angle of vision from which its beauties are visible.

Many critics do not realize their function. They aim not to appreciate, but to judge; they seek first to draw up laws about literature and then to bully readers into accepting these laws. In the nineteenth century Matthew Arnold sought elegantly to bully his readers into acquiescing in his view that Milton was a greater poet than Chaucer: recently I read a piece by a respected modern critic who sought, less elegantly, to bully me into agreeing with him that D. H. Lawrence was a greater writer than Thomas Hardy. Both efforts failed, and inevitably. You cannot force a taste on someone else, you cannot argue people into enjoyment. Many people continue to think Chaucer as great a poet as Milton; and I go on rating Lawrence much below Hardy.

Still less are these magisterial critics able to influence authors. Most authors agree with Turgenev, who said that criticism was 'a delightful pastime for critics and sometimes delightful for readers; but it had nothing at all to do with the process by which Art is achieved.'

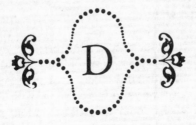

DEATH

It is therfore Death alone that can suddenly make man to know himselfe. He tells the proud and insolent, that they are but Abjects, and humbles them at the instant; makes them crie, complaine and repent, yea, even to hate their forepassed happinesse. He takes the account of the rich, and proves him a begger; a naked begger, which hath interest in nothing, but in the gravell that fills his mouth. He holds a Glasse before the eyes of the most beautifull, and makes them see therein, their deformitie and rottennesse; and they acknowledge it.

O eloquent, just and mightie Death! whom none could advise, thou hast persuaded; what none hath dared, thou hast done; and whom all the world hath flattered, thou only hath cast out of the world and despised: thou has drawne together all the farre stretched greatnesse, all the pride, crueltie, and ambition of man, and covered it all over with these two narrow words, *Hic iacet.*

Sir Walter Raleigh, The History of the World

... this day we're facing death, maybe, and death should be a poor, untidy thing, though it's a queen that dies.

J. M. Synge, Deirdre of the Sorrows

Two contrasting comments on death, but both just. Synge's remark is vividly true of the actual death of most of us. Man, however noble or wise, does in his last moments usually decline to the condition of a struggling animal. 'A poor untidy thing' well describes this condition. 'It is as natural to die as to be born', said Bacon; a process, he might have added, no prettier nor more dignified.

But if we turn from the spectacle of the individual dying man to contemplate it as a fact of human history, death grows to incarnate itself as a majestic king of terrors; and also as a revealer of truth; in particular of the stern but calming truth which says that not only individuals but human institutions and causes must at last come to an end – that, as much now as when Raleigh wrote, death will draw together all the purposeful vital manifestations of human energy, good and evil alike, and will cover their lifeless forms all over with the 'two narrow words *Hic iacet*'.

Death was Raleigh's most inspiring subject. Some years later – it is thought on the actual night before his execution – he wrote the following verse:

> Even such is time, which takes in trust
> Our youth, our joys, and all we have,
> And pays us but with age and dust:
> Who in the dark and silent grave
> When we have wandered all our ways
> Shuts up the story of our days.
> And from which earth and grave and dust
> The Lord shall raise me up I trust.

Now that I have grown old enough to see my contemporaries die, and after a reasonably long life, I often find myself repeating

> When we have wandered all our ways
> Shuts up the story of our days.

The life stories of these contemporaries of mine have not been cut off uncompleted. Rather they can now be read as a whole from the start to finish; and the book then shut.

DEMOCRACY, AUTOCRACY, BUREAUCRACY ETC

Mr. Chesterton once chid me, in a brilliant essay, for not cherishing in my heart the ideal of democracy. It is quite true that I don't believe at all firmly in (what has always been to Mr.

Chesterton a dark and mystical reality) the wisdom of the people. I would not stake sixpence on the people's capacity for governing itself, and not a penny on its capacity for governing me. Democracy, wherever it has been tried, has failed as a means of increasing the sum of human happiness. Autocracy, aristocracy, bureaucracy, and all the other modes of government have similarly failed. In theory they are all of them admirable, but they won't work in practice. They would, doubtless, if man were a rational and an unselfish animal. But man is not built that way, and cannot be trusted either to wield power wisely or to obey wise ordinances. He means well; but original sin and muddle-headedness, between them, make havoc of his good intentions. Political history is the term by which we dignify the record of his ludicrous flounderings. And the political history of the future will be just as amusing or depressing, you may be sure. And let us smile rather than be indignant, since we cannot hope to remedy the nature of things, and since, after all, there will be, as there has ever been, a general impression that life is worth living. The vitality of man will always rise superior to the circumstances of existence.

Max Beerbohm, Around Theatres

DENUNCIATION

. . . Carlyle, Froude, Ruskin, all bore me in their prophetic capacity. It is a cheap line to denounce, it satisfies the sense that something ought to be done: I am weary of denunciation. We of this generation all go about the world each abusing everybody else, and each forgetting to amend himself. The world's evils are many and patent. We can all do much to cure them, 'here a little and there a little,' but do not let us expend our energy in meaningless abuse. Mankind will not be saved by that. I remember listening with sorrow to Ruskin describing a railway journey from Carnforth to Oxford. He ridiculed everyone whom he had seen, described his fellow passengers without a touch of sympathy, and ended by saying 'I saw over 700 people on the way, and not one face had a look of happiness.' I looked at Ruskin's own face: that certainly had not. I should have like to ask him what contribution he had tried to make to the happiness of those whom he met.

Bishop Creighton, Life and Letters of Mandell Creighton

How admirably unsentimental is this plea for the tolerant spirit! It comes from no exaggerated opinion of human merit. On the contrary, it faces – and this without undue cynicism – the plain fact that man is incorrigibly imperfect. Denunciation is foolish because it is unhelpful. It implies that things can be improved more than in fact they can. As such it is disagreeable in itself; and it only makes worse a life already all too full of incurable evils.

DIALOGUE

Mrs. Millamant . . . Ah! I'll never marry, unless I am first made sure of my will and pleasure.

Mirabell. Would you have 'em both before marriage? or will you be contented with the first now, and stay for the other till after grace?

Mrs. Millamant. Ah! don't be impertinent. – My dear liberty, shall I leave thee? my faithful solitude, my darling contemplation, must I bid you then adieu? Ah-h, adieu – my morning thoughts, agreeable wakings, indolent slumbers, all ye *douceurs*, ye *sommeils du matin*, adieu? I can't do't, 'tis more than impossible – Positively, Mirabell, I'll lie abed in a morning as long as I please.

Mirabell. Then, I'll get up in a morning as early as I please.

Mrs. Millamant. Ah! idle creature, get up when you will – and d'ye hear, I won't be called names after I'm married; positively I won't be called names.

Mirabell. Names!

Mrs. Millamant. Ay, as wife, spouse, my dear, joy, jewel, love, sweetheart, and the rest of that nauseous cant, in which men and their wives are so fulsomely familiar – I shall never bear that – good Mirabell, don't let us be familiar or fond, nor kiss before folks, like my Lady Fadler and Sir Francis: nor go to Hyde Park together the first Sunday in a new chariot, to provoke eyes and whispers; and then never be seen there together again; as if we were proud of one another the first week, and ashamed of one another ever after. Let us never visit together, nor go to a play together; but let us be very strange and well bred; let us be as strange as if we had been married a great while; and as well bred as if we were not married at all.

William Congreve, The Way of the World

Pegeen. You should have had great people in your family, I'm thinking, with the little, small feet you have, and you with a kind of a quality name, the like of what you'd find on the great powers and potentates of France and Spain.

Christy. We were great, surely, with wide and windy acres of rich Munster land.

Pegeen. Wasn't I telling you, and you a fine, handsome young fellow with a noble brow?

Christy. Is it me?

Pegeen. Aye. Did you never hear that from the young girls where you come from in the west or south?

Christy. I did not, then. Oh, they're bloody liars in the naked parish where I grew a man.

Pegeen. If they are itself, you've heard it these days, I'm thinking, and you walking the world telling out your story to young girls or old.

Christy. I've told my story no place till this night, Pegeen Mike, and it's foolish I was here, maybe, to be talking free; but you're decent people, I'm thinking, and yourself a kindly woman, the way I wasn't fearing you at all.

Pegeen. You've said the like of that, maybe, in every cot and cabin where you've met a young girl on your way.

Christy. I've said it nowhere till this night, I'm telling you; for I've seen none the like of you the eleven long days I am walking the world, looking over a low ditch or a high ditch on my north or south, into stony, scattered fields, or scribes of bog, where you'd see young, limber girls, and fine, prancing women making laughter with the men.

Pegeen. If you weren't destroyed travelling, you'd have as much talk and streeleen, I'm thinking, as Owen Roe O'Sullivan or the poets of the Dingle Bay; and I've heard all times it's the poets are your like – fine, fiery fellows with great rages when their temper's roused.

J. M. Synge, The Playboy of the Western World

The author of a realistic play in prose is confronted with an immediate inescapable problem. If he is to please his audience, his dialogue must express his meaning clearly, and delightfully: but if it is to be convincing, it must also give the effect of spontaneous conversation. This might seem impossible: in real life people do not express themselves clearly, let alone delightfully. However some writers have achieved the apparently impossible. Congreve has done it in the passage quoted above. We almost hear the characters speaking, so exactly does the movement of the sentences suggest the intonations and inflexions and pauses and hesitations of their voices. Yet the whole composes into a piece of prose as melodious as an aria of Mozart. Congreve contrives to make his realistic dialogue not only delightful but beautiful. He said he was helped by the Earl of Montague who introduced him into high society where he was able to hear the best conversation.

Synge, though less exquisitely, also contrives to make his dialogue at once eloquent and realistic. But he found his models at the other end of the social scale. 'I got more aid,' he said, 'than any learning would have given me from a chink in the floor of the old Wicklow House, where I was staying, that let me hear what was being said by the servant girls in the kitchen.' If these authors spoke the truth, it appears that the standard of conversation, alike in kitchens and drawing-rooms, has sadly declined from what it was in the periods in which each lived.

This is less surprising in Synge's case; for the Wicklow girls he speaks of are likely to have been illiterate or nearly so. Words by them were learnt through the ear; and words learnt through the ear, for some reason unknown to me, stir a stronger imaginative and sensual response than words learnt through the eye. Children, before they learn to read, enjoy the sound and flavour of words as they seldom do later. Elizabethan literature shows a zest for language now lost; and, to most Elizabethans, language was something spoken rather than something written. It is a sad and bewildering truth that literary style has got worse since everyone has learned to read.

DOING GOOD

He who would do good to another must do it in Minute
Particulars:
  General Good is the plea of the scoundrel, hypocrite and
flatterer, . . .

William Blake, 'Jerusalem' : 111

Like many of Blake's remarks, this is too sweeping: like more of
Blake's remarks it is in essence true. We judge individuals to be
good, because of the 'minute particular' actions we see them do.
We judge them to be bad for the same reason. Fanatics and
terrorists often profess general good as their motive. But since
their particular actions are evil, they reveal themselves to be evil
persons.

DORSET

Very few people respond to a particular landscape for purely
aesthetic reasons; pleasure in its beauty is generally mixed with
and intensified by associations. Myself I realize that the Cotswolds
and the Yorkshire Dales are as beautiful, perhaps even more
beautiful, than Dorset. But they do not move me so deeply. For I
have known Dorset ever since I can remember and its downs and
woods, its chalky sea-coast and dark stretches of heathland, its
beech groves and clumps of immemorial yew trees are inextricably
intertwined with memories of childhood, of youth, of middle age;
and saturated with the sentiment awoken in me by these memories.
Now in old age the sight of them stirs me as no other landscape
does. It is lucky for me that Dorset has produced Thomas Hardy
who, since he is one of the greatest of authors that ever lived,
does it justice.

It was nearly midnight on the eve of St. Thomas's, the shortest
day in the year. A desolating wind wandered from the north
over the hill whereon Oak had watched the yellow waggon and
its occupant in the sunshine of a few days earlier.
  Norcombe Hill – not far from lonley Toller-Down – was one

of the spots which suggest to a passer-by that he is in the presence of a shape approaching the indestructible as nearly as any to be found on earth. It was a featureless convexity of chalk and soil – an ordinary specimen of those smoothly-outlined protuberances of the globe which may remain undisturbed on some great day of confusion, when far grander heights and dizzy granite precipices topple down.

The hill was covered on its northern side by an ancient and decaying plantation of beeches, whose upper verge formed a line over the crest, fringing its arched curve against the sky, like a mane. To-night these trees sheltered the southern slope from the keenest blasts, which smote the wood and floundered through it with a sound as of grumbling, or gushed over its crowning boughs in a weakened moan. The dry leaves in the ditch simmered and boiled in the same breezes, a tongue of air occasionally ferreting out a few, and sending them spinning across the grass. A group or two of the latest in date amongst this dead multitude had remained till this very mid-winter time on the twigs which bore them, and in falling rattled against the trunks with smart taps.

Between this half-wooded, half-naked hill, and the vague, still horizon that its summit indistinctly commanded, was a mysterious sheet of fathomless shade – the sounds from which suggested that what it concealed bore some humble resemblance to features here. The thin grasses, more or less coating the hill, were touched by the wind in breezes of differing powers, and almost of differing natures – one rubbing the blades heavily, another raking them piercingly, another brushing them like a soft broom. The instinctive act of human-kind was to stand and listen, and learn how the trees on the right and the trees on the left wailed or chaunted to each other in the regular antiphonies of a cathedral choir; how hedges and other shapes to leeward then caught the note, lowering it to the tenderest sob; and how the hurrying gust then plunged into the south, to be heard no more.

The sky was clear – remarkably clear – and the twinkling of all the stars seemed to be but throbs of one body, timed by a common pulse. The North Star was directly in the wind's eye, and since evening the Bear had swung round it outwardly to the east, till he was now at a right angle with the meridian. A difference of colour in the stars – oftener read of than seen in England – was really perceptible here. The kingly brilliancy of Sirius pierced the eye with a steely glitter, the star called Capella was yellow, Aldebaran and Betelgueux shone with a fiery red.

To persons standing alone on a hill during a clear midnight such as this, the roll of the world eastward is almost a palpable movement. The sensation may be caused by the panoramic glide of the stars past earthly objects, which is perceptible in a few minutes of stillness, or by the better outlook upon space that a hill affords, or by the wind, or by the solitude; but whatever be its origin, the impression of riding along is vivid and abiding. The poetry of motion is a phrase much in use, and to enjoy the epic form of that gratification it is necessary to stand on a hill at a small hour of the night, and, having first expanded with a sense of difference from the mass of civilised mankind, who are dreamwrapt and disregardful of all such proceedings at this time, long and quietly watch your stately progress through the stars. After such a nocturnal reconnoitre it is hard to get back to earth, and to believe that the consciousness of such majestic speeding is derived from a tiny human frame.

Far From the Madding Crowd

The sheep-washing pool was a perfectly circular basin of brickwork in the meadows, full of the clearest water. To birds on the wing, its glassy surface, reflecting the light sky, must have been visible for miles around as a glistening Cyclops' eye in a green face. The grass about the margin at this season was a sight to remember long – in a minor sort of way. Its activity in sucking the moisture from the rich damp sod was almost a process observable by the eye. The outskirts of this level water-meadow were diversified by rounded and hollow pastures, where just now every flower that was not a buttercup was a daisy. The river slid along noiselessly as a shade, the swelling reeds and sedge forming a flexible palisade along its moist brink. To the north of the mead were trees, the leaves of which were new, soft, and moist, not yet having stiffened and darkened under summer sun and drought, their colour being yellow beside a green – green beside a yellow. From the recesses of this knot of foliage the loud notes of three cuckoos were resounding through the still air.

Far From the Madding Crowd

. . . A tract of country unaltered from that sinister condition which made Caesar anxious every year to get clear of its glooms before the autumnal equinox, a kind of landscape and weather which leads travellers from the South to describe our Island as Homer's Cimmerian land, was not, on the face of it, friendly to women.

It might reasonably have been supposed that she was listening to the wind, which rose somewhat as the night advanced, and laid hold of the attention. The wind, indeed, seemed made for the scene, as the scene seemed made for the hour. Part of its tone was quite special; what was heard there could be heard nowhere else. Gusts in innumerable series followed each other from the northwest, and when each one of them raced past the sound of its progress resolved into three. Treble, tenor, and bass notes were to be found therein. The general ricochet of the whole over pits and prominences had the gravest pitch of the chime. Next there could be heard the baritone buzz of a holly tree. Below these in force, above them in pitch, a dwindled voice strove hard at a husky tune, which was the peculiar local sound alluded to. Thinner and less immediately traceable than the other two, it was far more impressive than either. In it lay what may be called the linguistic peculiarity of the heath; and being audible nowhere on earth off a heath, it afforded a shadow of reason for the woman's tenseness which continued as unbroken as ever.

Throughout the blowing of these plaintive November winds that note bore a great resemblance to the ruins of human song which remain to the throat of fourscore and ten. It was a worn whisper, dry and papery, and it brushed so distinctly across the ear that, by the accustomed, the material minutiae in which it originated could be realised as by touch. It was the united products of infinitesimal vegetable causes, and these were neither stems, leaves, fruit, blades, prickles, lichen, nor moss.

The Return of the Native

Hardy writes about Dorset towns as truthfully and imaginatively as he does about its countryside:

When Elizabeth-Jane opened the hinged casement next morning, the mellow air brought in the feel of imminent autumn almost as distinctly as if she had been in the remotest hamlet. Casterbridge was the complement of the rural life around; not its urban opposite. Bees and butterflies in the corn-fields at the top of the town, who desired to get to the meads at the bottom, took no circuitous course, but flew straight down High Street without any apparent consciousness that they were traversing strange latitudes. And in autumn airy spheres of thistledown floated into the same street, lodged upon the shop fronts, blew into drains; and innumerable tawny and yellow leaves skimmed along the pavement, and stole through people's doorways into their passages, with a hesitating scratch on the floor, like the skirts of timid visitors.

The Mayor of Casterbridge

DRESS

(1)

. . . The magic of art is that it inspires inanimate objects with some of the qualities of life, so that they can create pleasure, and satisfy obscure needs for colour, or rhythm, or form: the art of dress perhaps brings these qualities into the closest relationship with ourselves; and a woman who has no use for it must have some secret obliquity, arrogance or malady of soul. I suspect anyone self-satisfied enough to refuse lawful pleasure: we are not sufficiently rich in our separate resources to reject the graces of the universe when offered; it is bad manners, like refusing to eat when invited to dinner; and indeed I should call humility in religion the equivalent of good manners in ordinary life.

Freya Stark

. . . The beautiful woman expresses an aspect of the divine purpose, one of God's aims, as well as a man of genius does,

or a virtuous woman. She feels this, and hence her pride. . . .
Why forbid her to make the most of the gift bestowed upon
her, or to give the diamond allotted to her its due setting? By
adorning herself woman accomplishes a duty; she practises an
art, an exquisite art, in a sense the most charming of arts. Do
not let us be misled by the smile which certain words provoke
in the frivolous. We award the palm of genius to the Greek
artist who succeeded in solving the most delicate of problems,
that of adorning the human body, that is to say, adorning per-
fection itself, and yet some people wish to see nothing more
than an affair of chiffons in the attempt to collaborate with the
finest work of God – woman's beauty! Women's toilette with
all its refinements is a great art in its own way.

Ernest Renan

Serious thinkers, for the most part, have made little of dress.
Because, I suppose, of its connection with personal vanity, they
look on a concern with it as a sign of triviality. In fact, as Renan
and Dame Freya Stark rightly point out, the concern shows that
they realize dress to be a mode through which man and still more
woman expresses his or her aesthetic sense. It is therefore an art;
not an austere heavy-weight art but a light pleasure-loving,
pleasure-giving art. It is right that Herrick, the arch-poet of
pleasure, should write of it so often and so gaily:

> Whenas in silks my Julia goes,
> Then, then (me thinks) how sweetly flowes
> The liquefaction of her clothes.
>
> Next, when I cast mine eyes and see
> That brave Vibration each way free;
> O how that glittering taketh me!

'Upon Julia's Clothes'

> Thy Azure Robe, I did behold,
> As ayrie as the leaves of gold;
> Which erring here, and wand'ring there,
> Pleas'd with transgression ev'ry where:
> Sometimes 'two'd pant, and sigh, and heave,

As if to stir it scarce had leave:
But having got it; thereupon,
'Two'd make a brave expansion.
And pounc't with Stars, it shew'd to me
Like a *Celestial Canopie*.
Sometimes 'two'd blaze, and then abate,
Like to a flame growne moderate:
Sometimes away 'two'd wildly fling;
Then to thy thighs so closely cling,
That some conceit did melt me downe,
As Lovers fall into a swoone:

. . .

'Julia's Petticoat'

Three hundred years later Virginia Woolf, speaking of a ball dress, strikes a similar smiling delighted note.

Nancy, dressed at enormous expense by the greatest artists in Paris, stood there looking as if her body had merely put forth, of its own accord, a green frill.

Mrs. Dalloway

(11)

Dress also has significance as expressing not just an individual but an age and a civilization. As in any one period people speak and think, so also do they dress. This is why the performance of a Shakespeare play in modern dress, though interesting as an occasional experiment, is ultimately wrong. It is only girls dressed like Juliet who declare their love in words like Juliet, with the same mixtures of formality and richness, the same unselfconscious full-blooded delight in splendour. In Shakespeare's day people did not shrink from speaking splendidly. 'Your Majesty must go to bed to content the people', said Sir Robert Cecil to the dying Queen Elizabeth. 'Is *must* a word to be used to Princes!' she replied superbly. So might have spoken Shakespeare's Cleopatra or Webster's Duchess of Malfi: but not Queen Victoria. Nor did Queen Victoria dress herself as Queen Elizabeth did, with a hieratic magnificence, that was the visible expression of her sense of herself as the Lord's Anointed, the Regent of God on Earth.

Robert Cecil Himself, though not a poet like Raleigh or Sidney, could clothe his words, as he clothed his body, with an Elizabethan grandeur. During his last illness, he spoke to his friend Sir Walter Cope in the very accents of Shakespeare's John of Gaunt. 'Ease and pleasure quake to hear of death; but my life, full of cares and miseries, desireth to be dissolved.'

DRESSING TABLES

And now, unveiled, the toilet stands displayed,
Each silver vase in mystic order laid.
First; robed in white, the nymph intent adores,
With head uncovered, the cosmetic powers.
A heavenly image in the glass appears,
To that she bends, to that her eyes she rears;
The inferior priestess, at her altar's side,
Trembling begins the sacred rites of pride.
Unnumbered treasures ope at once, and here
The various offerings of the world appear;
From each she nicely culls with curious toil,
And decks the Goddess with the glittering spoil.
This casket India's glowing gems unlocks,
And all Arabia breathes from yonder box.
The tortoise here and elephant unite,
Transformed to combs, the speckled, and the white.
Here files of pins extend their shining rows.
Puffs, powders, patches, bibles, billet-doux.
Now awful beauty puts on all its arms;
The fair each moment rises in her charms,
Repairs her smiles, awakens every grace,
And calls forth all the wonders of her face;
Sees by degrees a purer blush arise,
And keener lightnings quicken in her eyes.

Pope, 'The Rape of the Lock'

I watched the Lady Caroline
Bind up her dark and beauteous hair;
Her face was rosy in the glass,
And 'twixt the coils her hands would pass
    White in the candleshine.

Her bottles on the table lay,
Stoppered, yet sweet of violet;
Her image in the mirror stooped
To view those locks as lightly looped
  As cherry-boughs in May.

The snowy night lay dim without,
I heard the Waits their sweet song sing;
The window smouldered keen with frost;
Yet still she twisted, sleeked and tossed
  Her beauteous hair about.

                             Walter De La Mare

These surely are the two prettiest dressing tables in English literature. But they are different. That of Pope's Belinda is an 18th-century Rococo confection, set firmly in London and surveyed with a satirical eye, whose pleasure in the prettiness of its appointments does not exclude amusement at its follies, the confused mixture it presents of 'Puffs, powders, patches, bibles, billet-doux'.

Lady Caroline's on the other hand is a 'Romantic' dressing table, given a touch of glamour and strangeness by the contrast between its candle-lit violet-scented tranquillity and the dark snow-bound winter night outside.

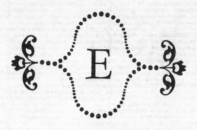

EIGHTEENTH CENTURY

My Dear William,

Our severest winter, commonly called the spring, is now
over, and I find myself seated in my favourite recess, the green-
house. In such a situation, so silent, so shady, where no human
foot is heard, and where only my myrtles presume to peep in
at the window, you may suppose I have no interruption to
complain of, and that my thoughts are perfectly at my com-
mand. But the beauties of the spot are themselves an interrup-
tion; my attention is called upon by those very myrtles, by a
double row of grass pinks just beginning to blossom, and by a
bed of beans already in bloom; and you are to consider it, if
you please, as no small proof of my regard that though you
have so many powerful rivals, I disengage myself from them all,
and devote this hour entirely to you . . .

Letters of William Cowper

. . . Nothing could have more of that melancholy which once
used to please me, than that day's journey: for after having
pass'd through my favourite woods in the forest, with a
thousand reveries of past pleasures, I rid over hanging hills,
whose tops were edged with groves, and whose feet water'd
with winding rivers, listening to the falls of cataracts below,
and the murmuring of winds above. The gloomy verdure of
Stonor succeeded to these, and then the shades of the evening
overtook me. The moon rose in the clearest sky I ever saw, by
whose solemn light I paced on slowly, without company, or any
interruption to the range of my thoughts. About a mile before

I reach'd Oxford, all the night bells toll'd, in different notes; the clocks of every college answer'd one another; and told me, some in a deeper, some in a softer voice, that it was eleven o'clock.

All this was no ill preparation to the life I have led since; among those old walls, venerable galleries, stone porticos, studious walks and solitary scenes of the University. I wanted nothing but a black gown and a salary, to be as mere a bookworm as any there. I conform'd myself to the college hours, was roll'd up in books and wrapt in meditation, lay in one of the most ancient, dusky parts of the University, and was as dead to the world as any hermit of the desert. If anything was awake or alive in me, it was a little vanity, such as even those good men us'd to entertain, when the monks of their own order extoll'd their piety and abstractedness. For I found myself receiv'd with a sort of respect, which this idle part of mankind, the Learned, pay to their own species; who are as considerable here, as the busy, the gay, and the ambitious are in your world. Indeed I was so treated, that I could not but sometimes ask myself in my mind, what college I was founder of, or what library I had built? Methinks, I do very ill to return to the world again, to leave the only place where I make a figure, and, from seeing myself seated with dignity on the most conspicuous shelves of a library, go to contemplate this wretched person in the abject condition of lying at a lady's feet in Bolton Street.

The Letters of Alexander Pope

Not knowing whether you are yet returned from your sea-water, I write at random to you. For me, I am come to my resting-place, and find it very necessary, after living for a month in a house with three women that laughed from morning to night, and would allow nothing to the sulkiness of my disposition. Company and cards at home, parties by land and water abroad, and (what they call) *doing something*, that is, racketting about from morning to night, are occupations, I find, that wear out my spirits; especially in a situation where one might sit still, and be alone with pleasure; for the place was a hill like Clifden, opening to a very extensive and diversified landscape, with the Thames, which is navigable, running at its foot.

I would wish to continue here (in a very different scene, it must be confessed) till Michaelmas; but I fear I must come to town much sooner. Cambridge is a delight of a place, now there is nobody in it. I do believe you would like it, if you knew what it was without inhabitants. It is they, I assure you, that get it an ill name and spoil all. Our friend Dr. * * (one of its nuisances) is not expected here again in a hurry. He is gone to his grave with five fine mackerel (large and full of roe) in his belly. He eat them all at one dinner; but his fate was a turbot on Trinity Sunday, of which he left little for the company besides bones. He had not been hearty all the week; but after this sixth fish he never held up his head more, and a violent looseness carried him off. They said he made a very good end.

The Letters of Thomas Gray

... Oh! my dear Sir, don't you find that nine parts in ten of the world are of no use but to make you wish yourself with that tenth part? I am so far from growing used to mankind by living amongst them, that my natural ferocity and wildness does but every day grow worse. They tire me, they fatigue me; I don't know what to do with them; I don't know what to say to them; I fling open the windows, and fancy I want air; and when I get by myself, I undress myself, and seem to have had people in my pockets, in my plaits, and on my shoulders! I indeed find this fatigue worse in the country than in town, because one can avoid it there and has more resources; but it is there too. I fear 'tis growing old; but I literally seem to have murdered a man whose name was Ennui, for his ghost is ever before me. They say there is no English word for *ennui*; I think you may translate it most literally by what is called 'entertaining people,' and 'doing the honours': that is, you sit an hour with somebody you don't know and don't care for, talk about the wind and the weather, and ask a thousand foolish questions, which all begin with, 'I think you live a good deal in the country', or, 'I think you don't love this thing or that'. Oh! 'tis dreadful!

The Letters of Horace Walpole

... It has just struck eleven, and the whole house, excepting

Sally and me, have been in bed near an hour, and we have set at the open window listening to the Nightingales and watching for the post man with the most eager impatience. I do not know what Sally expected; whatever it was she has got it, for she has two letters (I thought myself sure one was for me), and she is in as good a humour as I am bad. We had first to bribe the post-man to open his bag (for naturally they do not give them till morning), then to tie the letters to a string and draw them in at the window. All this was for you, Sir, and then not a line. I had four other foolish letters I might just as well have receiv'd tomorrow without any fuss at all.

Nothing can be a greater contrast than my life here and that I usually lead. As the clock strikes eight I am down at Prayers, then breakfast, then I give Caroline her lessons as usual, read or write for a little while till my Mother sends for me to help her in teaching her School Girls. I acquit myself tant bien que mal, and often wonder what you, and still more Sol, would say to see me stuck up in the midst of an old ruin'd Abbey teaching some little beggar Girls to spell and sing. We dine at three, are out all evening after tea, return generally to have some music, in which the Chaplain's wife principally shines. She has a very fine voice d'un très gros Volume; it makes the house echo again, and tho' I din the right note in her ears as loud as I can, she disdains such narrow limits, and with laudable perseverance keeps constantly a half note too high or too low the whole way thro'. At nine ye bell rings for Prayers, then supper, and at ten not a mouse is stirring in the whole House. I hope you are edified with the length of my letter and the importance of its contents.

Lady Bessborough to Granville Leveson Gower, 1797
Lord Granville Leveson Gower: Private Correspondence

The authors of these extracts lived different lives and were themselves very different people. Pope was a quarrelsome genius; Horace Walpole a brilliant young man of fashion, Cowper a gentle rural recluse, Gray a fastidious academic, Lady Bessborough a mature woman writing to her lover. Yet these extracts have something in common: unmistakably they all sound the 18th-century tone. It is the best possible tone for private and social intercourse, for letters and memoirs and conversation. In a way that no other period does, it blends the relaxed and the mannerly, the accomplished and the unselfconscious, the intimate and the stylish. Compared with it the Elizabethan tone sounds too ceremonious, the Victorian too earnest, that of our own day too self-conscious and slipshod. None of these others achieve the easy graceful agreeability of the 18th century.

Anyone starting a school of manners should make their pupils soak themselves in the informal literature of that sociable period.

ENDINGS

Those who know best how to begin a book or poem know best how to end it, Milton for example or Hardy. Milton is a master of the quiet ending, the 'dying fall'; as in the last lines of *Paradise Lost*:

> Some natural tears they dropp'd, but wiped them soon;
> The World was all before them, where to choose
> Their place of rest, and Providence their guide.
> They, hand in hand, with wandering steps and slow,
> Through Eden took their solitary way.

From *Samson Agonistes*:

> His servants he, with new acquist
> Of true experience from this great event,
> With peace and consolation hath dismiss'd,
> And calm of mind all passion spent.

Here are two of Hardy's endings: they also are quiet.

The candle held by his father shed its waving light upon John's face and uniform as with a farewell smile he turned on the doorstone, backed by the black night; and in another moment he had plunged into the darkness, the ring of his smart step dying away upon the bridge as he joined his companions-in-arms, and went off to blow his trumpet till silenced for ever upon one of the bloody battle-fields of Spain.

The Trumpet-Major

Immediately they had dropped down the hill she entered the churchyard, going to a secluded corner behind the bushes, where rose the unadorned stone that marked the last bed of Giles Winterborne. As this solitary and silent girl stood there in the moonlight, a straight slim figure, clothed in a plaitless gown, the contours of womanhood so undeveloped as to be scarcely perceptible in her, the marks of poverty and toil effaced by the misty hour, she touched sublimity at points, and looked almost like a being who had rejected with indifference the attribute of sex for the loftier quality of abstract humanism. She stooped down and cleared away the withered flowers, that Grace and herself had laid there the previous week, and put her fresh ones in their place.

'Now, my own, own love,' she whispered, 'you are mine, and only mine; for she has forgot 'ee at last, although for her you died! But I – whenever I get up I'll think of 'ee, and whenever I lie down, I'll think of 'ee again. Whenever I plant the young larches I'll think that none can plant as you planted; and whenever I split a gad, and whenever I turn the cider wring, I'll say none could do it like you. If ever I forget your name let me forget home and heaven! . . . But no, no, my love, I never can forget 'ee; for you was a good man, and did good things!'

The Woodlanders

These quiet endings, coming as they do after tense and tragic dramas, are designed to send us away, as Milton phrases it, in 'calm of mind all passion spent'.

Another memorable quiet ending is that of *Wuthering Heights*:

I sought, and soon discovered, the three headstones on the slope next the moor: the middle one grey, and half buried in heath: Edgar Linton's only harmonised by the turf and moss creeping up its foot; Heathcliff's still bare.

I lingered round them, under the benign sky; watched the moths fluttering among the heath and harebells, listened to the soft wind breathing through the grass, and wondered how any one could ever imagine unquiet slumbers for the sleepers in that quiet earth.

Here the quiet is not one of exhaustion but of harmony.

Wuthering Heights is often spoken of as a dark and terrible tragedy. Indeed it does include dark and terrible passages, for Emily Brontë faced life at its most alarming. But her drama does not end in disaster as Hardy's do. On the contrary, discord is resolved, harmony restored; and this not by the arbitrary will of the author but as the inevitable logical conclusion of all that has gone before. *Wuthering Heights* is one of the few great novels with a convincingly happy ending.

The most original ending I know is that of *Twelfth Night*. For two and a half hours in the golden Never-Never Land of Illyria, we have watched a gay company of romantic gallants and lovely ladies, and pert maids and motley-clad jesters and comical drunken knights frolic and fantasticate before us; at last they make their bows and curtsies and dance off. The jester is left alone to sing a song to the audience before he too says goodbye. But what he chooses to sing is no bright courtly Illyrian valediction but a sad mocking little English street song set to a sad minor-key little street tune which wafts us back, as with a rueful smile, to the commonplace imperfect world we have in reality to live in and whose refrain is 'Hey, ho, the wind and the rain, for the rain it raineth every day'.

Its last verse runs:

A great while ago the world begun,
    With hey, ho, the wind and the rain,
But that's all one, our play is done,
    And we'll strive to please you every day.

The most tremendous ending I know is that which closes Izaak Walton's life of John Donne: the spacious dead march of the penultimate paragraph and then, following it, like a trumpet call, the brief triumphant last sentence:

He was earnest and unwearied in the search of knowledge; with which, his vigorous soul is now satisfied, and employed in a continual praise of that God, that first breathed it into his active body; that body, which once was a Temple of the Holy Ghost, and is now become a small quantity of Christian dust.
    But I shall see it reanimated.

ENGLISH LANDSCAPE

The night was winter in his roughest mood;
The morning sharp and clear. But now at noon
Upon the southern side of the slant hills,
And where the woods fence off the northern blast,
The season smiles, resigning all its rage,
And has the warmth of May. The vault is blue
Without a cloud, and white without a speck
The dazzling splendour of the scene below.
Again the harmony comes o'er the vale;
And through the trees I view th' embattled tow'r
Whence all the music. I again perceive
The soothing influence of the wafted strains,
And settle in soft musings as It read
The walk, still verdant, under oaks and elms,
Whose outspread branches overarch the glade.
The roof, though moveable through all its length
As the wind sways it, has yet well suffic'd,
And, intercepting in their silent fall
The frequent flakes, has kept a path for me.
No noise is here, or none that hinders thought.
The redbreast warbles still, but is content
With slender notes, and more than half suppress'd:
Pleas'd with his solitude, and flitting light
From spray to spray, where'er he rests he shakes
From many a twig the pendent drops of ice,
That tinkle in the wither'd leaves below.
Stillness, accompanied with sounds so soft,
Charms more than silence . . .

William Cowper, 'The Task'

The snow has left the cottage top;
    The thatch-moss grows in brighter green;
And eaves in quick succession drop,
    Where grinning icicles have been,
Pit-patting with a pleasant noise
    In tubs set by the cottage-door;
While ducks and geese, with happy joys,
    Plunge in the yard-pond brimming o'er.

The sun peeps through the window-pane;
   Which children mark with laughing eye,
And in the wet street steal again
   To tell each other spring is nigh . . .

        John Clare, 'The Shepherd's Calendar – February'

So, some tempestuous morn in early June,
When the year's primal burst of gloom is o'er,
Before the roses and the longest day –
When garden-walks and all the grassy floor
With blossoms red and white of fallen May
And chestnut-flowers are strewn –
So have I heard the cuckoo's parting cry
From the wet field, through the vext garden-trees,
Come with the volleying rain and tossing breeze:
The bloom is gone and with the bloom go I.

        Matthew Arnold, 'Thyrsis'

The lonely season in lonely lands, when fled
Are half the birds, and mists lie low, and the sun
Is rarely seen, nor strayeth far from his bed;
The short days pass unwelcomed one by one.

   Out by the ricks the mantled engine stands
Crestfallen, deserted, – for now all hands
Are told to the plough – and ere it is dawn appear
The teams following and crossing far and near,
As hour by hour they broaden the brown bands
Of the striped fields; and behind them firk and prance
The heavy rooks, and daws grey-pated dance:
As awhile, surmounting a crest, in sharp outline
(A miniature of toil, a gem's design,)
They are pictured, horses and men, or now near by
Above the lane they shout lifting the share,
By the trim hedgerow bloom'd with purple air;
Where, under the thorns, dead leaves in huddle lie
Packed by the gales of Autumn, and in and out
The small wrens glide

With a happy note of cheer,
And yellow amorets flutter above and about,
Gay, familiar in fear.

And now, if the night shall be cold, across the sky
Linnets and twites, in small flocks, helter-skelter,
All the afternoon to the gardens fly,
From thistle-pastures hurrying to gain the shelter
Of American rhododendron or cherry-laurel:
And here and there, near chilly setting of sun,
In an isolated tree a congregation
Of starlings chatter and chide,
Thickset as summer leaves, in garrulous quarrel:
Suddenly they hush as one, –
The tree top springs, –
And off, with a whirr of wings,
They fly by the score
To the holly-thicket, and there with myriads more
Dispute for the roosts; and from the unseen nation
A babel of tongues, like running water unceasing,
Makes live the wood, the flocking cries increasing,
Wrangling discordantly, incessantly,
While falls the night on them self-occupied;
The long dark night, that lengthens slow,
Deepening with Winter to starve grass and tree,
And soon to bury in snow
The Earth, that, sleeping 'neath her frozen stole,
Shall dream a dream crept from the sunless pole
Of how her end shall be.

Robert Bridges, 'November'

Not wholly in the busy world, nor quite
Beyond it, blooms the garden that I love.
News from the humming city comes to it
In sounds of funeral or of marriage bells;
And, sitting muffled in dark leaves, you hear
The windy clanging of the minster clock;
Although between it and the garden lies
A league of grass, wash'd by a slow broad stream,
That, stirr'd with languid pulses of the oar,

Waves all its lazy lilies, and creeps on,
Barge-laden, to three arches of a bridge
Crown'd with the minster-towers.

                                The fields between
Are dewy-fresh, browsed by deep-udder'd kine,
And all about the large lime feathers low,
The lime a summer home of murmurous wings.

                       Tennyson, 'The Gardener's Daughter'

Now fades the last long streak of snow,
  Now burgeons every maze of quick
    About the flowering squares, and thick
By ashen roots the violets blow.

Now rings the woodland loud and long,
  The distance takes a lovelier hue,
    And drown'd in yonder living blue
The lark becomes a sightless song.

Now dance the lights on lawn and lea,
  The flocks are whiter down the vale,
    And milkier every milky sail
On winding stream or distant sea; . . .

                         Tennyson, 'In Memoriam'

It rains, and nothing stirs within the fence
Anywhere through the orchard's untrodden, dense
Forest of parsley. The great diamonds
Of rain on the grass blades there is none to break,
Or the fallen petals further down to shake . . .

                         Edward Thomas, 'It Rains'

The train. A hot July. On either hand
Our sober, fruitful, unemphatic land,
This Cambridge country plain beneath the sky
Where I was born, and grew, and hope to die.

Look! where the willows hide a rushy pool,
And the old horse goes squelching down to cool,
One angler's rod against their silvery green,
Still seen today as once by Bewick seen.

A cottage there, thatched sadly, like its earth,
Where crimson ramblers make a shortlived mirth;
Here, only flies the flick-tail cows disturb
Among the shaven meads and willow-herb.

There, rounded hay-ricks, solemn in the yard,
Barns gravely, puritanically tarred,
Next heavy elms that guard the ripening grain
And fields, and elms, and corn, and fields again . . .

Frances Cornford, 'Travelling Home'

There was a day, ere yet the autumn closed,
When, ere her wintry wars, the earth reposed,
When from the yellow weed the feathery crown,
Light as the curling smoke fell slowly down;
When the winged insect settled in our sight,
And waited wind to recommence her flight;
When the white river was a silver sheet,
And on the ocean slept th' unanchored fleet.

George Crabbe

At the same times the same dull views to see,
The bounding marsh-bank and the blighted tree;
The water only, when the tides were high,
When low, the mud half-cover'd and half-dry;
The sun-burnt tar that blisters on the planks,
And bank-side stakes in their uneven ranks;
Heaps of entangled weeds that slowly float,
As the tide rolls by the impeded boat.
    When tides were neap, and, in the sultry day,
Through the tall bounding mud-banks made their way,
Which on each side rose swelling, and below
The dark warm flood ran silently and slow;

There anchoring, Peter chose from man to hide,
There hang his head, and view the lazy tide
In its hot slimy channel slowly glide;
Where the small eels that left the deeper way
For the warm shore, within the shallows play;

Where gaping muscles, left upon the mud,
Slope their slow passage to the fallen flood; –
Here dull and hopeless he'd lie down and trace
How sidelong crabs had scrawl'd their crooked race;
Or sadly listen to the tuneless cry
Of fishing gull or clanging golden-eye;
What time the sea-birds to the marsh would come,
And the loud bittern, from the bull-rush home,
Gave from the salt-ditch side the bellowing boom:
He nursed the feelings these dull scenes produce,
And loved to stop beside the opening sluice;
Where the small stream, confined in narrow bound,
Ran with a dull, unvaried, sadd'ning sound;

George Crabbe, 'Peter Grimes'

Crabbe in the last quotation, unlike his fellow landscape painters,
describes a scene, which, so he says, displeased him. But the
reader enjoys the description. This is not only because Crabbe's
description is skilful but because natural landscape in England
always has something pleasant about it. Cowper was right, so far
as England was concerned, when he said 'God made the country,
and man made the town.'

EPITHETS

The universe, so far as we can observe it, is a wonderful and
immense engine; its extent, its order, its beauty, its cruelty,
make it alike impressive. If we dramatise its life and conceive
its spirit, we are filled with wonder, terror, and amusement, so
magnificent is that spirit, so prolific, inexorable, grammatical,
and dull. Like all animals and plants, the cosmos has its own
way of doing things, not wholly rational nor ideally best, but

patient, fatal, and fruitful. Great is this organism of mud and fire, terrible this vast, painful, glorious experiment. Why should we not look on the universe with piety? Is it not our substance? Are we made of other clay? All our possibilities lie from eternity hidden in its bosom. It is the dispenser of all our joys. We may address it without superstitious terrors; it is not wicked. It follows its own habits abstractedly; it can be trusted to be true to its word. Society is not impossible between it and us, and since it is the source of all our energies, the home of all our happiness, shall we not cling to it and praise it, seeing that it vegetates so grandly and so sadly, and that it is not for us to blame it for what, doubtless, it never knew that it did?

George Santayana, Reason in Religion

This splendid piece of prose depends for its effect on its epithets. I used to be told by my schoolmasters to use as few epithets as possible. For straightforward narrative this is a good enough rule; but meditative and descriptive prose needs adjectives. Such writing involves fine distinctions: the adjective is there to make distinctions. It qualifies its use of a noun in such a way as to distinguish it from other uses of the same noun. An adjective misused is either commonplace, adding nothing to the noun it qualifies, or so far-fetched as to confuse its meaning. A master of the adjective like Santayana always employs one which noticeably qualifies the noun: but in such a way as to enhance its meaning; it also indicates the author's individual sense of that meaning. If the author's is a complex spirit like Santayana's, the adjectives are particularly important, for it is only through them that he can communicate its complexity. How carefully he has chosen the adjectives in this passage! – 'prolific, inexorable, grammatical and dull', 'vast, painful, glorious', 'patient, fateful, fruitful'.

Henry James, another master of fine distinctions, is also a master of the epithet, as when he says of Mr Longman, the middle-aged dandy in *The Awkward Age*, 'Though he couldn't look young, he came near – strikingly and amusingly – to looking new.'

Conrad is also strong on the epithet. His special device is to link two seemingly incongruous adjectives together in order to achieve a more exact description: he speaks of the 'blinding and frigid' light of an arc lamp and of a negro's countenance 'pathetic and brutal'.

Some other examples of a similar use: Bridges speaks of the 'soft unchristened smile' of Eros, God of Love, and Ruth Pitter of 'the delicate fox with soft and savage feet' and the 'long blest eventless days' of a fine summer.

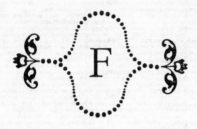

FAITH

Men must be saved in this world by their want of faith.

George Savile, Marquess of Halifax

A profound truth though seldom recognized. It is often said that mankind needs a faith, if the world is to be improved. In fact, unless the faith is vigilantly and regularly checked by a sense of man's fallibility it is likely to make the world worse. From Torquemada to Robespierre and Hitler, the men who have made mankind suffer the most have been inspired to do so by a strong faith; so strong that it led them to think their crimes were acts of virtue necessary to help them achieve their aim, which was to build some sort of an ideal kingdom on earth.

But, as we have been told on very good authority, the Kingdom of Heaven is not of this world. Those who think they can establish it here are more likely to create a hell on earth.

FAREWELL

King Arthur had been killed in a war that had arisen in consequence of the love between Guenever his Queen and his friend Sir Launcelot. The repentant Guenever became a nun and Launcelot, hearing of this, decided to go and see her:

> Then came Sir Bors de Ganis and said: 'My lord Sir Launcelot, what think ye for to do, now to ride in this realm? wit ye well ye shall find few friends.'
> 'Be as be may,' said Sir Launcelot, 'keep you still here, for I

will forth on my journey, and no man nor child shall go with me.'

So it was no boot to strive, but he departed and rode westerly, and there he sought a seven or eight days; and at the last he came to a nunnery, and then was Queen Guenever ware of Sir Launcelot as he walked in the cloister. And when she saw him there she swooned thrice, that all the ladies and gentlewomen had work enough to hold the queen up. So when she might speak she called her ladies and gentlewomen to her, and said: 'Ye marvel, fair ladies, why I make this fare. Truly,' she said, 'it is for the sight of yonder knight that yonder standeth; wherefore I pray you all call him to me.'

When Sir Launcelot was brought to her, then she said to all the ladies: 'Through this man and me hath all this war been wrought, and the death of the most noblest knights of the world; for through our love that we have loved together is my most noble lord slain. Therefore, Sir Launcelot, wit thou well I am set in such a plight to get my soul heal; and yet I trust through God's grace that after my death to have a sight of the blessed face of Christ, and at doomesday to sit on his right side, for as sinful as ever I was, now are saints in heaven. Therefore, Sir Launcelot, I require thee, and beseech thee heartily, for all the love that ever was betwixt us, that thou never see me more in the visage; and I command thee, on God's behalf, that thou forsake my company, and to thy kingdom thou turn again, and keep well thy realm from war and wrake; for as well as I have loved thee, mine heart will not serve me to see thee, for through thee and me is the flower of kings and knights destroyed; therefore, Sir Launcelot, go to thy realm, and there take thee a wife, and live with her with joy and bliss; and I pray thee heartily, pray for me to our Lord that I may amend my misliving.'

'Now, sweet madam,' said Sir Launcelot, 'would ye that I should now return again unto my country, and there to wed a lady? Nay, madam, wit you well that shall I never do, for I shall never be so false to you of that I have promised; but the same destiny that yet have taken you to, I will take me unto, for to please Jesu, and ever for you I cast me specially to pray.'

'If thou wilt do so,' said the queen, 'hold thy promise; but I may never believe but that thou wilt turn to the world again.'

'Well, madam,' said he, 'ye say as pleaseth you, yet wist you me never false of my promise, and God defend but I should forsake the world as ye have done. For in the quest of the Sangreal I had forsaken the vanities of the world had not your love been. And if I had done so at that time with my heart, will, and thought, I had passed all the knights that were in the Sangreal except Sir Galahad, my son. And therefore, lady, sithen ye have taken you to perfection, I must needs take me to perfection, of right. For I take record of God, in you I have had mine earthly joy; and if I had found you now so disposed, I had cast to have had you into mine own realm. But sithen I find you thus disposed, I ensure you faithfully, I will ever take me to penance, and pray while my life lasteth, if I may find any hermit, either gray or white, that will receive me. Wherefore, madam, I pray you kiss me and never no more.'

'Nay,' said the queen, 'that shall I never do, but abstain you from such works.'

And they departed. But there was never so hard an hearted man but he would have wept to see the dolour that they made; for there was lamentation as they had been stung with spears; and many times they swooned, and the ladies bare the queen to her chamber.

And Sir Launcelot awoke, and went and took his horse, and rode all that day and all night in a forest weeping. And at the last he was ware of an hermitage and a chapel stood betwixt two cliffs; and then he heard a little bell ring to mass, and thither he rode and alit, and tied his horse to the gate and heard mass.

And he that sang mass was the Bishop of Canterbury. Both the Bishop and Sir Bedivere knew Sir Launcelot, and they spake together after mass. But when Sir Bedivere had told his tale all whole, Sir Launcelot's heart almost brast for sorrow, and Sir Launcelot threw his arms abroad, and said: 'Alas, who may trust this world!'

And when he kneeled down on his knee, and prayed the Bishop to shrive him and assoil him. And then he besought the Bishop that he might be his brother. Then the Bishop said: 'I will gladly', and there he put an habit upon Sir Launcelot. And there he served God day and night with prayers and fastings.

Thomas Malory, Morte d'Arthur

The highest tragic tension can only come when two goods are in conflict with one another. The love of Guenever and Launcelot was not an ignoble love: on the contrary it was tender, chivalrous, self-forgetful. But for them it was a sin against the Divine Law and also a betrayal of King Arthur, who they both loved and honoured above all other human beings. Thus it was bound to end unhappily and finally, in a parting that both accepted as right though agonizing. All this is brought out in this wonderful passage. Malory lived in a naive and savage age and was, it appears, a ruffianly sort of man. Yet his version of the love story of Launcelot and Guenever is marked by a nobility and refinement of moral feeling hardly to be equalled in any subsequent English fiction.

FATHERLY FEELING

No man can tell but he that loves his children how many delicious accents make a man's heart dance in the pretty conversation of these dear pledges: their childishness, their stammering, their little angers, their innocence, their imperfections, their necessities, are so many emanations of joy and comfort to him that delights in their persons and society; but he that loves not his wife and children feeds a lioness at home, and broods a nest of sorrows.

Jeremy Taylor, XXV Sermons, 1653

FEAR

... I am told that I am wild by nature. Whether or no this is so I cannot tell. But the thought has made me wonder what the difference is between the wild and the tame, and I have come to the conclusion that one of the main differences it that of habitually making or not making up one's mind. Every wild animal lives in a state of danger, which means deciding all the time, while the very essence of tameness is the absence of any need for decision. The wild soul is perhaps conscious – as I certainly am always conscious – of the intrinsic danger of life, which is hidden from the domesticated, whether animal or human, by the fact that their necessities are provided for them, and only a strong imagination or accident can make them realize the precarious nature of what they rely on.

It is hard to say which is the better of the two states of mind: but it does not do to assume the domestic alone to be laudable in a world where all the chances of survival are with wildness. On the other hand it would be unfair to assume that wildness alone is brave: there is a slow and steady noble courage needed to face, sustain and conquer domestic life. The wild are perhaps the more fearless as opposed to courageous; their minds are more mobile and their instincts more ready, by necessity, to face the unexpected when it comes; and whether they are bedawin, untamed birds and beast, or eccentrics like ourselves, mere captivity is likely to kill them.

Freya Stark

This is true and, by implication, a criticism of those reformers who hope to achieve 'freedom from fear' simply by doing away with things that are likely to frighten people. As Dame Freya Stark says life is of its nature dangerous: disappointment and misfortune lie in wait for us at every turn in our journey through it, with cruel death at the end of all. It is courage, not security, that frees us from fear.

FISH

Shakespearean fish swam the sea, far away from land;
Romantic fish swam in nets coming to the hand;
What are all those fish that lie gasping on the strand?

W. B. Yeats, 'Three Movements'

What indeed, we may ask, as we turn over, one after another, the pages of the little magazines devoted to the work of present-day poets? The world of the later twentieth century does not provide a natural and congenial element for poets to live in; with the result that the utterances of the poor creatures are, many of them, little better than gasps; brief, breathless, effortful and cacophonous!

FLOWERS

'I detest the vegetable world', remarked urban Baudelaire; but, for the most part, poets have liked flowers and found in them a source of inspiration. Many have given us passages in which they catalogue one flower after the other. The catalogues in *Lycidas* and *A Winter's Tale* are especially famous. Here are some lesser known flower lists:

> Too quick despairer, wherefore wilt thou go?
>   Soon will the high Midsummer pomps come on,
>   Soon will the musk carnations break and swell,
>   Soon shall we have gold-dusted snapdragon,
>   Sweet-William with his homely cottage-smell,
>   And stocks in fragrant blow;
>   Roses that down the alleys shine afar,
>   And open, jasmine-muffled lattices,
>   And groups under the dreaming garden-trees,
>   And the full moon, and the white evening-star.

Matthew Arnold, 'Thyrsu'

>   . . . Laburnum, rich
> In streaming gold; syringa, iv'ry pure;
> The scentless and the scented rose; this red
> And of an humbler growth, the other tall,
> And throwing up into the darkest gloom
> Of neighb'ring cypress, or more sable yew,
> Her silver globes, light as the foamy surf
> That the wind severs from the broken wave;
> The lilac, various in array, now white,
> Now sanguine, and her beauteous head now set
> With purple spikes pyramidal, as if,
> Studious of ornament, yet unresolv'd
> Which hue she most approv'd, she chose them all;
> Copious of flow'rs the woodbine, pale and wan,
> But well compensating her sickly looks
> With never-cloying odours, early and late;
> Hypericum, all bloom, so thick a swarm

Of flow'rs, like flies clothing her slender rods,
That scarce a leaf appears; mezerion, too,
Though leafless, well attir'd, and thick beset
With blushing wreaths, investing ev'ry spray;
Althaea with the purple eye; the broom,
Yellow and bright, as bullion unalloy'd,
Her blossoms; and, luxuriant above all,
The jasmine, throwing wide her elegant sweets,
The deep dark green of whose unvarnish'd leaf,
Makes more conspicuous, and illumines more
The bright profusion of her scatter'd stars.

William Cowper, 'The Task', Book VI

Dark-leaved arbutus blooms with wax-pale bells
And their faint honey-smells,
The velvety syringa with smooth leaves,
Gloxinia with a green shade in the snow,
Jasmine and moon-clear orange-blossoms and green blooms
Of the wild strawberries from the shade of woods.

Edith Sitwell, 'The Swans'

Edith Sitwell mentions the gloxinia. Such flowers are seldom named in poetry because these names are too unromantic and scientific-sounding. However, if a poet does take the risk, he often gets away with it. Edith Sitwell does; so also do Dalmon, Mary Coleridge and Hardy who wrote about the fuchsia, the cyclamen and the cotoneaster respectively. The associations roused by these names are different to those raised by what may be called the classic flowers, the rose or the lily. These last are vague inclusive names that serve to stand for beauty in general. The others are particular and precise and carry with them a suggestion of some localized specific event, some personal private recollection.

O what if the fowler my blackbird has taken?
  The roses of dawn blossom over the sea;
Awaken, my blackbird, awaken, awaken,
  And sing to me out of my red fuchsia tree!

O what if the fowler my blackbird has taken?
 The sun lifts his head from the lap of the sea –
Awaken, my blackbird, awaken, awaken,
 And sing to me out of my red fuchsia tree!

O what if the fowler my blackbird has taken?
 The mountain grows white with the birds of the sea;
But down in my garden forsaken, forsaken,
 I'll weep all the day by my red fuchsia tree!

          Charles Dalmon

Some hang above the tombs,
Some weep in empty rooms,
I, when the iris blooms,
 Remember.

I, when the cyclamen
Opens her buds again,
Rejoice a moment – then
 Remember.

          Mary Coleridge

Around the house flakes fly faster,
And all the berries are now gone
From holly and cotoneaster
Around the house. The flakes fly! – faster
Shutting indoors that crumb-outcaster
We used to see upon the lawn
Around the house. Flakes fly faster
And all the berries now are gone.

    Thomas Hardy, 'Birds at Winter Nightfall'

FOOD AND DRINK

And still she slept an azure-lidded sleep,
In blanchèd linen, smooth, and lavender'd,
While he from forth the closet brought a heap

Of candied apple, quince, and plum, and gourd;
With jellies soother than the creamy curd,
And lucent syrops, tinct with cinnamon;
Manna and dates, in argosy transferr'd
From Fez; and spicèd dainties, every one,
From silken Samarcand to cedar'd Lebanon.

These delicates he heap'd with glowing hand
On golden dishes and in baskets bright
Of wreathèd silver: sumptuous they stand
In the retirèd quiet of the night,
Filling the chilly room with perfume light.

John Keats, 'The Eve of St Agnes'

... the lunch on this occasion began with soles, sunk in a deep dish, over which the College cook had spread a counterpane of the whitest cream, save that it was branded here and there with brown spots as on the flanks of a doe. After this came the partridges, but if this suggests a couple of bald brown birds on a plate you are mistaken. The partridges, many and various, came with all their retinue of sauces and salads, the sharp and the sweet, each in its order; their potatoes, thin as coins but not so hard; their sprouts foliated as rosebuds but more succulent. And no sooner had the roast and its retinue been done with than the silent serving man . . . set before us, wreathed in napkins, a confection which rose all sugar from the waves. To call it pudding and so relate it to rice and tapioca would be an insult.

Virginia Woolf, A Room of One's Own

The pleasures given by food and drink are very hard to put into words. Just to say that a drink is 'refreshing' or that a dish is 'savoury' conveys little of the particular satisfaction each gives. This can only be done by analogy and suggestion. The writer however must be careful not to choose too grand an analogy or the effect is unintentionally comical as it often is in the description of their wares given by wine merchants: for instance

Château Lynch-Bages, Grand Cru Classé Pauillac, Château-Bottled.

Just the wine for those who like the smell of Verdi. Dark colour, swashbuckling bouquet and ripe flavour. Ready for drinking, but will hold well showing a gradual shift in style as it ages into graceful discretion.

My earlier quotations, however, show that literature can successfully describe the pleasures of the table. Keats does it in 'The Eve of St Agnes', in his account of the refreshments spread out in Madeline's bedroom; and Virginia Woolf does it in her description of the luncheon given in what I take to be King's College, Cambridge. Of the two, hers makes the mouth water the most. Her description is more specific; and she is also helped by the fact that she is describing a solid three-course meal while Keats's Porphyro only provided a light dessert for his Madeline, before starting on their wintry elopement.

FORMALITY

. . . My mother when I learn'd that thou wast dead,
Say, wast thou conscious of the tears I shed?
Hover'd thy spirit o'er thy sorrowing son,
Wretch even then, life's journey just begun?
Perhaps thou gav'st me, though unseen, a kiss;
Perhaps a tear, if souls can weep in bliss –
Ah that maternal smile! it answers – Yes.
I heard the bell toll'd on thy burial day,
I saw the hearse that bore thee slow away,
And, turning from my nurs'ry window, drew
A long, long sigh, and wept a last adieu!
But was it such? – It was – Where thou art gone
Adieus and farewells are a sound unknown.
May I but meet thee on that peaceful shore,
The parting sound shall pass my lips no more!
Thy maidens griev'd themselves at my concern,
Oft gave me promise of a quick return.
What ardently I wish'd, I long believ'd,
And, disappointed still, was still deceiv'd;
By disappointment every day beguil'd,
Dupe of *to-morrow* even from a child.

Thus many a sad to-morrow came and went,
Till, all my stock of infant sorrow spent,
I learn'd at last submission to my lot;
But, though I less deplor'd thee, ne'er forgot.
　Where once we dwelt our name is heard no more,
Children not thine have trod my nurs'ry floor;
And where the gard'ner Robin, day by day,
Drew me to school along the public way,
Delighted with my bauble coach, and wrapt
In scarlet mantle warm, and velvet capt,
'Tis now become a history little known,
That once we call'd the past'ral house our own.
Short-liv'd possession! but the record fair
That mem'ry keeps of all thy kindness there,
Still outlives many a storm that has effac'd
A thousand other themes less deeply trac'd.
Thy nightly visits to my chamber made,
That thou might'st know me safe and warmly laid;
Thy morning bounties ere I left my home,
The biscuit, or confectionary plum;
The fragrant waters on my cheeks bestow'd
By thy own hand, till fresh they shone and glow'd;
All this, and more endearing still than all,
Thy constant flow of love, that knew no fall,
Ne'er roughen'd by those cataracts and brakes
That humour interpos'd too often makes;
All this still legible in mem'ry's page,
And still to be so, to my latest age,
Adds joy to duty, makes me glad to pay
Such honours to thee as my numbers may;
Perhaps a frail memorial but sincere,
Not scorn'd in heav'n though little notic'd here.
　Could time, his flight revers'd, restore the hours,
When, playing with thy vesture's tissued flow'rs,
The violet, the pink, and jessamine,
I prick'd them into paper with a pin,
(And thou wast happier than myself the while,
Would'st softly speak, and stroke my head and smile)
Could those few pleasant hours again appear,
Might one wish bring them, would I wish them here?

I would not trust my heart – the dear delight
Seems so to be desir'd, perhaps I might –
But no – what here we call our life is such,
So little to be lov'd, and thou so much,
That I should ill requite thee to constrain
Thy unbound spirit into bonds again.

William Cowper, 'Lines to his mother's picture'

Cowper's is the best poem I know about the love of parent and child, the tenderest, the most moving. This might be thought surprising considering it was written in the formal mode of the 18th century. In fact this mode was a help to the author. Tender feelings present a difficult problem to the poet; it is so difficult to express them without appearing sentimental, and as if exploiting them publicly in order to make the reader shed tears. Formality of manner especially when lightened, as it is here, by a touch of humour, acts as a filter of reticence and good manners through which the emotion comes to us purged of any taint of sentimentality or exhibitionism. Cowper's poem is an outstanding example of this; but other 18th-century poets illustrate it too. There are greater poems about the death of a friend than Thomas Gray's sonnet on the death of Richard West but none that, for me, expresses so well what the ordinary person feels on such an occasion; and here too formality of manner helps to make the words ring true.

In vain to me the smiling mornings shine,
    And reddening Phoebus lifts his golden fire:
The birds in vain their amorous descant join;
    Or cheerful fields resume their green attire:
These ears, alas! for other notes repine;
    A different object do these eyes require:
My lonely anguish melts no heart but mine;
    And in my breast the imperfect joys expire.
Yet morning smiles the busy race to cheer,
    And new-born pleasure brings to happier men:
The fields to all their wonted tribute bear:
    To warm their little loves the birds complain:
I fruitless mourn to him, that cannot hear,
    And weep the more, because I weep in vain.

Good manners – and good manners involve a touch of formality – are necessary if only to make articulate man's intimate and tender personal feelings. I note that nowadays when manners both in life and literature have become more and more informal, poets seem unable to express the tender emotions. Parents and children are just as fond of each other as in the past and men are just as sad when their friends die. But what poet of today writes about these feelings?

FRAGMENTS

Why thinks King Henry's son that Margaret's love
Hangs in th'uncertain balance of proud time?

Robert Greene, 'Friar Bacon and Friar Bungay'

So with Division infinite and Trill
On would the nightingale have warbled still,
And all the World have listen'd; but a Note
Of sterner Import, check'd the love-sick Throat.

Edward Fitzgerald, 'Bird Parliament'

I died; and for my winding-sheet a wave
I had, and all the ocean for my grave . . .

Dryden, 'The Conquest of Granada'

And on the beech-bole, smooth and grey
Some lover of an older day
Has carved in time-blurred lettering
One word only: 'Alas.'

Aldous Huxley, 'Philoclea' in the Forest'

O fret not after knowledge. I have none,
And yet my song comes native with the warmth.

O fret not after knowledge! I have none,
And yet the evening listens . . .

Keats, 'What the Thrush Said'

Hot, shining, swift, light and aspiring things
Are of immortal and celestial nature.
George Chapman, 'The Conspiracy of Charles, Duke of Byron'

In youth's first bloom reluctantly he dies.

Pope's translation of the Iliad

I call these 'fragments' because I became acquainted with them
all for the first time in the fragmentary form in which they are
printed here, either quoted in a book or in conversation.

I traced them to their sources only to find that they lost by being
seen in their original context. They were all the better for being
'fragments'. Keats's lines in particular are equal to anything that
he ever wrote.

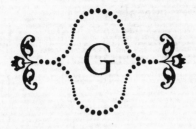

GOLD

... No gold, no Holy Ghost ...

Samuel Butler, Note Books

This is a half truth. Saints – and saints do exist – can attain high virtue without money: poverty may even assist them to do so. But persons with an average capacity for virtue are better for possessing a competence. Moreover high civilizations have always rested on a foundation of wealth. St Peter's at Rome was not built on a shoe-string; nor were the cultures rich and spacious enough to inspire Shakespeare or Titian.

Not that the presence of gold necessarily ensures the presence of the Holy Ghost. This can bring a sour comfort to those who feel themselves poorer than they deserve to be. 'It is a foolish thing,' writes Thomas Gray to a friend, 'that one can't, not only not live as one pleases, but where and with whom one pleases, without money. Swift somewhere says that money is liberty: and I fear money is friendship too, and society, and almost every external blessing. It is a great, though ill-natured comfort to see most of those who have it in plenty, without pleasure, without liberty, and without friends.'

GOLDEN BALLS

The critic's aim should be to encourage every writer to do what he can do best, what is most natural to him; not to implore him to persist in tasks which (be they never so superior) he will never accomplish. To every artist that form of art to which his own talent is best suited should seem the highest form of art.

It is curious how often the artist is ignorant of his own true bent. . . . How many charming talents have been spoiled by the instilled desire to do 'important' work! Some people are born to lift heavy weights. Some are born to juggle with golden balls. The lifters are far more numerous in England than are the jugglers.

Max Beerbohm

True of literature, Max's words are equally true of life. The art of living consists largely in discovering your own bent, realizing its possibilities and limitations and, so far as circumstances allow, designing your way of life in the light of this knowledge. Max makes his point using terms drawn from juggling; card games provide just as good a metaphor. Life is a card game in which everyone is dealt a hand which he must accept. His success will depend on his playing it as well as it can be played. A very large proportion of failures in life are made by men who refuse to do this and instead insist on playing the hand they think that they should have been dealt.

THE GOVERNMENT OF THE WORLD

The Government of the World is a great thing; but it is a very coarse one, too, compared to the fineness of Speculative Knowledge.

Halifax

This is a truth not generally acknowledged. People often talk of the life of thought, as lived in universities and libraries, as 'unreal' and therefore inferior to the life of action lived by politicians and captains of industry and trade union leaders and so on: and the thinkers and academics are infected with a sense of inferiority and become apologetic about their mode of living. They have no need to do so. A life spent in a library is as 'real' as a life spent in a government office or on the factory floor: it exists just as much and is concerned with subjects that are as important; often more important, for they are of more permanent interest. The problems of practical politics in the ancient world do not interest us any more; but we are still moved by the sentiments of ancient poets and set thinking by the speculations of ancient philosophers.

GREAT HOUSES

(1)

Surely among a rich man's flowering lawns,
Amid the rustle of his planted hills,
Life overflows without ambitious pains;
And rains down life until the basin spills,
And mounts more dizzy high the more it rains
As though to choose whatever shape it wills
And never stoop to a mechanical
Or servile shape, at others' beck and call.

Mere dreams! mere dreams! Yet Homer had not sung
Had he not found it certain beyond dreams
That out of life's own self-delight had sprung
The abounding glittering jet; though now it seems
As if some marvellous empty sea-shell flung
Out of the obscure dark of the rich streams,
And not a fountain, were the symbol which
Shadows the inherited glory of the rich.

Some violent bitter man, some powerful man
Called architect and artist in, that they,
Bitter and violent men, might rear in stone
The sweetness that all longed for night and day,
The gentleness none there had ever known;
But when the master's buried mice can play,
And maybe the great-grandson of that house,
For all its bronze and marble, 's but a mouse.

O what if gardens where the peacock strays
With delicate feet upon old terraces,
Or else all Juno from an urn displays
Before the indifferent garden deities;
O what if levelled lawns and gravelled ways
Where slippered Contemplation finds his ease
And Childhood a delight for every sense,
But take our greatness with our violence?

What if the glory of escutcheoned doors,
And buildings that a haughtier age designed,
The pacing to and fro on polished floors
Amid great chambers and long galleries, lined
With famous portraits of our ancestors;
What if those things the greatest of mankind
Consider most to magnify, or to bless,
But take our greatness with our bitterness?

W. B. Yeats, 'Meditations in Time of Civil War –
Ancestral Houses'

Yeats at his superb best: noble and exquisite as a building of
Palladio, this poem shows him the only modern master of the
grand manner. What he says, too, sets one thinking. Myself,
wandering through the halls and galleries of a great English
country house, I have wondered at the discrepancy between its
stately beauty so exalting and tranquillizing to the spirit and the
fierce, restless, unscrupulous character of the men who were so
often responsible for its original building. Or was it a discrepancy?
Perhaps, as Yeats suggests, a gentler more contented spirit would
not have felt the urge and the vitality to create these buildings.
But I do not think this is the reason why later generations have
not built such houses. There are still fierce and unscrupulous rich
persons about, and none of them show any signs of wishing to
leave behind them such monuments. No – where the builders of
the past differed from their successors today is that they took a
more uninhibited delight in the beautiful along with a conviction
of its spiritual significance. For all its approval of 'permissiveness',
the twentieth century is a Puritan age. Beauty is created by those
who believe both in the body and the soul and delight in both. The
present age believes in the body but does not delight in it; and it
is not sure whether it believes in the soul at all.

(11)

. . . You stumble upon them in a drive or a walk. You catch a
glimpse of an ivied front at some midmost point of wide acres,
and taking your way, by leave of a serious old woman at a

lodge-gate, along an over-arching avenue, you find yourself introduced to an edifice so human-looking in its beauty that it seems for the occasion fairly to reconcile art and morality.

To Broughton Castle, the first seen in this beautiful group, I must do no more than allude; but this is not because I failed to think it, as I think every house I see, the most delightful habitation in England. It lies rather low, and its woods and pastures slope down to it; it has a deep, clear moat all round it, spanned by a bridge that passes under a charming old gate-tower, and nothing can be sweeter than to see its clustered walls of yellow-brown stone so sharply islanded while its gardens bloom on the other side of the water. . . . After this we paid our respects to another old house which is full of memories and suggestions of that most dramatic period of English history. But of Compton Wyniates (the name of this seat of enchantment) I despair of giving any coherent or adequate account. It belongs to the Marquis of Northampton, and it stands empty all the year round. It sits on the grass at the bottom of a wooded hollow, and the glades of a superb old park go wandering upward away from it. When I came out in front of the house from a short and steep but stately avenue I said to myself that here surely we had arrived at the farthest limits of what ivy-smothered brick-work and weather-beaten gables, conscious old windows and clustered mossy roofs can accomplish for the eye. It is impossible to imagine a more finished picture. And its air of solitude and delicate decay – of having been dropped into its grassy hollow as an ancient jewel is deposited upon a cushion, and being shut in from the world and back into the past by its circling woods – all this drives the impression well home. The house is not large, as great houses go, and it sits, as I have said, upon the grass, without even a flagging or a footpath to conduct you from the point where the avenue stops to the beautiful sculptured doorway which admits you into the small, quaint inner court. From this court you are at liberty to pass through the crookedest series of oaken halls and chambers, adorned with treasures of old wainscotting and elaborate doors and chimneypieces. Outside, you may walk all round the house on a grassy bank which is raised above the level on which it stands, and find it from every point of view a more charming composition. I should not omit to mention that Compton

Wyniates is supposed to have been in Scott's eye when he des-
cribed the dwelling of the old royalist knight in *Woodstock*. In
this case he simply transferred the house to the other side of the
county. He has indeed given several of the features of the place,
but he has not given what one may call its colour. I must add
that if Sir Walter could not give the colour of Compton Wyniates,
it is useless for any other writer to try. It is a matter for the
brush and not for the pen.

And what shall I say of the colour of Wroxton Abbey, which
we visited last in order and which in the thickening twilight,
as we approached its great ivy-muffled face, laid on the mind
the burden of its felicity? Wroxton Abbey, as it stands, is a
house of about the same period as Compton Wyniates – the
latter years, I suppose of the sixteenth century. But it is quite
another affair. The place is inhabited, 'kept up', full of the most
interesting and most splendid detail. . . . Everything that in the
material line can render life noble and charming has been
gathered into it with a profusion which makes the whole place
a monument to past opportunity. As I wandered from one rich
room to another and looked at these things that intimate
appeal to the romantic sense which I just mentioned was
mercilessly emphasised. But who can tell the story of the
romantic sense when that adventure really rises to the occasion
– takes its ease in an old English country-house while the twi-
light darkens the corners of expressive rooms and the victim of
the scene, pausing at the window, turns his glance from the
observing portrait of a handsome ancestral face and sees the
great soft billows of the lawn melt away into the park?

Henry James, English Hours

No one describes old English country houses so well as Henry
James. To artistic sensibility and historic sense he added the ad-
vantage of being a foreigner: so that he was able to see his subject
in a wider perspective and, contrasting it with its foreign counter-
parts, could note its distinguishing characteristics with a sharper
clearer eye. Broughton and Wroxton are real houses; but Henry
James's novels contain invented ones just as convincing and
memorable. There is charming intimate Jacobean Gardencourt,
where Isabel Archer got her first sight of the English traditional

scene; there is Lord Warburton's galleried castle at Lockleigh: there is romantic Mellows, home of unromantic Lionel Berrington with its wainscotted parlour and Shakespearean garden. There is Harsh Place, Julia Dallow's Palladian mansion, 'high, square, grey and clean', standing among parterres and fountains: there is Summersoft where Paul Overt first met Henry St George:

. . . Overt remained at the head of the wide double staircase, saying to himself that the place was sweet and promised a pleasant visit, while he leaned on the balustrade of fine old ironwork which, like all the other details, was of the same period as the house. It all went together and spoke in one voice – a rich English voice of the early part of the eighteenth century. It might have been church-time on a summer's day in the reign of Queen Anne: the stillness was too perfect to be modern, the nearness counted so as distance, and there was something so fresh and sound in the originality of the large smooth house, the expanse of beautiful brickwork that showed for pink rather than red and that had been kept clear of messy creepers by the law under which a woman with a rare complexion disdains a veil . . . he turned back through the open doors into the great gallery which was the pride of the place. It marched across from end to end and seemed – with its bright colours, its high panelled windows, its faded flowered chintzes, its quickly-recognised portraits and pictures, the blue-and-white china of its cabinets and the attenuated festoons and rosettes of its ceiling – a cheerful upholstered avenue into the other century.

Henry James, The Lesson of the Master

or classical Longlands, where Waterville visited Sir Arthur Demesne:

It was agreeable to him to arrive at an English country house at the close of the day. He liked the drive from the station in the twilight, the sight of the fields and copses and cottages, vague and lonely in contrast to his definite lighted goal; the sound of the wheels on the long avenue, which turned and wound repeatedly without bringing him to what he reached however at last – the wide, grey front, with a glow in its scattered windows and a sweep of still firmer gravel up to the door. The front of Longlands, which was of this sober complexion, had a grand, pompous air; it was attributed to the genius of Sir Christopher Wren. There were wings curving forward in a semi-circle, with statues placed at intervals on the cornice; so that in the flattering dusk it suggested a great Italian villa dropped by some monstrous hand in an English park.

Henry James, The Siege of London

Most memorable of all is Medley the 16th-century house, rented by the Princess Casamassima, where Hyacinth Robinson the poor little bookbinder got his first fatal glimpse of the charm of traditional aristocratic life:

Hyacinth got up early – an operation attended with very little effort, as he had scarce closed his eyes all night. What he saw from his window made him dress as quickly as a young man might who desired more than ever that his appearance shouldn't give strange ideas about him: an old garden with parterres in curious figures and little intervals of lawn that seemed to our hero's cockney vision fantastically green. At one end of the garden was a parapet of mossy brick which looked down on the other side into a canal, a moat, a quaint old pond (he hardly knew what to call it) and from the same standpoint showed a considerable part of the main body of the house – Hyacinth's room belonging to a wing that commanded the extensive irregular back – which was richly grey wherever clear of the ivy and the other dense creepers, and everywhere infinitely a picture: with a high-piled ancient russet roof broken by huge chimneys and queer peep-holes and all manner of odd gables and windows on different lines, with all manner of antique patches and protrusions and with a particularly fascinating architectural excrescence where a wonderful clock-face was lodged, a clock-face covered with gilding and blazonry but showing many traces of the years and the weather. He had never in his life been in the country – the real country, as he called it, the country which was not the mere ravelled fringe of London – and there entered through his open casement the breath of a world enchantingly new and after his recent feverish hours unspeakably refreshing; a sense of sweet sunny air and mingled odours, all strangely pure and agreeable, and of a musical silence that consisted for the greater part of the voices of many birds. There were tall quiet trees near by and afar off and everywhere; and the group of objects that greeted his eyes evidently formed only a corner of larger spaces and of a more complicated scene. There was a world to be revealed to him: it lay waiting with the dew on it under his windows, and he must go down and take of it such possession as he might.

He rambled an hour in breathless ecstasy, brushing the dew from the deep fern and bracken and the rich borders of the garden, tasting the fragrant air and stopping everywhere, in murmuring rapture, at the touch of some exquisite impression. His whole walk was peopled with recognitions; he had been dreaming all his life of just such a place and such objects, such a morning and such a chance. It was the last of April and everything was fresh and vivid; the great trees in the early air, were a blur of tender shoots. Round the admirable house he revolved repeatedly, catching every aspect and feeling every value, feasting on the whole expression. . . . There was something in the way the grey walls rose from the green lawn that brought tears to his eyes; the spectacle of long duration unassociated with some sordid infirmity or poverty was new to him; he had lived with people among whom old age meant for the most part a grudged and degraded survival. In the favoured resistance of Medley was a serenity of success, an accumulation of dignity and honour.

Henry James, The Princess Casamassima

There is as much about the garden as about the house in this extract. Rightly; in such places the gardens are equally important and Henry James realized it. Like Hyacinth, his creator 'caught every aspect and felt every value and feasted on the whole expression'.

GREAT THINGS

Great things are done when men and mountains meet;
This is not done by jostling in the street.

William Blake

This admirable couplet should be posted up in conspicuous places all over England. The truth it embodies is threatened by two parties of opinion: on the one hand by those who hold it as a sin against nature to try and control the increase of population in any way and on the other by those who believe in 'growth', the pursuit at all costs of a standard of living which entails more and more industrialization and urbanization. If the believers in nature have their way, England will in the end be so full of people that they will be jostling each other even on mountains: if the believers in 'growth' have their way, the whole country will be covered with streets and we shall hardly be aware that mountains exist.

GREEK ART

. . . he left her alone in the glorious room, among the shining antique marbles. She sat down in the centre of the circle of these presences, regarding them vaguely, resting her eyes on their beautiful blank faces; listening as it were, to their eternal silence. It is impossible, in Rome at least, to look long at a great company of Greek sculptures without feeling the effect of their noble quietude; which, as with a high door closed for the ceremony, slowly drops on the spirit the large white mantle of peace. I say in Rome especially, because the Roman air is an exquisite medium for such impressions. The golden sunshine mingles with them, the deep stillness of the past, so vivid yet, though it is nothing but a void full of names, seems to throw a solemn spell upon them. The blinds were partly closed in the windows of the Capitol, and a clear, warm shadow rested on the figures and made them more mildly human. Isabel sat there a long time, under the charm of their motionless grace, wondering to what, of their experience, their absent eyes were open, and how, to our ears, their alien lips would sound. The dark red walls of the room threw them into relief; the polished marble floor reflected their beauty. She had seen them all before, but her enjoyment repeated itself . . .

Henry James, The Portrait of a Lady

The yellow columns of the Parthenon are to be seen at all

hours of the day firmly planted upon the Acropolis; though at sunset, when the ships in the Piraeus fire their guns, a bell rings, a man in uniform (the waistcoat unbuttoned) appears; and the women roll up the black stockings which they are knitting in the shadow of the columns, call to the children, and troop off down the hill back to their houses.

There they are again, the pillars, the pediment, the Temple of Victory and the Erechtheum, set on a tawny rock cleft with shadows, directly you unlatch your shutters in the morning and, leaning out, hear the clatter, the clamour, the whip cracking in the street below. There they are.

The extreme definiteness with which they stand, now a brilliant white, again yellow, and in some lights red, imposes ideas of durability, of the emergence through the earth of some spiritual energy elsewhere dissipated in elegant trifles. But this durability exists quite independently of our admiration. Although the beauty is sufficiently humane to weaken us, to stir the deep deposit of mud – memories, abandonments, regrets, sentimental devotions – the Parthenon is separate from all that; and if you consider how it has stood out all night, for centuries, you begin to connect the blaze (at midday the glare is dazzling and the frieze almost invisible) with the idea that perhaps it is beauty alone that is immortal.

Added to this, compared with the blistered stucco, the new love songs rasped out to the strum of guitar and gramophone, and the noble yet insignificant faces of the street, the Parthenon is really astonishing in its silent composure; which is so vigorous that, far from being decayed, the Parthenon appears, on the contrary, likely to outlast the entire world.

Virginia Woolf, Jacob's Room

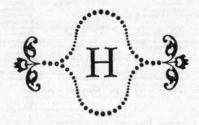

GEORGE SAVILE, 1ST MARQUIS OF HALIFAX

The end-papers of my copy of Halifax's works are black with page references. Of all English authors he is surely the most underrated. He was a supreme master of the aphorist's art and a supremely intelligent observer of his fellow men. In addition, he had a unique advantage over rival aphorists in that, unlike them, he was also a distinguished statesman who spent much of his life in active politics; so that he can speak of them with the authority and understanding born of experience.

From *Political Thoughts and Reflections*:

The best Definition of the best Government is, that it hath no Inconveniences but such as are supportable; but Inconveniences there must be.

The lower Sort of Men must be indulged the Consolation of finding fault with those above them; without that, they would be so melancholy, that it would be dangerous, considering their Numbers.

They are too many to be told of their Mistakes, and for that reason they are never to be cured of them.

There is an accumulative Cruelty in a number of Men, though none in particular are ill-natured.

There are as many apt to be angry as being well, as at being ill governed: for most Men to be well governed must be scurvily used.

If none were to have Liberty but those who understand what it is, there would not be many freed Men in the World.

When the People contend for their Liberty, they seldom get anything by their Victory but new Masters.

Liberty can neither be got, nor kept, but by so much Care, that Mankind generally are unwilling to give the Price for it ...

The best Party is but a kind of a Conspiracy against the rest of the Nation. They put everybody else out of their Protection. Like the Jews to the Gentiles, all others are the Offscourings of the World.

Ignorance maketh most Men go into a Party, and Shame keepeth them from getting out of it.

These sayings are as true of modern politics and politicians as they were of those of Halifax's time. Equally true nowadays are his sayings about subjects not political.

Time hath thrown a Vail upon the Faults of former Ages, or else we should see the same Deformities we condemn in the present Times.

The uncertainty of what is to come, is such a dark Cloud, that neither Reason nor Religion can quite break through it; and the Condition of Mankind is to be weary of what we do know, and afraid of what we do not.

The Follies of grave Men have the Precedence of all others, a ridiculous Dignity, that gives them a Right to be laughed at in the first place.

Weak Men are apt to be cruel, because they stick at nothing that may repair the ill Effect of their Mistakes.

Explaining is generally half confessing.

Friendship cannot live with Ceremony, nor without Civility.

A rooted Disease must be stroked away, rather than kicked away.

Desiring to have anything mended is venturing to have it spoiled: To know when to let Things alone, is a high pitch of good Sense . . .

When a Man is very kind or very angry, there is no sure Guide but Silence upon that Subject.

A wise Man, in trusting another, must not rely upon his promise against his Nature.

Where Sense is wanting, every thing is wanting.

Good manners is such a part of good sense that they cannot be divided.

The best way to suppose what may come, is to remember what is past.

If Men would think more, they would act less.

Nothing has an uglier Look to us than Reason, when it is not of our side.

We think our children part of ourselves, though as they grow up they might very well undeceive us.

Halifax said 'To understand the world and to like it are two things not easily to be reconciled.' His judgement is detached, disenchanted, and alarming: often it comes upon us like a sudden douche of cold water.

But it is not always cold. No amount of disillusionment could chill his love for his country, his passion for liberty, for learning and for truth. When he speaks of them his cool laconic style changes and his words begin to glow and expand under the pressure of a strong though controlled emotion.

There is a smell in our native earth better than all the perfumes in the East; there is something in a mother, though never so angry, that the children will more naturally trust her than the studied civilities of strangers.

Liberty is the Mistress of Mankind, she hath powerful Charms which do so dazzle us, that we find Beauties in her which perhaps are not there, as we do in other Mistresses; yet if she was not a Beauty, the World would not run mad for her.

The struggling for knowledge hath a pleasure in it like that of wrestling with a fine Woman.

Our Trimmer adoreth the Goddess Truth, tho' in all Ages she hath been scurvily used, as well as those that Worshipped her; 'tis of late become such a ruining Virtue, that Mankind seemeth to be agreed to commend and avoid it; yet the want of Practice which Repealeth the other Laws, hath no influence upon the Law of Truth, because it hath a root in Heaven, and an Intrinsick value in it self, that can never be impaired . . . All the power upon earth can never extinguish her; she hath lived in all ages; and let the Mistaken Zeal of prevailing Authority christen any opposition to it with what Name they please, she maketh it not only an ugly and unmannerly, but a dangerous thing to persist. She hath lived very retired indeed, nay sometimes so buried, that only some few of the discerning part of Mankind could have a Glimpse of her. With all that, she hath Eternity in her, she knoweth not how to die. . .

The Character of a Trimmer

HAPPINESS

There is nothing Sir, so little for so little a creature as man. It is by studying little things that we attain the great art of having as little misery and as much happiness as possible.

Dr Johnson

How charming is divine philosophy, when it is really divine, when it descends to earth from a higher sphere, and loves the things of earth without needing or collecting them! What the gay Aristippus said of his mistress: I possess, I am not possessed, every spirit should say of an experience that ruffles it like a breeze playing on the summer sea. A thousand ships sail over it in vain, and the worst of tempests is in a teapot. This once acknowledged and inwardly digested, life and happiness can honestly begin. Nature is innocently fond of puffing herself out, spreading her peacock feathers, and saying, What a fine bird am I! And so she is; to rave against this vanity would be to imitate it. On the contrary, the secret of a merry carnival is that Lent is at hand. Having virtually renounced our follies, we are for the first time able to enjoy them with a free heart in their ephemeral purity. When laughter is humble, when it is not based on self-esteem, it is wiser than tears. Conformity is wiser than hot denials, tolerance wiser than priggishness and puritanism. It is not what earnest people renounce that makes me pity them, it is what they work for. No possible reform will make existence adorable or fundamentally just. . . . Wealth is dismal and poverty cruel unless both are festive. There is no cure for birth and death save to enjoy the interval. The easier attitudes which seem more frivolous are at bottom infinitely more spiritual and profound than the tense attitudes; they are nearer to understanding and to renunciation.

George Santayana, Soliloquies in England

It is not in experience that our lives are poor, though sometimes, it would seem so. If they appear to us limited and monotonous, it is because we do not watch what is happening to us or what we are feeling about it. Montaigne is a good master in the art of life because he teaches that detachment which enables us to be more conscious of life as it passes. Each day contains moments which could not be more pleasant or interesting even if our heart's desire had been fulfilled, or some longed-for piece of good fortune had befallen us. We do not wake up to this until our desires have been met or the luck is actually ours when we are astonished to find after all how little difference that has made. The daily texture of our lives remains what it was, and in amazement we cry out that all is vanity! Since fortune is fickle and many things may come between a man and his desire, it is wise to make the most of those resources which good fortune cannot increase and only the worst calamities destroy. This is the lesson of Montaigne. Have not even the stricken sometimes marvelled to find themselves enjoying a fine day, a joke, a meal? There is comfort in this. Why dwell only on the humiliation in it? We may smile ironically with Montaigne at human nature, its 'flexibility and diversity', but unless we learn from him to smile also gratefully, we have not caught his message.

Desmond MacCarthy

Happiness must come unsought in this hard world: pursued, it eludes us. But these three quotations indicate how to make the most of such happiness as chances to come our way.

HAZLITT

Can Hazlitt be called a 'wise' man? Certainly his sayings do not add up to compose a considered, coherent philosophy of living as do those of Halifax and Sidney Smith. Yet I find myself noting his words as much as theirs. These words are extraordinarily penetrating – flashes of lightning that shed a revealing light on all manner of places. Hazlitt is most characteristically at his best on literature and art; but he is stimulating about life too. He sets one thinking, even if only about why one disagrees with him.

Man is the only animal that laughs and weeps; for he is the only animal that is struck with the difference between what things are, and what they ought to be.

No wise man can have a contempt for the prejudices of others; and he should even stand in a certain awe of his own, as if they were aged parents and monitors. They may in the end prove wiser than he.

Those who are the loudest and bitterest in their complaints of persecution and ill-usage are the first to provoke it.

We are not satisfied to be right, unless we can prove others to be quite wrong.

If mankind had wished for what is right, they might have had it long ago.

Those who are fond of setting things to rights have no great objection to seeing them wrong.

We grow tired of ourselves, much more of other people. Use may in part reconcile us to our own tediousness, but we do not adopt that of others on the same paternal principle. We may be willing to tell a story twice, never to hear one more than once.

Insignificant people are a necessary relief in Society. Such characters are extremely agreeable and even favourites, if they appear satisfied with the part they have to perform.

The youth is better than the old age of friendship.

To be capable of steady friendship or lasting love, are the two greatest proofs, not only of goodness of heart but strength of mind.

The discussing the characters and foibles of common friends is a great sweetener and cement of friendship.

The least pain in our little finger gives us more concern and uneasiness than the destruction of millions of our fellow-beings.

Our intercourse with the dead is better than our intercourse with the living. There are only three pleasures in life pure and lasting, and all derived from inanimate things – books, pictures, and the face of nature.

Literature has its piety, its conscience; it cannot long forget, without forfeiting all dignity, that it serves a burdened and perplexed creature, a human animal struggling to persuade the universal Sphinx, to propose a more intelligible riddle.

You cannot change your own character, and you can never be sure about other peoples'.

Nothing keeps so well as a decoction of spleen. We grow tired of everything but turning others into ridicule and congratulating ourselves on their defects.

Hazlitt's was not a tolerant mind – indeed he was notable among his acquaintances for his intolerance – but it was a free mind, which is something rarer and as precious. He did not allow his convictions to imprison him. All his life he was a fervent radical and a supporter of the French Revolution: but he is ready to reflect.

I am by education and conviction inclined to republicanism and puritanism. In America they have both; but I confess I feel a little staggered . . . when I ask myself, 'Can they throughout the United States, from Boston to Baltimore, produce a single head like one of Titian's Venetian nobles, nurtured in all the pride of aristocracy and all the blindness of popery?'

Moreover he can take a cheerful holiday from his graver sentiments.

Could I have had my will, I should have been born a lord: but one would not be a booby lord neither. I am haunted by an odd fancy of driving down the Great North Road in a chaise and four, about fifty years ago, and coming to the inn at Ferrybridge, with outriders, white favours, and a coronet on the panels; and then, too, I choose my companion in the coach. Really there is a witchcraft in all this that makes it necessary to turn away from it, lest, in the conflict between imagination and impossibility, I should grow feverish and lightheaded! But, on the other hand, if one was a born lord, should one have the same idea (that everyone else has) of *a peeress in her own right?* Is not distance, giddy elevation, mysterious awe, an impassible gulf, necessary to form this idea in the mind, that fine ligament of 'ethereal braid, sky-woven', that lets down heaven upon earth, fair as enchantment, soft as Berenice's hair, bright and garlanded like Ariadne's crown; and is it not better to have had this idea all through life – to have caught but glimpses of it, to have known it but in a dream – than to have been born a lord ten times over, with twenty pampered menials at one's beck, and twenty descents to boast of?

On Personal Identity

'Earnestness,' said Samuel Butler, 'is the last enemy to be overcome.' Vehement, opinionated Hazlitt could overcome it.

HEAVEN

The spirit of the dead Protesilaus appears for a moment before his bereaved and loving wife Laodomia:

... In his deportment, shape, and mien, appeared
Elysian beauty, melancholy grace,
Brought from a pensive though a happy place.

He spake of love, such love as Spirits feel
In worlds whose course is equable and pure;
No fears to beat away – no strife to heal –
The past unsighed for, and the future sure;
Spake of heroic arts in graver mood
Revived, with finer harmony pursued;

Of all that is most beauteous – imagined there
In happier beauty; more pellucid streams,
An ampler ether, a diviner air,
And fields invested with purpureal gleams;
Climes which the sun, who sheds the brightest day
Earth knows, is all unworthy to survey.

Wordsworth, 'Laodomia'

Wordsworth is speaking of the Greek Elysium: yet I know of no description in our literature of the Christian heaven that communicates such a sense of ineffable bliss, as do these lines: and, paradoxically, the words 'pensive' and 'melancholy' seem to intensify the blissful effect.

THE HEBRIDES

Or, where the Northern Ocean in vast whirls
Boils round the naked melancholy isles

Of farthest Thule, and the Atlantic surge
Pours in among the stormy Hebrides . . .

James Thomson, 'Autumn'; The Seasons

Ay me! whilst thee the shores and sounding seas
Wash far away, where'er thy bones are hurled;
Whether beyond the stormy Hebrides,
Where thou perhaps under the whelming tide
Visit'st the bottom of the monstrous world; . . .

Milton, 'Lycidas'

No Nightingale did ever chaunt
More welcome notes to weary bands
Of travellers in some shady haunt,
Among Arabian sands:
A voice so thrilling ne'er was heard
In spring-time from the Cuckoo-bird,
Breaking the silence of the seas
Among the farthest Hebrides.

Wordsworth, 'The Solitary Reaper'

From the lone sheiling of the misty island
Mountains divide us, and the waste of seas –
Yet still the blood is strong, the heart is Highland,
And we in dreams behold the Hebrides!

J. G. Lockhart

The name Hebrides has a peculiar and potent magic, denied, so far as I know, to other groups of islands. It is its presence that makes these four quotations spellbinding. Why?

THE HEROIC

I have heard it said that readers no longer respond to the heroic in literature. It is more likely that they are quicker and more fastidi-

ous to detect the pseudo-heroic or the heroic chord jarred by a
false note. It is all too easy to make the hero, or he who praises
him, sound self-admiring and self-advertising. Simplicity and self-
restraint are necessary for the heroic note to tell. Shakespeare
himself illustrates this. I do not find Henry V's speeches deeply
stirring; their fine florid rhetoric seems too conscious of itself.
Kipling's heroes too, for all that they are often made to talk in
colloquial cockney, have a touch of staginess about them; and
their creator is too obviously pleased with himself for admiring
them. The fact that they are represented as inarticulate seems to
enhance his admiration. He seems to be saying 'how splendidly
manly and homely it is of these men not to be able to express
themselves and how manly and democratic of me it is to appreciate
this!' Such carefully staged inarticulateness exhales a disagreeable
smell of self-admiration. All this it is – and the grim experience of
two world wars – that has produced the impression that people
no longer respond to the heroic. But since, as Dr Johnson said,
courage is the first of virtues because without it we cannot be sure
of maintaining any others, the heroic, well expressed, still stirs the
heart. Well-expressed means articulately but simply. Shakespeare
can show an example of the right as well as of the wrong. He may
fail with King Henry V, but not with Feeble the women's tailor,
conscripted by Falstaff to leave his peaceful life in a country village
to join the army. His tougher-looking neighbours Wart and
Bullcalf hang back. Not so Feeble.

> 'By my troth, I care not:' [he says], 'a man can die but once: we
> owe God a death: I'll ne'er bear a base mind: an't be my
> destiny, so: a'nt be not, so. No man's too good to serve's
> prince; and, let it go which way it will, he that dies this year,
> is quit for the next.'
>
> *Henry IV, pt. II*

It is from Feeble, not from King Henry V, that we hear the true
accents of a hero. So also in the work of Scott, the novelist likest
to Shakespeare, the humble Highland gillie Evan outshines the
lordly head of his clan, Vich Ian Vohr Fergus McIvor. Both are
on trial for their lives, as Jacobite rebels after the failure of the
1745 rebellion:

Fergus, as the Presiding Judge was putting on the fatal cap of judgment, placed his bonnet upon his head, regarded him with a steadfast and stern look, and replied in a firm voice, 'I cannot let this numerous audience suppose that to such an appeal I have no answer to make. But what I have to say, you would not bear to hear, for my defence would be your condemnation. Proceed, then, in the name of God, to do what is permitted to you. Yesterday, and the day before, you have condemned loyal and honourable blood to be poured forth like water. Spare not mine. Were that of all my ancestors, in my veins, I would have peril'd it in this quarrel.'

Evan Maccombich looked at him with great earnestness, and, rising up, seemed anxious to speak; but the confusion of the court, and the perplexity arising from thinking in a language different from that in which he was to express himself, kept him silent. There was a murmur of compassion among the spectators, from the idea that the poor fellow intended to plead the influence of his superior as an excuse for his crime . . .

'I was only ganging to say, my lord,' said Evan, in what he meant to be an insinuating manner, 'that if your excellent honour, and the honourable Court, would let Vich Ian Vohr go free just this once, and let him gae back to France, and no to trouble King George's government again, that ony six o' the very best of his clan will be willing to be justified in his stead; and if you'll just let me gae down to Glennaquoich, I'll fetch them up to ye mysell, to head or hang, and you may begin wi' me the very first man.'

Notwithstanding the solemnity of the occasion, a sort of laugh was heard in the court at the extraordinary nature of the proposal. The Judge checked this indecency, and Evan, looking sternly around, when the murmur abated, 'If the Saxon gentlemen are laughing,' he said, 'because a poor man, such as me, thinks my life, or the life of six of my degree, is worth that of Vich Ian Vohr, it's like enough they may be very right; but if they laugh because they think I would not keep my word, and come back to redeem him, I can tell them they ken neither the heart of a Hielandman, nor the honour of a gentleman.'

There was no farther inclination to laugh among the audience, and a dead silence ensued.

Sir Walter Scott, Waverley

For me, the greatest heroic speech in English literature is that
of Mr Valiant-for-truth, in *Pilgrim's Progress*, about to enter the
river of Death:

After this it was noised abroad that Mr. Valiant-for-truth
was taken with a Summons by the same Post as the other.
When he understood it, he called for his friends, and told them
of it. Then, he said, 'I am going to my Father's; and though
with great difficulty I am got hither, yet now I do not repent
me of all the trouble I have been at to arrive where I am. My
sword I give to him that shall succeed me in my pilgrimage,
and my courage and skill to him that can get it. My marks and
scars I carry with me, to be a witness for me, that I have fought
his battle who now will be my rewarder.' When the day that he
must go hence was come, many accompanied him to the river
side, into which as he went he said 'Death, where is thy sting?'
And as he went down deeper, he said 'Grave, where is thy
victory?' So he passed over, and all the trumpets sounded for
him on the other side.

John Bunyan

All these passages are fictional. I know one true sentence that is
their equal. It is from a letter written during the Civil War by
Lord Ormonde in answer to one condoling with him on the death
of his young son killed in battle. 'I would rather have my dead son
than any living son in Christendom.'

All these passages, except that from *Waverley*, were written in
the 16th and 17th centuries. In the age that extended to include
Shakespeare at the beginning and Bunyan at the end, people were
not, as they became later, self-conscious about expressing noble
sentiments. Moreover, the language to express them in had not
been devalued by misuse and over-use. I do not know if the same
is true of other literatures. But certainly in 1940, during the heroic
days of the Battle of Britain, I found myself recalling the words of
17th-century La Fontaine:

Tu murmures, vieillard! vois ces jeunes mourir,
Vois-les marcher, vois-les courir
A des morts, il est vrai, glorieuses et belles
Mais sures cependant, et quelquefois cruelles.

HUMOUR

I

My end-papers are scrawled all over with references to passages marked because they made me laugh. Here are some of them. Are they distinguished by some common quality? I find it impossible to say. Humour is as hard to define as beauty is; and it is as various. There is satirical humour and sympathetic humour, verbal humour and nonsense humour, humour that springs from preposterous flights of fancy, and humour that springs from sharp accurate observation of life in the real world: there is also humour that comes from combinations and permutations of these different categories. Nothing is to be gained, I suggest, from trying to impose an order on a scene so complex and confusing: there is also something absurd in trying seriously and strenuously to analyse the nature of jokes. It is better to enjoy them. Below are some diverse and, to me, irresistibly entertaining examples:

... in the course of my long residence in London, I did entertain friends. But the memory of those occasions is not dear to me – especially not the memory of those that were in the more distinguished restaurants. Somewhere in the back of my brain, while I tried to lead the conversation brightly, was always the haunting fear that I had not brought enough money in my pocket. I never let this fear master me. I never said to anyone 'Will you have a liqueur?' – always 'What liqueur will you have?' But I postponed as far as possible the evil moment of asking for the bill. When I had, in the proper casual tone (I hope and believe), at length asked for it, I wished always it were not brought to me *folded* on a plate, as though the amount were so hideously high that I alone must be privy to it. So soon as it was laid beside me, I wanted to know the worst at once. But I pretended to be so occupied in talk that I was unaware of the bill's presence; and I was careful to be always in the middle of a sentence when I raised the upper fold and took my not (I hope) frozen glance. In point of fact, the amount was always much less than I had feared. Pessimism does win us great happy moments.

Max Beerbohm, Hosts and Guests

Mr Pooter and his wife Carrie pay a Sunday afternoon visit to Mr Finsworth:

We found Watney Lodge farther off than we anticipated, and only arrived as the clock struck two, both feeling hot and uncomfortable. To make matters worse, a large collie dog pounced forward to receive us. He barked loudly and jumped up at Carrie, covering her light skirt, which she was wearing for the first time, with mud. Teddy Finsworth came out and drove the dog off and apologised. We were shown into the drawing room, which was beautifully decorated. It was full of knick-knacks, and some plates hung up on the wall. There were several little wooden milk-stools with paintings on them; also a white wooden banjo painted by one of Mr. Paul Finsworth's nieces – a cousin of Teddy's.

Mr. Paul Finsworth seemed quite a distinguished-looking elderly gentleman, and was most gallant to Carrie. There were a great many water-colours hanging on the walls, mostly different views of India, which were very bright . . .

There was also a large picture in a very handsome frame done in coloured crayons. It looked like a religious subject. I was very much struck with the lace collar, it looked so real, but I unfortunately made the remark that there was something about the expression of the face that was not quite pleasing. It looked pinched. Mr. Finsworth sorrowfully replied: 'Yes, the face was done after death – my wife's sister.'

I felt terribly awkward and bowed apologetically, and in a whisper said I hoped I had not hurt his feelings. We both stood looking at the picture for a few minutes in silence, when Mr. Finsworth took out a handkerchief and said: 'She was sitting in our garden last summer,' and blew his nose violently. He seemed quite affected, so I turned to look at something else and stood in front of a portrait of a jolly-looking middle-aged gentleman, with a red face and straw hat. I said to Mr. Finsworth: 'Who is this jovial-looking gentleman? Life doesn't seem to trouble him much.' Mr. Finsworth said: 'No, it doesn't. *He is dead too – my brother.*'

I was absolutely horrified at my own awkwardness. Fortunately at this moment Carrie entered with Mrs. Finsworth, who had taken her upstairs to take off her bonnet and brush her skirt. Teddy said: 'Short is late,' but at that moment the gentle-man referred to arrived, and I was introduced to him by Teddy, who said: 'Do you know Mr. Short?' I replied, smiling, that I had not that pleasure, but I hoped it would not be *long* before I knew Mr. *Short*. He evidently did not see my little joke, although I repeated it twice with a little laugh. I suddenly re-membered it was Sunday, and Mr. Short was perhaps *very particular*.

In this I was mistaken, for he was not at all particular in several of his remarks after dinner. In fact I was so ashamed of one of his observations that I took the opportunity to say to Mrs. Finsworth that I feared she found Mr. Short occasionally a little embarrassing. To my surprise she said: 'Oh! he is privileged you know.' I did *not* know as a matter of fact, and so I bowed apologetically. I fail to see why Mr. Short should be privileged.

George and Weedon Grossmith, The Diary of a Nobody

It is a fact that not once in all my life have I gone out for a walk. I have been taken out for walks; but that is another matter. Even while I trotted prattling by my nurse's side I regretted the good old days when I had, and wasn't, a perambu-lator. When I grew up it seemed to me that the one advantage of living in London was that nobody ever wanted me to come out for a walk. London's very draw-backs – its endless noise and hustle, its smoky air, the squalor ambushed everywhere in it – assured this one immunity. Whenever I was with friends in the country, I knew that at any moment, unless rain were actually falling, some man might suddenly say 'Come out for a walk!' in that sharp imperative tone which he would not dream of using in any other connexion. People seem to think there is something inherently noble and virtuous in the desire to go for a walk. Any one thus desirous feels that he has a right to impose his will on whomever he sees comfortably settled in an arm-chair, reading. It is easy to say simply 'No' to an old friend. In the case of a mere acquaintance one wants some excuse. 'I wish I could, but' – nothing ever occurs to me except 'I have some letters to write.' This formula is unsatisfactory in three ways. (1) It isn't believed. (2) It compels you to rise from your chair, go to the writing-table, and sit improvising a letter to somebody until the walkmonger (just not daring to call you liar and hypocrite) shall have lumbered out of the room. (3) It won't operate on Sunday mornings. 'There's no post out till this evening' clinches the matter; and you may as well go quietly.

Walking for walking's sake may be as highly laudable and exemplary a thing as it is held to be by those who practise it. My objection to it is that it stops the brain. Many a man has professed to me that his brain never works so well as when he is swinging along the high road or over hill and dale. This boast is not confirmed by my memory of anybody who on a Sunday morning has forced me to partake of his adventure. Experience teaches me that whatever a fellow-guest may have of power to instruct or to amuse when he is sitting on a chair, or standing on a hearth-rug, quickly leaves him when he takes one out for a walk. The ideas that came so thick and fast to him in any room, where are they now? where that encyclopaedic knowledge which he bore so lightly? where the kindling fancy that played like summer lightning over *any* topic that was started? The man's face that was so mobile is set now; gone is the light from his fine eyes. He says that A. (our host) is a thoroughly good fellow. Fifty yards further on, he adds that A. is one of the best fellows he has ever met. We tramp another furlong or so, and he says that Mrs. A. is a charming woman. Presently he adds that she is one of the most charming women he has ever known. We pass an inn. He reads vapidly aloud to me: 'The King's Arms. Licensed to sell Ales and Spirits.' I foresee that during the rest of the walk he will read aloud any inscription that occurs. We pass a milestone. He points at it with his stick, and says, 'Uxminster. 11 Miles.' We turn a sharp corner at the foot of a hill. He points at the wall, and says, 'Drive Slowly'. I see far ahead, on the other side of the hedge bordering the high road, a small notice-board. He sees it too. He keeps his eye on it. And in due course 'Trespassers,' he says, 'Will Be Prosecuted.' Poor man! – mentally a wreck.

Luncheon at the A.s', however, salves him and floats him in full sail. Behold him once more the life and soul of the party. Surely he will never, after the bitter lesson of this morning, go out for another walk. An hour later, I see him striding forth, with a new companion. I watch him out of sight. I know what

he is saying. He is saying that I am rather a dull man to go a
walk with. He will presently add that I am one of the dullest
men he ever went a walk with. Then he will devote himself to
reading out the inscriptions.

Max Beerbohm, 'Going for a Walk'

Some difficulties in English usage:

Where to use 'only' in a sentence is a moot question, one of the
mootest questions in all rhetoric. The purist will say that the
expression: 'He only died last week,' is incorrect, and that it
should be: 'He died only last week.' The purist's contention is
that the first sentence, if carried to a natural conclusion, would
give us something like this: 'He only died last week, he didn't
do anything else, that's all he did.' It isn't a natural conclusion,
however, because nobody would say that and if anybody did it
would be likely to lead to stomping of feet and clapping of
hands, because it is one of those singy-songy expressions which
set a certain type of person to acting rowdy and becoming un-
manageable. It is better just to let the expression go, either
one way or the other, because, after all, this particular sentence
is of no importance except in cases where one is breaking the
news to a mother. In such cases one should begin with: 'Mrs.
Gormley, your son has had an accident,' or, 'Mrs. Gormley,
your son is not so good,' and then lead up gently to: 'He died
only last week.'

The best way is often to omit 'only' and use some other
expression. Thus, instead of saying: 'He only died last week,'
one could say: 'It was no longer ago than last Thursday that
George L. Wodolgoffing became an angel.' Moreover, this is
more explicit and eliminates the possibility of a misunderstand-
ing as to who died. The greatest care in this regard, by the way,
should be taken with the verbs 'to die,' 'to love,' 'to embezzle,'
and the like. In this connection, it is well never to use 'only' at
the beginning of a sentence – 'Only one person loves me,' for
example. This of course makes it necessary to capitalize 'Only'
and there is the risk of a hurried reader taking it for a proper
noun and confusing it with the late Richard Olney, who was
Secretary of State under Cleveland.

The indefinite 'one' is another source of trouble and is frequently the cause of disagreeable scenes. Such a sentence as 'One loves one's friends' is considered by some persons to be stilted and over-formalized, and such persons insist that 'One loves his friends' is permissible. It is not permissible, however, because 'one' is indefinite and 'his' is definite and the combination is rhetorically impossible. This is known as hendiadys and was a common thing in Latin. Rare examples of it still exist and are extremely valuable as antiques, although it is usually unsafe to sit or lie down on one.

The chief objection to a consistent, or 'cross-country' use of 'one' is that it tends to make a sentence sound like a trombone solo – such as: 'One knows one's friends will help one, if one is in trouble, or at least one trusts one's friends will help one.' Even though this is correct, to the point of being impeccable, there is no excuse for it. The 'one' enthusiast should actually take up the trombone and let it go at that.

'One' is, as a matter of fact, too often used for the personal pronoun. What, for example, could be sillier than to write a lady like this: 'One loves you and one wonders if you love one.' Such a person is going to get nowhere. 'I love you. Do you love me?' is a much simpler and better way to say it, except, of course, that there is always the danger here of drifting into a popular ballad of the 'Ramona' type.

Some persons use neither the indefinite 'one' nor the definite pronoun, but substitute a pet name and get some such result as 'Mopsy loves Flopsy and wonders if Flopsy loves Mopsy.' This usage frequently gets into the newspapers and becomes famous, particularly if Flopsy is an ambitious blonde and Mopsy a wealthy mop-handle manufacturer. The fault here, however, is not so much with the nouns or pronouns as with the verb, 'to love'. Nothing can be done about the verb 'to love'.

James Thurber, 'The Owl in the Attic'

A correspondent has asked me to give some details of the new religions I mentioned the other day. I will do so as briefly as I can.

Oblong Movement: Belief in Goodness as a Vital Urge.

Gaga, Ltd. (See also Neo-Cretinism): Rejects belief in Sin or Hope. All things exist only in so far as they are selfconscious.

Mrs. Barlington's Top-Notchers: Rejects belief in death. Nothing is what it really is. Object of Life is Self-Expression.

Sadie's Ethical Boys: Belief in love as a be-all. Men wear no waistcoats. Women bishops.

Juggo: Transrhenanism under another name. Rejects belief in everything.

Upandup: Has been called transcendental rotarianism. One thing is as good as another. Doesn't matter what you do, so long as you don't do it.

The Caeruleans: Rejects belief in Life as an entity. Members call each other 'Pard.' The Big Chief Pard elected for life. No laughing.

Dr. Grant Armitage's Sky-Fans: Sometimes called the Song-birds. Firm belief in hymns. Eat nothing. Drink nothing. Wear no clothes. Simplification-urge is a major tenet.

Beachcomber, By the Way

(II)

These pieces are all from specifically humorous works. But some of the most amusing passages in English literature occur in the course of books not exclusively or even mainly comic.

'. . . I wouldn't have believed it, Mr. Chuzzlewit,' declared Mr. Pecksniff magnificently, 'if a Fiery Serpent had proclaimed it from the top of Salisbury Cathedral. I would have said that the Serpent lied. Such was my faith in Thomas Pinch that I would have cast the falsehood back into the Serpent's teeth, and would have taken Thomas to my heart. But I am not a Serpent, sir, myself, I grieve to say, and no excuse or hope is left me.'

Charles Dickens, Martin Chuzzlewit

. . . 'What a delightful place Bath is!' said Mrs. Allen, as they sat down near the great clock, after parading the room till they were tired; 'and how pleasant it would be if we had any acquaintance here'.

This sentiment had been uttered so often in vain that Mrs. Allen had no particular reason to hope it would be followed with more advantage now; but we are told to 'despair of nothing we would attain', as 'unwearied diligence our point would gain'. And the unwearied diligence with which she had every day wished for the same thing was at length to have its just reward; for hardly had she been seated ten minutes, before a lady of about her own age, who was sitting by her, and had been looking at her attentively for several minutes, addressed her with great complaisance in these words: 'I think, madam, I cannot be mistaken; it is a long time since I had the pleasure of seeing you, but is not your name Allen?' This question answered, as it readily was, the stranger pronounced hers to be Thorpe, and Mrs. Allen immediately recognized the features of her former schoolfellow and intimate, whom she had seen only once since their respective marriages, and that many years ago. Their joy on this meeting was very great, as well it might, since they had been contented to know nothing of each other for the last fifteen years. Compliments on good looks now passed; and, after observing how time had slipped away since they were last together, how little they had thought of meeting in Bath, and what a pleasure it was to see an old friend, they proceeded to make enquiries and give intelligence as to their families, sisters and cousins, talking both together, far more ready to give than to receive information, and each hearing very little of what the other said. Mrs. Thorpe, however, had one great advantage as a talker, over Mrs. Allen, in a family of children; and when she expatiated on the talents of her sons, and the beauty of her daughters – when she related their different situations and views – that John was at Oxford, Edward at Merchant-Taylors', and William at sea, and all of them more beloved and respected in their different stations than any other three beings ever were – Mrs. Allen had no similar information to give, no similar triumphs to press on the unwilling and unbelieving ear of her friend, and was forced to sit and appear to listen to all these material effusions, consoling herself, however, with the discovery, which her keen eye soon made, that the lace on Mrs. Thorpe's pelisse was not half so handsome as that on her own.

Jane Austen, Northanger Abbey

Mrs. Linnet had become a reader of religious books since Mrs. Tryan's advent, and as she was in the habit of confiding her perusal to the purely secular portions, which bore a very small proportion to the whole, she could make rapid progress through a large number of volumes. On taking up the biography of a celebrated preacher, she immediately turned to the end to see what disease he died of; and if his legs swelled, as her own occasionally did, she felt a stronger interest in ascertaining any earlier facts in the history of the dropsical divine – whether he had ever fallen off a stage-coach, whether he had married more than one wife, and, in general, any adventures or repartees recorded of him previous to the epoch of his conversion. She then glanced over the letters and diary, and wherever there was a predominance of Zion, the River of Life, and notes of exclamation, she turned over to the next page; but any passage in which she saw such promising nouns as 'smallpox', 'pony', 'boots and shoes', at once arrested her.

George Eliot, Janet's Repentance

. . . Mrs. Farrinder . . . was a copious, handsome woman, in whom angularity had been corrected by the air of success; she had a rustling dress (it was evident what *she* thought about taste), abundant hair of a glossy blackness, a pair of folded arms, the expression of which seemed to say that rest, in such a career as hers, was as sweet as it was brief, and a terrible regularity of feature. I apply that adjective to her fine placid mask because she seemed to face you with a question of which the answer was preordained, to ask you how a countenance could fail to be noble of which the measurements were so correct. You could contest neither the measurements nor the nobleness, and had to feel that Mrs. Farrinder imposed herself. There was a lithographic smoothness about her and a mixture of the American matron and the public character. There was something public in her eye, which was large, cold and quiet; it had acquired a sort of exposed reticence from the habit of looking down from a lecture-desk, over a sea of heads, while its distinguished owner was eulogised by a leading citizen. Mrs. Farrinder, at almost any time, had the air of being introduced by a few remarks. She talked with great slowness and distinctness and evidently had a high sense of responsibility; she pronounced every syllable of every word and insisted on being explicit. If in conversation with her, you attempted to take anything for granted, or to jump two or three steps at a time, she paused, looking at you with a cold patience, as if she knew that trick, and then went on at her own measured pace. She lectured on temperance and the rights of women; the ends she laboured for were to give the ballot to every woman in the country and to take the flowing bowl from every man. She was held to have a very fine manner, and to embody the domestic virtues and the graces of the drawing-room; to be a shining proof, in short, that the forum, for ladies, is not necessarily hostile to the fireside. She had a husband, and his name was Amariah.

Henry James, The Bostonians

. . . 'But this deceiving of folks is nothing unusual in matrimony,' said Farmer Cawtree. 'I know'd a man and wife – faith, I don't mind owning, as there's no strangers here, that the pair were my own relations – they'd be at it that hot one hour that you'd hear the poker, and the tongs, and the bellows, and the warming-pan, flee across the house with the movements of their vengeance; and the next hour you'd hear 'em singing "The Spotted Cow" together, as peaceable as two holy twins; yes – and very good voices they had, and would strike in like street ballet-singers to one another's support in the high notes.

. . . 'I knowed a woman, and the husband o' her went away for four-and-twenty-year,' [said the bark-ripper]. 'And one night he came home when she was sitting by the fire, and thereupon he sat down himself on the other side of the chimney-corner. "Well," says she, "have ye got any news?" "Don't know as I have," says he; "have you?" "No" says she, "except that my daughter by the husband that succeeded 'ee was married last month, which was a year after I was made a widow by him." "Oh! Anything else?" he says. "No," says she. And there they sat, one on each side of that chimney-piece, and were found by the neighbours sound asleep in their chairs, not having known what to talk about at all.'

Thomas Hardy, The Woodlanders

(III)

Finally some more sentences from Dickens and from a letter of Charles Lamb:

Mrs Gamp improves on the Bible:

'Rich folk may ride on camels,' said Mrs. Gamp, 'but it ain't so easy for 'em to see out of a needle's eye.'

'And which of all them smoking monsters is the Ankworks boat, I wonder. Goodness me!' cried Mrs. Gamp.
'What boat do you want?' asked Ruth.
'The Ankworks package,' Mrs. Gamp replied. 'I will not deceive you, my sweet. Why should I?'
'That is the Antwerp packet in the middle,' said Ruth.
'And I wish it was in Jonadge's belly, I do,' cried Mrs. Gamp; appearing to confound the prophet with the whale in this miraculous aspiration.

Martin Chuzzlewit

What Mr Dombey provided for the guests who had attended his son's christening:

. . . a cold collation, set forth in a cold pomp of glass and silver, and looking more like a dead dinner lying in state than a social refreshment . . .

Dombey and Son

I made a pun the other day, and palmed it upon Holcroft, who grinned like a Cheshire cat. (Why do cats grin in Cheshire? – Because it was once a country palatine and the cats cannot help laughing whenever they think of it, though I see no joke in it.)

Charles Lamb, Letters

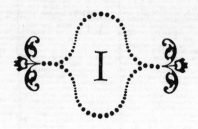

IMPRESSIONS

Perhaps, and when all is said and done, the criticisms most helpful to readers are impressionistic; those in which the critic – in a paragraph, a sentence, sometimes only a phrase – sums up and articulates the quality or blend of qualities that for him give a work its unique and precious flavour.

For instance Hazlitt on Wordsworth:

... There is a lofty philosophic tone, a thoughtful humanity, infused into his pastoral vein. Remote from the passions and events of the great world, he has communicated interest and dignity to the primal movements of the heart of man, and in-grafted his own conscious reflections on the casual thoughts of hinds and shepherds. Nursed amidst the grandeur of mountain scenery, he has stooped to have a nearer view of the daisy under his feet, or plucked a branch of white-thorn from the spray: but in describing it, his mind seems imbued with the majestic and solemnity of the objects around him – the tall rock lifts its head in the erectness of his spirit; the cataract roars in the sound of his verse; and in its dim and mysterious meaning, the mists seem to gather in the hollows of Helvellyn, and the forked Skiddaw hovers in the distance. There is little mention of mountainous scenery in Mr. Wordsworth's poetry; but by internal evidence one might be almost sure that it was written in a mountainous country, from its bareness, its simplicity, its loftiness and its depth!

The Spirit of the Age

or Charles Lamb on the dirge in Webster's *The White Devil*:

I never saw anything like the funeral dirge in this play, for the death of Marcello, except the ditty which reminds Ferdinand of his drowned father in the Tempest. As that is of the water, watery; so this is of the earth, earthy. Both have that intentness of feeling, which seems to resolve itself into the element which it contemplates.

Criticisms of Dramatic Writers

or Pater on Wordsworth:

. . . A sort of biblical depth and solemnity hangs over this strange, new, passionate pastoral world of which he first raised the image.

. . . the sudden passage from lowly thoughts and places to the majestic forms of philosophical imagination, the play of these forms over a world so different, enlarging so strangely the bounds of its humble churchyards, and breaking such a wild light on the graves of christened children.

Appreciations

or De La Mare on Bridges:

. . . he is the poet of happiness – not of mirth, gaiety, joviality, Bacchic abandon, but that of a mood, or, rather, a state of being in which mind and heart are at one, a balance between joy and solemnity such as delights and solaces us in the music of Handel . . .

Private View

or on the characters in Hardy's poems.

. . . these characters are mysterious, and touched with a kind of strangeness or romance, as indeed all humanity is mysterious when, viewed searchingly, it is off its guard . . .

Private View

or Virginia Woolf on Sophocles:

. . . Sophocles gliding like a shoal of trout smoothly and quietly, apparently motionless, and then, with a flicker of fins, off and away. . .

The Common Reader

or C. S. Lewis's description of what is at once the first and the final impression made on the imagination by Hamlet, that impression which remains in the memory when all discussions about its philosophic significance and the motives of its characters have grown dim:

> . . . night, ghosts, a castle, a lobby where a man can walk four hours together, a willow-fringed brook and a sad lady drowned, a graveyard and a terrible cliff above the sea, and amidst all these a pale man in black clothes . . . with his stockings coming down, a dishevelled man whose words make us at once think of loneliness and doubt and dread, of waste and dust and emptiness, and from whose hands, or from our own, we feel the richness of heaven and earth and the comfort of human affection slipping away.

They Asked for a Paper

INFLUENCES

We have done with dogma and divinity,
    Easter and Whitsun past,
The long, long Sundays after Trinity
    Are with us at last,
The passionless Sundays after Trinity,
    Neither feast-day nor fast.

Christmas comes with plenty,
    Lent spreads out its pall,
But these are five and twenty,
    The longest Sundays of all;
The placid Sundays after Trinity,
    Wheat-harvest, fruit-harvest, Fall.

Spring with its burst is over,
    Summer has had its day,
The scented grasses and clover
    Are cut, and dried into hay;
The singing birds are silent,
    And the swallows flown away.

Post pugnam pausa fiet;
   Lord, we have made our choice;
In the stillness of autumn quiet,
   We have heard the still, small voice.
We have sung *Oh where shall Wisdom?*
   Thick paper, folio, Boyce.

Let it not all be sadness,
   Not *omnia vanitas,*
Stir up a little gladness
   To lighten the *Tibi cras*;
Send us that little summer.
   That comes with Martinmas.

When still the cloudlet dapples
   The windless cobalt blue,
And the scent of gathered apples
   Fills all the store-rooms through,
The gossamer silvers the bramble,
   The lawns are gemmed with dew.

An end of tombstone Latinity,
   Stir up sober mirth,
Twenty-fifth after Trinity,
   Kneel with the listening earth,
Behind the Advent trumpets,
   They are singing Emmanuel's birth.

              John Meade Falkner, 'After Trinity'

This agreeable poem was written at least sixty years ago. But, alike in subject and spirit and manner it is so like the work of Sir John Betjeman that any literary historian might take for granted that its author had had a direct and major influence on it. In fact Sir John has only come across Meade Falkner's poems in later life and long after his own work had achieved its characteristic form.

   This should teach literary historians to beware of laying down the law about influences.

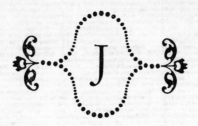

JANE AUSTEN'S LETTERS

Jane Austen's letters are not so amusing as her novels. They are too unpretentiously concerned to give the local news rather than to entertain her correspondent. But she cannot repress herself completely; now and again her robust and exquisite sense of fun breaks out – all the more gaily when she is writing to her sister Cassandra and can be as mischievous as she likes. Here are some examples:

At a ball in Bath:

> . . . there were people enough I suppose to have made five or six very pretty Basingstoke assemblies. I then got Mr. Evelyn to talk to, & Miss Twisleton to look at; and I am proud to say that I have a very good eye at an Adultress, for tho' repeatedly assured that another in the same party was the *She*, I fixed upon the right one from the first. A resemblance to Mrs. Leigh was my guide. She is not so pretty as I expected; her face has the same defect of baldness as her sister's, & her features not so handsome; she was highly rouged, & looked rather quietly & contentedly silly than anything else. Mrs. Badcock & two young Women were of the same party, except when Mrs. Badcock thought herself obliged to leave them to run round the room after her drunken Husband. His avoidance, and her pursuit, with the probable intoxication of both, was an amusing scene.

> *To Cassandra Austen: 12 May 1801*

Only think of Mrs. Holder being dead! Poor woman, she has done the only thing in the world she could possibly do to make one cease to abuse her.

The death of Mrs. W. K. we had seen. I had no idea that anybody liked her, & therefore felt nothing for any survivor, but I am now feeling sorry on her husband's account, and think he had better marry Miss Sharpe.

Mr. Hall is in such a very deep mourning that either his mother, his wife, or himself must be dead.

Mr. Richard Harvey is going to be married; but as it is a great secret, and only known to half the neighbourhood, you must not mention it.

Some of these remarks have shocked Jane Austen's Victorian and Edwardian critics as flippant and hard-hearted. She was neither but rather a child of the eighteenth century, an age less squeamish and more high-spirited than theirs. Indeed her tone was not peculiar to herself. We find it in the letters of two other women, contemporaries of her though living in a different world. Miss Emily Eden and Harriet, Lady Granville, observed Whig high society with the same agreeable sharp-tongued amusement as Jane Austen observed the country gentry. Moreover the crisp stylishness of their letters is noticeably like hers and unlike that of earlier or later generations.

Here is Lady Granville on her cousin Caroline, wife of William Lamb, enjoying herself in Paris after the Battle of Waterloo:

Nobody is agissant but Caroline William in a purple riding habit, tormenting everybody, but, I am convinced, ready primed for an attack upon the Duke of Wellington, and I have no doubt but that she will to a certain extent succeed, as no dose of flattery is too strong for him to swallow or her to administer. Poor William hides in a small room, while she assembles lovers and tradespeople in another. He looks worn to the bone. She arrived dying by her own account, having had French apothecaries at most of the towns through which she passed. She sent here immediately for a doctor, but by mistake they went for the Duke of Wellington . . .

on Lord and Lady Jersey:

The Jerseys go tomorrow. If I was handsome, and he not frivolous, we should certainly have a little affair together. 'La sympathie, doux lien des ames,' would unite us, but as it is we flag amazingly when left to ourselves. He has a mind composed of ennui and jokes, to me the most wearying of all compositions. They both like me as much as they can the person in the whole world who suits them least, and I am sure we feel at moments equal remorse at finding our affections towards each other so cold and dead in the midst of so many efforts and acts of kindness. I would risk my life for them rather than spend a week with them . . .

Now Emily Eden:

Lady Melville and her children were here for five days last week. I do not know exactly what I thought of her. She is too clever not to be rather pleasant, and too argumentative not to be very tiresome, and altogether I do not think I liked her . . .

To Lady Buckinghamshire, 1818

Miss P. is something of a failure in every way, except in intrinsic goodness; but she was terrified here, and at all times dull, and as nearly ugly as is lawful . . .

To Miss Villiers, 1821

We have had a spirt of company for the last three days, but they all very kindly walked off yesterday, and as it is wrong to dwell upon past evils, I spare you an account of most of them.

There were a Mr and Mrs Winyard amongst them who were very pleasant. He was in the army and is now in the Church, and though they are the sort of people who have a child every year, and talk about their governess, and though she very naturally imagined, that because she was absent, the high wind would blow away the little tittupy parsonage, and the ten precious children, yet they really were very agreeable.

To the Dowager Lady Buckinghamshire, 1819

Provided one was English and born in comfortable circum-
stances, there was a lot to be said for living in a period that could
produce this kind of entertaining lady.

DOCTOR JOHNSON

(1)

Life is barren enough surely with all her trappings; let us
therefore be cautious how we strip her.

No man is much regarded by the rest of the world. He that
considers how little he dwells upon the condition of others,
will learn how little the attention of others is attracted by
himself. While we see multitudes passing before us, of whom
perhaps not one appears to deserve our notice or excite our
sympathy, we should remember, that we likewise are lost in the
same throng; that the eye which happens to glance upon us is
turned in a moment on him that follows us, and that the utmost
which we can reasonably hope or fear, is to fill a vacant hour
with prattle, and be forgotten.

The man who threatens the world is always ridiculous; for
the world can easily go on without him, and in a short time
will cease to miss him.

His scorn of the great is repeated too often to be real; no man
thinks much of that which he despises.

To tell of disappointment and misery, to thicken the darkness
of futurity, and perplex, the labyrinth of uncertainty, has been
always a delicious employment of the poets.

The reciprocal civility of authors is one of the most risible
scenes in the farce of life.

The only end of writing is to enable the readers better to
enjoy life or better to endure it.

Histories of the downfall of kingdoms and revolutions of
empires, are read with great tranquility.

The perceptions as well as the senses may be improved to our own disquiet, and we may, by diligent cultivation of the powers of dislike, raise in time an artificial fastidiousness, which shall fill the imagination with phantoms of turpitude.

Were it not for imagination, Sir, a man would be as happy in the arms of a chambermaid as of a Duchess.

Marriage is not commonly unhappy, otherwise than as life is unhappy.

That which is to be loved long must be loved with reason rather than with passion.

Every one in this world has as much as they can do in caring for themselves and few have leisure really to think of their neighbour's distresses, however they may delight their tongues with talking of them.

. . . Sir, all the arguments which are brought to represent poverty as no evil, show it to be evidently a great evil. You never find people labouring to convince you that you may live very happily upon a plentiful fortune.

. . . Melancholy, indeed, should be diverted by every means but drinking . . .

Let no man's felicity depend on the death of his aunt.

Wigs and boots and snuff boxes are vain without a resolute determination to be merry.

[To someone lamenting exaggeratedly and insincerely over a bereavement] We must either outlive our friends or our friends outlive us; and I see no man that would hesitate about the choice.

[After his first and only day out hunting] The dogs had less sagacity than I could have prevailed upon myself to suppose. It is very strange and very melancholy that the paucity of human pleasures should persuade us ever to call hunting one of them.

If I had no duties, and no reference to futurity, I would spend my life in driving briskly in a post-chaise with a pretty woman.

Johnson is not to be resisted: even the Johnsonians cannot put one off him. He is an outstanding example of the charm that comes from an unexpected combination of qualities. In general, odd people are not sensible and sensible people are not odd. Johnson is both and often both at the same time. Like the child in the tale of the Emperor's New Clothes, he startles by saying something that no one has said before, but which we instantly recognize to be true.

Though, as a matter of fact, his odd untrue remarks have a special charm, just because they are so outrageously odd; as when he says of *Lycidas* 'its form is that of a pastoral, easy, vulgar, and therefore disgusting', or dogmatizes about the winter habits of the swallow.

. . . Swallows certainly sleep all winter. A number of them conglobulate together, by flying round and round, and then all in a heap throw themselves under water and lie in the bed of a river.

What perverse line of thought could have led him to assert that this preposterous flight of fancy was a certainty!

(11)

Johnson is equally good at greater length. His account of a philosophic discussion in *Rasselas* is as amusing as it is true to life and as true to life now as it was in the eighteenth century. The occasion of the discussion is the return of a hermit to the world in search of the happiness he has failed to find in his hermitage.

Prince Rasselas went often to an assembly of learned men, who met at stated times to unbend their minds, and compare their opinions. Their manners were somewhat coarse, but their conversation was instructive, and their disputations acute, though sometimes too violent, and often continued till neither controvertist remembered upon what question they began. Some faults were almost general among them: every one was desirous to dictate to the rest, and every one was pleased to hear the genius or knowledge of another depreciated.

In this assembly Rasselas was relating his interview with the hermit, and the wonder with which he heard him censure a course of life which he had so deliberately chosen, and so laudably followed. The sentiments of the hearers were various. Some were of the opinion, that the folly of his choice had been justly punished by condemnation to perpetual perseverance. One of the youngest among them, with great vehemence, pronounced him a hypocrite. Some talked of the right of society to the labour of individuals, and considered retirement as a desertion of duty. Others readily allowed, that there was a time when the claims of the publick were satisfied, and when a man might properly sequester himself, to review his life, and purify his heart.

One, who appeared more affected with the narrative than the rest, thought it likely, that the hermit would, in a few years, go back to his retreat, and, perhaps, if shame did not restrain, or death intercept him, return once more from his retreat into the world: 'For the hope of happiness, said he, is so strongly impressed, that the longest experience is not able to efface it. Of the present state, whatever it be, we feel, and are forced to confess, the misery, yet when the same state is again at a distance, imagination paints it as desirable. But the time will surely come, when desire will be no longer our torment, and no man shall be wretched but by his own fault.'

'This,' said a philosopher, who had heard him with tokens of great impatience, 'is the present condition of a wise man. The time is already come, when none are wretched but by their own fault. Nothing is more idle, than to enquire after happiness, which nature has kindly placed within our reach. The way to be happy is to live according to nature, in obedience to that universal and unalterable law with which every heart is originally impressed; which is not written on it by precept, but engraven by destiny, not instilled by education, but infused at our nativity. He that lives according to nature will suffer nothing from the delusions of hope, or importunities of desire: he will receive and reject with equability of temper; and act or suffer as the reason of things shall alternately prescribe. Other men may amuse themselves with subtle definitions, or intricate ratiocination. Let them learn to be wise by easier means: let them observe the hind of the forest, and the linnet of the grove: let them consider the life of animals, whose motions are regulated by instinct; they obey their guide and are happy. Let us therefore, at length, cease to dispute, and learn to live, throw away the incumbrance of precepts, which they who utter them with so much pride and pomp do not understand, and carry with us this simple and intelligible maxim. That deviation from nature is deviation from happiness.'

When he had spoken, he looked around him with a placid air, and enjoyed the consciousness of his own beneficence. 'Sir,' said the prince, with great modesty, 'as I, like all the rest of mankind, am desirous of felicity, my closest attention has been fixed upon your discourse: I doubt not the truth of a position which a man so learned has so confidently advanced. Let me only know what it is to live according to nature.'

'When I find young men so humble and so docile,' said the philosopher, 'I can deny them no information which my studies have enabled me to afford. To live according to nature, is to act always with due regard to the fitness arising from the relations and qualities of causes and effects; to concur with the great and unchangeable scheme of universal felicity; to co-operate with the general disposition and tendency of the present system of things.'

The prince soon found that this was one of the sages whom he should understand less as he heard him longer. He therefore bowed and was silent, and the philosopher, supposing him satisfied, and the rest vanquished, rose up and departed, with the air of a man that had co-operated with the present system.

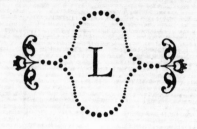

THE LAST LAP OF LIFE

The present is a fleeting moment, the past is no more; and our prospect of futurity is dark and doubtful. This day may *possibly* be my last: but the laws of probability, so true in general, so fallacious in particular, still allow about fifteen years. I shall soon enter into the period which, as the most agreeable of his long life, was selected by the judgement and experience of the sage Fontenelle. His choice is approved by the eloquent historian of nature, who fixes our moral happiness to the mature season in which our passions are supposed to be calmed, our duties fulfilled, our ambition satisfied, our fame and fortune established on a solid basis. In private conversation, that great and amiable man added the weight of his own experience; and this autumnal felicity might be exemplified in the lives of Voltaire, Hume, and many other men of letters. I am far more inclined to embrace than to dispute this comfortable doctrine. I will not suppose any premature decay of the mind or body; but I must reluctantly observe that two causes, the abbreviation of time, and the failure of hope, will always tinge with a browner shade the evening of life.

The proportion of a part to the whole is the only standard by which we can measure the length of our existence. At the age of twenty, one year is a tenth perhaps of the time which has elapsed within our consciousness and memory; at the age of fifty it is no more than the fortieth, and this relative value continues to decrease till the last sands are shaken by the hand of death. This reasoning may seem metaphysical; but on a trial it will be found satisfactory and just. The warm desires, the long expectations of youth, are founded on the ignorance of themselves and of the world: they are gradually damped by time and experience, by disappointment or possession; and after the middle season the crowd must be content to remain at the foot of the mountain; while the few who have climbed the summit aspire to descend or expect to fall. In old age, the consolation of hope is reserved for the tenderness of parents, who commence a new life in their children; the faith of enthusiasts, who sing Hallelujahs above the clouds; and the vanity of authors, who presume the immortality of their name and writings.

Edward Gibbon, Autobiography

. . . as the time of rest, or of departure, approaches me, not only do many of the evils I had heard of, and prepared for, present themselves in more grievous shapes than I had expected; but one which I had scarcely ever heard of, torments me increasingly every hour.

I had understood it to be in the order of things that the aged should lament their vanishing life as an instrument they had never used, now to be taken away from them; but not as an instrument, only then perfectly tempered and sharpened, and snatched out of their hands at the instant they could have done some real service with it. Whereas, my own feeling, now, is that everything which has hitherto happened to me, or been done by me, whether well or ill, has been fitting me to take greater fortune more prudently, and do better work more thoroughly. And just when I seem to be coming out of school – very sorry to have been such a foolish boy, yet having taken a prize or two, and expecting to enter now upon some more serious business than cricket, – I am dismissed by the Master I hoped to serve, with a – 'That's all I want of you, sir.'

John Ruskin, St Mark's Rest

. . . the charm I find in old age – for I was never happier than I am now – comes of having learned to live in the moment, and thereby in eternity; and this means recovering a perpetual youth, since nothing can be fresher than each day as it dawns and changes. When we have no expectations, the actual is a continual free gift, but much more placidly accepted than it could be when we were children; for then the stage was full of trap doors and unimaginable transformations that kept us always alarmed, eager and on the point of tears; whereas now we have wept our tears out, we know what can pop [out] of those trap doors, and what kind of shows those transformations can present; and we remember many of them with affection, and watch the new ones that come with interest and good will, but without false claims for our own future.

George Santayana, Letters

These vital links that bind the present to the past – how many of them have already been broken and how increasingly often, as one grows older, does one receive the news of yet another break. And the questions keep multiplying. How are we related to what we were? who are we now and what were we then? And who were the others – in our minds, in their minds, in the minds of omniscience. There are no answers of course – only the fact of living, changing, remembering and at last dying.

Aldous Huxley, Letters

I

That is no country for old men. The young
In one another's arms, birds in the trees,
– Those dying generations – at their song,
The salmon-falls, the mackerel-crowded seas,
Fish, flesh, or fowl, commend all summer long
Whatever is begotten, born, and dies.
Caught in that sensual music all neglect
Monuments of unageing intellect.

II

An aged man is but a paltry thing,
A tattered coat upon a stick, unless
Soul clap its hands and sing, and louder sing
For every tatter in its mortal dress,
Nor is there singing school but studying
Monuments of its own magnificence;

And therefore I have sailed the seas and come
To the holy city of Byzantium.

III

O sages standing in God's holy fire
As in the gold mosaic of a wall
Come from the holy fire, perne in a gyre,
And be the singing-masters of my soul.
Consume my heart away; sick with desire
And fastened to a dying animal
It knows now what it is; and gather me
Into the artifice of eternity.

IV

Once out of nature I shall never take
My bodily form from any natural thing,
But such a form as Grecian goldsmiths make
Of hammered gold and gold enamelling
To keep a drowsy Emperor awake;
Or set upon a golden bough to sing
To lords and ladies of Byzantium
Of what is past, or passing, or to come.

W. B. Yeats, 'Sailing to Byzantium'

Five comments on life as it appears to five men who have reached
its last phase. They are all contemplatives – writers and authors –
which means that old age is better for them than for men of
action. For, so long as they retain the use of their mental faculties,
they can still go on doing the work which gives value and signifi-
cance to their lives; whereas men of action in old age are liable to
feel their lives useless and without purpose.

All the same, three of these contemplatives regard old age as
casting a shadow. Huxley is sad and bewildered, Gibbon calm but
unhopeful, Ruskin resentful and disappointed that there may not
be time left for him in which to do what he expected to be his
best work. Yeats, on the other hand, has turned from the transient
world of human beings to find a deeper reality in the timeless and

invulnerable world of art; while Santayana is glad to be able, for the first time, to live contentedly in the moment, freed by the prospect of approaching death from any anxiety about the future.

For me, the actual sense of old age and the new strange light, in which it reveals the long perspective of past years, is best expressed by some sentences from the later diaries of Walter Scott. 'What is this world? A dream within a dream – as we grow older, each step is an awakening. The youth awakes, as he thinks, from childhood – the full-grown man despises the pursuits of youth as visionary – the old man looks on manhood as a feverish dream. The grave, the last sleep? – No; it is the last and final awakening.'

LAWS

How small, of all that human hearts endure,
That part which laws or kings can cause or cure!
Still to ourselves in every place consigned
Our own felicity we make or find . . .

Lines from Oliver Goldsmith's 'The Traveller'
(said to have been composed by Samuel Johnson)

These lines are not so true now as when they were first published in 1765. Centralization, technology and all the complex inter-dependent paraphernalia of modern life have increased the power of governments to affect the lives of the average person. Yet, in Western Europe at any rate, they are still a great deal truer than politicians and social scientists would have us believe. Except in moments of international and national crisis, people are happy or unhappy, not by will of the government but according as to whether or not they are good-humoured and sensible, unegotistic and adaptable.

The sooner they realize this the better. People are much given to lamenting that the English are losing faith in the capacity of politicians and political parties to better their lives. If true, this is an excellent thing. It means that they are learning to recognize a basic truth about the human condition.

LOVE LETTERS

. . . You are as much pleased, you say, with writing to me as I can be to receive your letters. Why should you not think the same of me? In earnest you may, and if you love me, you will, but then how much more satisfied should I be if there were no need of these and we might talk all that we write and more. Shall we ever be so happy?

Last night I was in the garden until eleven o'clock. It was the sweetest night that e'er I saw. The garden looked so well and the jessamine smelt beyond all perfume. And yet I was not pleased. The place had all the charms it used to have when I was most satisfied with it, and had you been there I should have liked it much more than ever I did; but that not being, it was no more to me than the next field . . .

Dorothy Osborne to William Temple

. . . The morning is the only proper time for me to write to a beautiful Girl whom I love so much: for at night, when the lonely day has closed, and the lonely, silent, unmusical Chamber is waiting to receive me as into a Sepulchre, then believe me my passion gets entirely the sway, then I would not have you see those rhapsodies which I once thought it impossible I should ever give way to, and which I have often laughed at in another; for fear you should think me either too unhappy or perhaps a little mad. I am now at a very pleasant Cottage window, looking onto a beautiful hilly country, with a glimpse of the sea; the morning is very fine. I do not know how elastic my spirit might be, what pleasure I might have in living here and breathing and wandering as free as a stag about this beautiful Coast if the remembrance of you did not weigh so upon me . . . Ask yourself my love whether you are not very cruel to have so entrammelled me, so destroyed my freedom. Will you confess this in the letter you must write immediately and do all you can to console me in it – make it rich as a draught of poppies to intoxicate me – write the softest words and kiss them that I may at least touch my lips where yours have been. For myself I know not how to express my devotion to so fair a form: I want a brighter word than bright, a fairer word than fair. I almost wish we were butterflies and liv'd but three summer days – three such days with you I could fill with more delight than fifty common years could ever contain. . . .

John Keats to Fanny Brawne

LOVESOME

Adjectives ending in 'some' have come to be regarded with suspicion; 'gladsome', 'winsome', 'fearsome', 'lovesome'. 'Lovesome is one of the most suspect on account of its association with T. E. Brown's unpleasing line 'a garden is a lovesome thing, God wot'. But no word can be good or bad in itself; to think it can be, is to be a word-snob, like those French writers of classical tragedy who refused to use the word '*chien*' on the ground that it lacked tragic dignity. Tennyson was a word-snob when he spoke of 'the knightly growth that fringed the lip' of one of his heroes rather than bring into a poem such an unromantic word as moustache. It should be possible for a good poet to use the word 'lovesome' and make the reader like it. In fact a good poet has done so. Sir George Etherege, in the reign of King Charles the Second, beautifully describes a girl as

'wild, witty, lovesome, beautiful and young'.

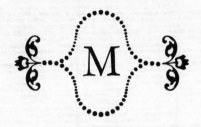

MACHINERY

How was November's melancholy endear'd to me
in the effigy of plowteams following and recrossing
patiently the desolate landscape from dawn to dusk,
as the slow-creeping ripple of their single furrow
submerged the sodden litter of summer's festival!
They are fled, those gracious teams; high on the headland now
squatted, a roaring engin toweth to itself
a beam of bolted shares, that glideth to and fro
combing the stubbled glebe: and agriculture here,
blotting out with such daub so rich a pictur of grace,
hath lost as much of beauty as it hath saved in toil.

Again where reapers, bending to the ripen'd corn,
were wont to scythe in rank and step with measured stroke,
a shark-tooth'd chariot rampeth biting a broad way,
and, jerking its high swindging arms around in the air,
swoopeth the swath. Yet this queer Pterodactyl is well,
that in the sinister torpor of the blazing day
clicketeth in heartless mockery of swoon and sweat,
as 'twer the salamandrine voice of all parch'd things:
and the dry grasshopper wondering knoweth his God.

Or what man feeleth not a new poetry of toil,
whenas on frosty evenings 'neath its clouding smoke
the engin hath huddled-up its clumsy threshing-coach
against the ricks, wherefrom laborers standing aloft
toss the sheaves on its tongue; while the grain runneth out,
and in the whirr of its multitudinous hurry
it hummeth like the bee, a warm industrious boom

that comforteth the farm, and spreadeth far afield
with throbbing power; as when in a cathedral awhile
the great diapason speaketh, and the painted saints
feel their glass canopies flutter in the heav'nward prayer.

Robert Bridges, 'The Testament of Beauty'

Tree-leaves labour up and down,
　And through them the fainting light
　Succumbs to the crawl of night.
Outside in the road the telegraph wire
　To the town from the darkening land
Intones to travellers like a spectral lyre
　Swept by a spectral hand.

A car comes up, with lamps full-glare,
　That flash upon a tree:
　It has nothing to do with me,
And whangs along in a world of its own,
　Leaving a blacker air;
And mute by the gate I stand again alone,
　And nobody pulls up there.

Thomas Hardy, 'Nobody Comes'

It was a clear still night and every tree in the square was
visible; some were black, others were sprinkled with strange
patches of green artificial light. Above the arc lamps rose shafts
of darkness. Although it was close on midnight, it scarcely
seemed to be night; but rather some ethereal disembodied day,
for there were so many lamps in the streets; cars passing; men
in white mufflers with their light overcoats open walking along
the clean dry pavements, and many houses were still lit up, for
everyone was giving parties. The town changed as they drew
smoothly through Mayfair. The public houses were closing;
here was a group clustered round a lamp-post at the corner . . .
Now they had turned, and the car was gliding at full speed up
a long bright avenue of great shuttered shops. The streets were
almost empty. The yellow station clock showed that they had
five minutes to spare.

Just in time, she said to herself. The usual exhilaration mounted in her as she walked along the platform. Diffused light poured down from a great height. Men's cries and the clangour of shunting carriages echoed in the immense vacancy. The train was waiting; travellers were making ready to start. Some were standing with one foot on the step of the carriage drinking out of thick cups as if they were afraid to go far from their seats. She looked down the length of the train and saw the engine sucking water from a hose. It seemed all body, all muscle; even the neck had been consumed into the smooth barrel of the body. This was 'the' train; the others were toys in comparison. She snuffed up the sulphurous air, which left a slight tinge of acid at the back of the throat, as if it already had a tang of the north.

Virginia Woolf, The Years

The coming of the machine age presented, perhaps still presents, a problem to poets. They must mention machines for they are as much basic and controlling features of our life as were ploughs and spades in the past. But the passage of centuries have endowed the words 'plough' and 'spade' with imaginative associations, they have become poetical; whereas the machines of today – cars and tractors etc. – have not had much time yet for this to happen. How then are the poets to make them poetical? Bridges and Hardy represent two ways of doing this. Bridges openly admits the problem. He describes the immemorial English landscape in traditional poetic terms and then plants modern machines in it, pointing out how incongruous they seem there. After this he sets to work to blend them into the ancient scene and thus give them imaginative associations. The result is beautiful but artificial. Hardy, simpler and bolder, is inspired to write a lyric about an experience which involves his mentioning a car and a telegraph wire. But he speaks of them as spontaneously and unselfconsciously as a poet of the past spoke of spades and ploughs. The result is beautiful and natural.

Both writers have been helped by the fact that the machines are presented in an ancient and beautiful natural setting. It is a harder task to acclimatize them to poetry, if they have to appear in a setting without such associations. But it can be done and even without the help of metre. Nothing could be further from beautiful nature than King's Cross railway station and the streets leading to it. Yet Virginia Woolf's description of them is both realistically accurate and aglow with poetry.

MAGIC

Look not thou on beauty's charming,
Sit thou still when kings are arming,
Taste not when the wine-cup glistens,
Speak not when the people listens,
Stop thine ear against the singer,
From the red gold keep thy finger;
Vacant heart and hand and, eye,
Easy live and quiet die.

Sir Walter Scott, 'The Bride of Lammermoor'

This is an extraordinary poem. The word 'magic' is for once strictly applicable: there is something spell-like and supernatural in the way it utters its mysterious message, its chill repudiation of all human passion and action. This is the more surprising when we remember its author was the warm-hearted, action-loving Walter Scott. But Scott was a stranger man than is generally thought. Intertwined with the firm sane fabric of his personality was a wild and unpredictable strain. It is heard again in Madge Wildfire's snatch of ballad:

My banes are buried in yon kirk-yard
  Sae far ayont the sea,
And it is but my blithesome ghaist
  That's speaking now to thee.

The Heart of Midlothian

MANNER

... As the Frenchman said, *'Il y a toujours le manière'*. Very true. Yes. There is the manner. The manner in laughter, in tears, in irony, in indignations and enthusiasms, in judgements – and even in love. Manner in which, as in the features and character of a human face, the inner truth is foreshadowed for those who know how to look at their kind.

Joseph Conrad, A Personal Record

Conrad is right. 'How' is just as important as 'what', especially in what Conrad calls enthusiasms. No cause seems wholly bad, if it is supported scrupulously, honourably, magnanimously and with a recognition that nothing human is perfect. Pursued unscrupulously, ungenerously and arrogantly, the best cause becomes a bad one.

MARRIED LOVE

'Our sweetest songs', wrote Shelley in 'To a Skylark', 'are those that tell of saddest thought.' Poems about marriage confirm, for the most part, this discouraging statement. Successful marriages have seldom inspired successful poetry. The happily married poets, like Browning and Patmore, appear all too anxious to advertise their happiness: to quote Oscar Wilde, 'they wash their clean linen in public'. Wordsworth and Stevenson have sung the praises of their wives; but hardly in a way to make them sound attractive. 'Mrs. Wordsworth', wrote her husband, was:

A perfect Woman, nobly planned
To warn, to comfort, and command.

Comfort sounds well enough; but who would want a wife noted for her ability to warn and to command!
Mrs Stevenson sounds equally formidable:

Trusty, dusky, vivid, true,
With eyes of gold and bramble-dew,
Steel-true and blade-straight,
The great artificer
Made my mate.

Honour, anger, valour, fire;
A love that life could never tire,

Death quench or evil stir,
The mighty master
Gave to her . . .

R. L. *Stevenson, 'My Wife'*

Yet happy married love is the best thing life has to give. It would be sad indeed if it had never been an inspiration to poets. The two poems printed below show that it can be.

So sweet love seemed that April morn,
When first we kissed besides the thorn
So strangely sweet, it was not strange
We thought that love could never change.

But I can tell – let truth be told –
That love will change in growing old;
Though day by day is nought to see,
So delicate his motions be.

And in the end 'twill come to pass
Quite to forget what once he was
Nor even in fancy to recall
The pleasure that was all in all.

His little spring, that sweet we found,
So deep in summer floods is drowned
I wonder, bathed in joy complete,
How love so young could be so sweet.

Robert Bridges

This is tender and beautiful and authentic. It fades into insignificance, however, when set beside Donne's triumphant paean of fulfilled and mutual love – all the more triumphant, one would imagine, since he had achieved it after many troubled amorous adventures.

All Kings, and all their favorites,
All Glory of Honors, beauties, wits,
The Sun itselfe, which makes times, as they passe,
Is elder by a yeare now, than it was

When thou and I first one another saw:
All other things, to their destruction draw,
   Only our love hath no decay;
This, no tomorrow hath, nor yesterday,
Running it never runs from us away,
But truly keepes his first, last, everlasting day.

   Two graves must hide thine and my coarse,
   If one might, death were no divorce.
Alas, as well as other Princes, wee,
(Who Prince enough in one another bee,)
Must leave at last in death, these eyes, and eares,
Oft fed with true oathes, and with sweet salt teares;
   But soules where nothing dwells but love
(All other thoughts being inmates) then shall prove
This, or a love increased there above,
When bodies to their graves, soules from their
   graves remove.

And then wee shall be throughly blest,
But wee no more, than all the rest;
Here upon earth, we'are Kings, and none but wee
Can be such Kings, nor of such subjects bee.
Who is so safe as wee? where none can doe
Treason to us, except one of us two.
   True and false feares let us refraine,
Let us love nobly, and live, and adde againe
Yeares and yeares unto yeares, till we attaine
To write threescore: this is the second of our raigne.

                                  'The Anniversarie'

Milton unexpectedly – for he was notoriously hard to please as
a husband – was far better at praising his wife than were Words-
worth and Stevenson.

Methought I saw my late espousèd saint
   Brought to me like Alcestis from the grave,
   Whom Jove's great son to her glad husband gave,
   Rescued from Death by force, though pale and faint.

Mine, as whom washed from spot of childbed taint
   Purification in the Old Law did save,
   And such as yet once more I trust to have
Full sight of her in Heaven without restraint,
Came vested all in white, pure as her mind.
   Her face was veiled; yet to my fancied sight
   Love, sweetness, goodness, in her person shined
So clear as in no face with more delight.
   But O! as to embrace me she inclined,
   I waked, she fled, and day brought back my night.

Milton, 'On His Deceased Wife'

'Love, sweetness, goodness, in her person shined' – this line is surely the most beautiful tribute paid to a wife by a husband in all English poetry. 'Shined' is the operative word, suggesting, as it does, that goodness, sweetness and love lit up her whole figure with a near visible radiance.

MELBOURNE

The second Viscount Melbourne was an amateur writer; his aphorisms lack the professional stylishness and concentration of Johnson's or Hazlitt's. But he was observant and humorous and independent-minded, and now and again he hits the nail sharply on the head.

Never disregard a book because the author of it is a foolish fellow.

Nobody ever did anything very foolish except from some strong principle.

This is too sweeping: to be unprincipled does not save a man from being foolish. All the same, to read history is to realize that there is a good deal in Melbourne's words.

It wounds a man less to confess that he has failed in any pursuit through idleness, neglect, the love of pleasure, etc.,

etc., which are his own faults, than through incapacity and unfitness which are the faults of his nature.

If you make an estimate of your expenses for the coming year, and upon that estimate you find that they exactly amount to or fall little short of your income, you may be sure that you are an embarrassed, if not a ruined man.

You should never assume contempt for that which it is not very manifest that you have it in your power to possess . . .

This last is very true. How often has one heard personal charm or a gift for social success spoken of contemptuously by people conspicuous for a lack of either!

MEMORIES

Do you remember – can we e'er forget? –
How, in the coiled perplexities of youth,
In our wild climate, in our scowling town,
We gloomed and shivered, sorrowed, sobbed and feared?
The belching winter wind, the missile rain,
The rare and welcome silence of the snows,
The laggard morn, the haggard day, the night,
The grimy spell of the nocturnal town,
Do you remember? – Ah, could one forget!

As when the fevered sick that all night long
Listed the wind intone, and hear at last
The ever-welcome voice of chanticleer
Sing in the bitter hour before the dawn, –
With sudden ardour, these desire the day:
So sang in the gloom of youth the bird of hope;
So we, exulting, hearkened and desired.
For lo! as in the palace porch of life
We huddled with chimeras, from within –
How sweet to hear! – the music swelled and fell,
And through the breach of the revolving doors
What dreams of splendour blinded us and fled!

I have since then contended and rejoiced;
Amid the glories of the house of life
Profoundly entered, and the shrine beheld:
Yet when the lamp from my expiring eyes
Shall dwindle and recede, the voice of love
Fall insignificant on my closing ears,
What sound shall come but the old cry of the wind
In our inclement city? what return
But the image of the emptiness of youth,
Filled with the sound of footsteps and that voice
Of discontent and rapture and despair?
So, as in darkness, from the magic lamp,
The momentary pictures gleam and fade
And perish, and the night resurges – these
Shall I remember, and then all forget.

Robert Louis Stevenson, 'To My Old Familiars'

Often I think of the beautiful town
    That is seated by the sea;
Often in thought go up and down
The pleasant streets of that dear old town,
    And my youth comes back to me.
        And a verse of a Lapland song
        Is haunting my memory still:
        'A boy's will is the wind's will,
And the thoughts of youth are long, long thoughts.'

I can see the shadowy lines of its trees,
    And catch in sudden gleams,
The sheen of the far-surrounding seas,
And islands that were the Hesperides
    Of all my boyish dreams.
        And the burden of that old song,
        It murmurs and whispers still:
        'A boy's will is the wind's will,
And the thoughts of youth are long, long thoughts.'

I remember the black wharves and the slips
    And the sea-tides tossing free;
And Spanish sailors with bearded lips,

And the beauty and mystery of the ships,
    And the magic of the sea.
      And the voice of that wayward song
      Is singing and saying still:
'A boy's will is the wind's will,
And the thoughts of youth are long, long thoughts.'

I remember the bulwarks by the shore,
    And the fort upon the hill;
The sunrise gun, with its hollow roar,
The drum-beat repeated o'er and o'er,
    And the bugle wild and shrill.
      And the music of that old song
      Throbs in my memory still:
      'A boy's will is the wind's will,
And the thoughts of youth are long, long thoughts.' . . .

        Henry Wadswoth Longfellow, 'My Lost Youth'

The Greeks were right in making memory the mother of the
Muses. Neither Stevenson nor Longfellow were among the great
poets. But in these two poems, the mingled sweetness and sadness
of recollection – recollection of happy youth, now for ever
vanished – stirs them to rise above themselves and achieve a
poignancy of utterance, which makes their words unforgettable.

MOON

No word has been used more often in poetry than Moon but it
has never lost its evocative force; no amount of misuse by bad
poets has, so to speak, worn it out. Even its recent invasion by
American astronauts has failed to dim its literary magic.

    The nature of this magic differs for different poets. To Ben
Jonson the moon is serene and regal:

Queen and huntress, chaste and fair,
    Now the sun is laid to sleep,
Seated in thy silver chair,
      State in wonted manner keep:
        Hesperus entreats thy light,
        Goddess excellently bright.

Earth, let not they envious shade
   Dare itself to interpose;
Cynthia's shining orb was made
   Heaven to clear when day did close:
      Bless us when with wishèd sight,
      Goddess excellently bright.

Lay thy bow of pearl apart,
   And thy crystal-shining quiver;
Give unto the flying hart
   Space to breathe, how short soever:
      Thou that mak'st a day of night –
      Goddess excellently bright.

                                        'Hymn to Diana'

In contrast Sir Philip Sidney sees the moon as melancholy, restless, haunted:

With how sad steps, O Moon, thou climb'st the skies!
How silently and with how wan a face!

Shelley's vision, over two hundred years later, was much the same.

Art thou pale for weariness
Of climbing heaven and gazing on the earth,
   Wandering companionless
Among the stars that have a different birth,
And ever changing, like a joyless eye
That finds no object worth its constancy?

Omar, interpreted by Edward Fitzgerald, portrays the moon as lonely and wistfully aware of the Earth and its transient inhabitants.

Ah, Moon of my Delight who know'st no wane,
The Moon of Heav'n is rising once again:
   How oft hereafter rising shall she look
Through this same Garden after me – in vain!

For Byron the moon is a symbol of passion, rising, as the day wanes, to usher in the night, the time for lovers. Expectantly, ardently, impatiently he cries:

The moon is up and yet it is not night.

In contrast, Burns sees the fading of the moon before daybreak as a symbol of approaching death:

The wan moon is setting ayont the white wave,
And Time is setting with me, O!

MUSIC

All art constantly aspires towards the condition of music. For while in all other kinds of art it is possible to distinguish the matter from the form, and the understanding can always make this distinction, yet it is the constant effort of art to obliterate it. That the mere matter of a poem, for instance, its subject, namely, its given incidents or situation – that the mere matter of a picture, the actual circumstances of an event, the actual topography of a landscape – should be nothing without the form, the spirit, of the handling, that this form, this mode of handling, should become an end in itself, should penetrate every part of the matter: this is what all art constantly strives after and achieves in different degrees. . . . Art then, is thus always striving to be independent of the mere intelligence, to become a matter of pure perception, to get rid of its responsibilities to its subject or material; the ideal examples of poetry and painting being those in which the constituent elements of the composition are so welded together, that the material or subject no longer strikes the intellect only; nor the form, the eye or the ear only; but form and matter, in their union or identity, present one single effect to the 'imaginative reason,' that complex faculty for which every thought and feeling is twin-born with its sensible analogue or symbol.

It is the art of music which most completely realises this artistic ideal, this perfect identification of matter and form. In its consummate moments, the end is not distinct from the means, the form from the matter, the subject from the expression; they inhere in and completely saturate each other; and to it, therefore, to the condition of its perfect moments, all the arts may be supposed constantly to tend and aspire. In music, then, rather than in poetry, is to be found the true type or measure of perfected art. Therefore, although each art has its incommunicable element, its untranslatable order of impressions, its unique mode of reaching the 'imaginative reason,' yet the arts may be represented as continually struggling after the law or principle of music, to a condition which music alone completely realises; and one of the chief functions of aesthetic criticism, dealing with the products of art, new or old, is to estimate the degree in which each of those products approaches, in this sense, to musical law.

Walter Pater, The Renaissance: 'The School of Giorgione'

I do not know if this passage is still famous. But it used to be, and it does contain a crucial truth, namely that music is the quintessential art. This is not to say that musical achievements are the highest achievements, that Mozart is greater than Shakespeare or Beethoven than Michelangelo, but that music is the one art that compels you to take it on its own terms, asking from it only what it can give.

This means that it is very hard to write about. Pater and Ruskin can convey in words the impression made on them by a picture; but attempts to do the same thing about a piece of music nearly always fail; witness E. M. Forster's dreadful whimsical little fantasy in *Howard's End* about sinister goblins and dancing elephants and purporting to represent its author's reactions to Beethoven's Fifth Symphony.

As usual however one comes across a rare exception. L. P. Hartley's few brief sentences in *Sixth Heaven* about the slow movement of Bach's concerto for two violins does beautifully succeed in evoking its subject:

The music went on, establishing in his mind its convention – if a mood so living could be called a convention – of flawless intellectual sympathy, of the perfected manners of the heart. The beauty was founded on the reasonableness of each utterance; it was born miraculously out of a kind of logic; the notes were not the parents of beauty, as with Schubert, but the children . . .

Sixth Heaven

It would appear easier to suggest the effect made by imaginary pieces of music than by real ones. Turgenev does this marvellously in his account of Lemm's piano sonata in *A House of Gentlefolk* or of the two songs in the singing competition in *A Sportsman's Sketches*. I suppose Jane's song on her guitar to Shelley was a real song. But, since Shelley does not specify what it was, it counts as imaginary. Certainly he manages eloquently to convey its sentiment.

> The keen stars were twinkling,
> And the fair moon was rising among
>   them.
>   Dear Jane!
>   The guitar was tinkling,
> But the notes were not sweet till you
>   sung them
>   Again.

> As the moon's soft splendour
> O'er the faint cold starlight of Heaven
>   Is thrown,
>   So your voice most tender
> To the strings without soul had then
>   given
>   Its own.

> The stars will awaken,
> Though the moon sleep a full hour later,
>   To-night;
>   no leaf will be shaken
> Whilst the dews of your melody
>   scatter
>   Delight.

> Though the sound overpowers,
> Sing again, with your dear voice
>   revealing

        A tone
      Of some world far from ours,
    Where music and moonlight and
              feeling
          Are one.

Shelley

MUTABILITY

An extraordinary number of the most beautiful pieces of prose have been inspired by a sense of the mutability of things human.

Time hath his revolutions. There must be a period and an end of all temporal things, finis rerum, an end of names and dignities and whatsoever is terrene; and why not of De Vere? For where is Bohun; where is Mowbray; where is Mortimer; nay, which is more and most of all, where is Plantagenet? They are entombed in the urns and sepulchres of mortality.

Lord Chief Justice Crewe

Laodameia died; Helen died; Leda, the beloved of Jupiter went before. It is better to repose in the earth betimes than to sit up late; better, than to cling pertinaciously to what we feel crumbling under us, and to protract an inevitable fall. We may enjoy the present while we are insensible of infirmity and decay: but the present, like a note in music, is nothing but as it appertains to what is past and what is to come. There are no fields of amaranth on this side of the grave: there are no voices, O Rhodopè, that are not soon mute, however tuneful: there is no name, with whatever emphasis of passionate love repeated, of which the echo is not faint at last.

Walter Savage Landor,
Imaginary Conversations: Aesop and Rhodope

I will not argue the matter: Time wastes too fast: every letter I trace tells me with what rapidity Life follows my pen; the days and hours of it, more precious, my dear Jenny! than the rubies about thy neck, are flying over our heads like light clouds of a windy day, never to return more – every thing presses on – whilst thou art twisting that lock, – see! it grows grey; and every time I kiss thy hand to bid adieu, and every absence which follows it, are preludes to that eternal separation which we are shortly to make.

Heaven have mercy upon us both!

Laurence Sterne, Tristram Shandy

This was the time, perhaps, when Kenyon first became sensible what a dreary city is Rome, and what a terrible weight is there imposed on human life, when any gloom within the heart corresponds to the spell of ruin that has been thrown over the site of ancient empire. He wandered, as it were, and stumbled over the fallen columns and among the tombs, and groped his way into the sepulchral darkness of the catacombs, and found no path emerging from them. The happy may well enough continue to be such, beneath the brilliant sky of Rome. But, if you go thither in melancholy mood – if you go with a ruin in your heart, or with a vacant site there where once stood the airy fabric of happiness, now vanished – all the ponderous gloom of the Roman Past will pile itself upon that spot, and crush you down as with the heaped-up marble and granite, the earth-mounds and multitudinous bricks, of its material decay.

It might be supposed that a melancholy man would here make acquaintance with a grim philosophy. He should learn to bear patiently his individual griefs, that endure only for one little lifetime, when here are the tokens of such infinite misfortune on an imperial scale, and when so many far landmarks of time all around him, are bringing the remoteness of a thousand years ago into the sphere of yesterday. But it is in vain that you seek this shrub of bitter sweetness among the plants that root themselves on the roughness of massive walls, or trail downward from the capitals of pillars, or spring out of the green turf in the palace of the Caesars. It does not grow in Rome; not even among the five hundred various weeds which deck the grassy arches of the Coliseum. You look through a vista of century beyond century – through much shadow, and a little sunshine – through barbarism and civilization, alternating with one another, like actors that have pre-arranged their parts – through a broad pathway of progressive generations bordered by palaces and temples, and bestridden by old, triumphal arches, until, in the distance, you behold the obelisks, with their unintelligible inscriptions, hinting at a past infinitely more remote than history can define. Your own life is as nothing, when compared with that immeasurable distance; but still you demand, none the less earnestly, a gleam of sunshine, instead of a speck of shadow, on the step or two that will bring you to your quiet rest.

How exceedingly absurd! All men, from the date of the earliest obelisk – and of the whole world, moreover, since that far epoch, and before – have made a similar demand, and seldom had their wish. If they had it, what are they the better now? But, even while you taunt yourself with this sad lesson, your heart cries out obstreperously for its small share of earthly happiness, and will not be appeased by the myriads of dead hopes that lie crushed into the soil of Rome. How wonderful that this our narrow foothold of the Present should hold its own so constantly, and, while every moment changing, should still be like a rock betwixt the encountering tides of the long Past and the infinite To-come!

Nathaniel Hawthorne, The Marble Fawn

Man, so far as natural science by itself is able to teach us, is no longer the final cause of the universe, the Heaven-descended heir of all the ages. His very existence is an accident, his story a brief and transitory episode in the life of one of the meanest of the planets. Of the combination of causes which first converted a dead organic compound into the living progenitors of humanity, science, indeed, as yet knows nothing. It is enough that from such beginnings, famine, disease, and mutual slaughter, fit nurses of the future lords of creation, have gradually evolved, after infinite travail, a race with conscience enough to feel that it is vile, and intelligence enough to know that it is insignificant. We survey the past, and see that its history is of blood and tears, of helpless blundering, of wild revolt, of stupid acquiescence, of empty aspirations. We sound the future, and learn that after a period, long compared with the individual life, but short indeed compared with the divisions of time open to our investigation, the energies of our system will decay, the glory of the sun will be dimmed, and the earth, tideless and inert, will no longer tolerate the race which has for a moment disturbed its solitude. Man will go down into the pit, and all his thoughts will perish. The uneasy consciousness which in this obscure corner has for a brief space broken the contented silence of the universe, will be at rest. Matter will know itself no longer. 'Imperishable monuments' and 'immortal deeds', death itself, and love stronger than death, will be as though they had never been. Nor will anything that is be better, or be worse for all that the labour, genius, devotion and suffering of man have striven through countless generations to effect.

A. J. Balfour, The Foundations of Belief

This, incidentally, is the best piece of prose written by a British Prime Minister that I have ever read.

Poets also have written eloquently about mutability.

When I bethinke me on that speech whyleare,
  Of Mutability, and well it way:
Me seemes, that though she all unworthy were
  Of the Heav'ns Rule; yet very sooth to say,
  In all things else she beares the greatest sway.
Which makes me loath this state of life so tickle
  And love of things so vaine to cast away,
Whose flowering pride, so fading and so fickle,
Short Time shall soon cut down with his consuming sickle.

Edmund Spenser, 'The Faerie Queene'

I do love these ancient ruins:
We never tread upon them but we set
Our foot upon some reverend history:
And, questionless, here in this open court,
Which now lies naked to the injuries
Of stormy weather, some men lie interred
Loved the church so well, and gave so largely to't,
They thought it should have canopied their bones
Till doomsday. But all things have their end.

Churches and cities, which have diseases like to men,
Must have like death that we have.

John Webster, The Duchess of Malfi

These are very fine. All the same, prose with its varying, lingering, reverberating cadences, seems an especially appropriate mode in which to give a voice to the spirit of man meditating wistfully on his mortality.

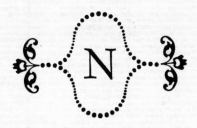

NEGLECTED

The neglected works of distinguished writers are for the most part rightly neglected. This becomes apparent when attempts are made to rescue them from neglect. But there are exceptions to this rule. I have not seen the poems printed below referred to by critics or quoted in anthologies. But each shows its author at his or her best – which is saying a great deal.

The sun upon the Weirdlaw Hill,
   In Ettrick's vale, is sinking sweet;
The westland wind is hush and still,
   The lake lies sleeping at my feet.
Yet not the landscape to mine eye
   Bears those bright hues that once it bore;
Though evening, with her richest dye,
   Flames o'er the hills of Ettrick's shore.

With listless look along the plain,
   I see Tweed's silver current glide,
And coldly mark the holy fane
   Of Melrose rise in ruin'd pride.
The quiet lake, the balmy air,
   The hill, the stream, the tower, the tree –
Are they still such as once they were,
   Or is the dreary change in me?

Alas, the warp'd and broken board,
   How can it bear the painter's dye!
The harp of strain'd and tuneless chord,
   How to the minstrel's skill reply!

To aching eyes each landscape lowers,
  To feverish pulse each gale blows chill;
And Araby's or Eden's bowers
  Were barren as this moorland hill.

Sir Walter Scott

Come not, when I am dead,
  To drop thy foolish tears upon my grave,
To trample round my fallen head,
  And vex the unhappy dust thou wouldst not save.
There let the wind sweep and the plover cry;
    But thou, go by.

Child, if it were thine error or thy crime
  I care no longer, being all unblest:
Wed whom thou wilt, but I am sick of Time,
  And I desire to rest.
Pass on, weak heart, and leave me where I lie:
    Go by, go by.

Alfred Tennyson

Oh tell me once and tell me twice
  And tell me thrice to make it plain,
When we who part this weary day,
  When we who part shall meet again.

When windflowers blossom on the sea
  And fishes skim along the plain
Then we who part this weary day,
  Then you and I shall meet again.

Yet tell me once before we part,
  Why need we part who part in pain?
If flowers must blossom on the sea,
  Why, we shall never meet again.

My cheeks are paler than a rose,
  My tears are salter than the main,
My heart is like a lump of ice
  If we must never meet again.

Oh weep or laugh, but let me be,
    And live or die, for all's in vain;
For life's in vain since we must part,
    And parting must not meet again.

Till windflowers blossom on the sea
    And fishes skim along the plain;
Pale rose of roses, let me be, –
    Your breaking heart breaks mine again.

Christina Rossetti

The wood is bare: a river-mist is steeping
    The trees that winter's chill of life bereaves:
Only their stiffened boughs break silence, weeping
    Over their fallen leaves;

That lie upon the dank earth brown and rotten,
    Miry and matted in the soaking wet:
Forgotten with the spring, that is forgotten
    By them that can forget.

Yet it was here we walked when ferns were springing,
    And through the mossy bank shot bud and blade: –
Here found in summer, when the birds were singing
    A green and pleasant shade.

'Twas here we loved in sunnier days and greener;
    And now, in this disconsolate decay,
I come to see her where I most have seen her,
    And touch the happier day.

For on this path, at every turn and corner,
    The fancy of her figure on me falls:
Yet walks she with the slow step of a mourner,
    Nor hear my voice that calls.

So through my heart there winds a track of feeling
    A path of memory, that is all her own:
Whereto her phantom beauty ever stealing
    Haunts the sad spot alone.

About her steps the trunks are bare, the branches
  Drip heavy tears upon her downcast head;
And bleed from unseen wounds that no sun stanches,
  For the year's sun is dead.

And dead leaves wrap the fruits that summer planted:
  And birds that love the South have taken wing.
The wanderer, loitering o'er the scene enchanted,
  Weeps, and despairs of spring.

Robert Bridges

There were three cherry trees once,
Grew in a garden all shady;
And there for delight of so gladsome a sight
  Walked a most beautiful lady,
  Dreamed a most beautiful lady.

Birds in those branches did sing,
Blackbird and throstle and linnet,
But she walking there was by far the most fair –
  Lovelier than all else within it,
  Blackbird and throstle and linnet.

But blossoms to berries do come,
And hanging on stalks light and slender,
And one long summer's day charmed that lady away,
  With vows sweet and merry and tender;
  A lover with voice low and tender.

Moss and lichen the green branches deck;
Weeds nod in its paths green and shady:
Yet a light footstep seems there to wander in dreams,
  The ghost of that beautiful lady,
  That happy and beautiful lady.

Walter De La Mare

NONSENSE

'Now one can breathe more easily,' said the Knight, putting back his shaggy hair with both hands, and turning his gentle face and large mild eyes to Alice. She thought she had never seen such a strange-looking soldier in all her life.

He was dressed in tin armour, which seemed to fit him very badly, and he had a queer-shaped little deal box fastened across his shoulders, upside-down, and with the lid hanging open. Alice looked at it with great curiosity.

'I see you're admiring my little box,' the Knight said in a friendly tone. 'It's my own invention – to keep clothes and sandwiches in. You see I carry it upside-down, so that the rain can't get in.'

'But the things can get *out*,' Alice gently remarked. 'Do you know the lid's open?'

'I didn't know it,' the Knight said, a shade of vexation passing over his face. 'Then all the things must have fallen out! And the box is no use without them.' He unfastened it as he spoke, and was just going to throw it into the bushes, when a sudden thought seemed to strike him, and he hung it carefully on a tree. 'Can you guess why I did that?' he said to Alice. Alice shook her head.

'In hopes some bees may make a nest in it – then I should get the honey.'

'But you've got a bee-hive – or something like one – fastened to the saddle,' said Alice.

'Yes, it's a very good bee-hive,' the Knight said in a discontented tone, 'one of the best kind. But not a single bee has come near it yet. And the other thing is a mousetrap. I suppose the mice keep the bees out – or the bees keep the mice out, I don't know which.'

'I was wondering what the mouse-trap was for,' said Alice. 'It isn't very likely there would be any mice on the horse's back.'

'Not very likely, perhaps,' said the Knight; 'but if they *do* come, I don't choose to have them running all about.'

'You see,' he went on after a pause, 'it's as well to be provided for *everything*. That's the reason the horse has all those anklets round his feet.'

'But what are they for?' Alice asked in a tone of great
curiosity.

'To guard against the bites of sharks,' the Knight replied.
'It's an invention of my own. And now help me on. I'll go with
you to the end of the wood – What's that dish for?'

'It's meant for plum-cake,' said Alice.

'We'd better take it with us,' the Knight said. 'It'll come in
handy, if we find any plum-cake. Help me to get it into this bag.'

This took a long time to manage, though Alice held the bag
open very carefully, because the knight was so *very* awkward in
putting in the dish: the first two or three times that he tried, he
fell in himself instead. 'It's rather a tight fit, you see,' he said,
as they got it in at last; 'there are so many candlesticks in the
bag.' And he hung it to the saddle, which was already loaded
with bunches of carrots, and fire-irons, and many other things.

'I hope you've got your hair well fastened on?' he continued
as they set off.

'Only in the usual way,' Alice said, smiling.

'That's hardly enough,' he said, anxiously. 'You see the wind
is so *very* strong here. It's as strong as soup.'

'Have you invented a plan for keeping the hair from being
blown off?' Alice enquired.

'Not yet,' said the Knight. 'But I've got a plan for keeping it
from *falling* off.'

'I should like to hear it, very much.'

'First you take an upright stick,' said the Knight, 'then you
make your hair creep up it, like a fruit-tree. Now the reason hair
falls off is because it hangs *down* – things never fall *upwards*,
you know. It's a plan of my own invention. You may try it if
you like.'

It didn't sound a comfortable plan, Alice thought, and for a
few minutes she walked on in silence . . .

Lewis Carroll, Alice Through the Looking Glass

Two receipts for Domestic Cookery.

(1) To make an Amblongus Pie.
Take 4 pounds (say 4½ pounds) of fresh Amblongusses, and put
them in a small pipkin.

Cover them with water and boil them for 8 hours incessantly, after which add 2 pints of new milk, and proceed to boil for 4 hours more.

When you have ascertained that the Amblongusses are quite soft, take them out and place them in a wide pan, taking care to shake them well previously.

Grate some nutmeg over the surface, and cover them carefully with powdered gingerbread, curry-powder, and a sufficient quantity of Cayenne pepper.

Remove the pan into the next room, and place it on the floor. Bring it back again, and let it simmer for three-quarters of an hour. Shake the pan violently till all the Amblongusses have become of a pale purple colour.

Then, having prepared the paste, insert the whole carefully, adding at the same time a small pigeon, 2 slices of beef, 4 cauliflowers, and any number of oysters.

Watch patiently till the crust begins to rise, and add a pinch of salt from time to time.

Serve up in a clean dish, and throw the whole out of the window as fast as possible.

(II) To make Gosky Patties.

Take a Pig, three or four years of age, and tie him by the off-hind leg to a post. Place 5 pounds of currants, 3 of sugar, 2 pecks of peas, 18 roast chestnuts, a candle, and six bushels of turnips, within his reach; if he eats these, constantly provide him with more.

Then procure some cream, some slices of Cheshire cheese, four quires of foolscap paper, and a packet of black pins. Work the whole into a paste, and spread it out to dry on a sheet of clean brown water-proof linen.

When the paste is perfectly dry, but not before, proceed to beat the Pig violently, with the handle of a large broom. If he squeals, beat him again.

Visit the paste and beat the Pig alternately for some days, and ascertain if at the end of that period the whole is about to turn into Gosky Patties.

If it does not then, it never will; and in that case the Pig may be let loose, and the whole process may be considered as finished.

Edward Lear, Nonsense Cookery

He thought he saw an Elephant,
  That practised on a fife:
He looked again, and found it was
  A letter from his wife.
'At length I realise', he said,
  'The bitterness of Life!'

       • • •

He thought he saw a Rattlesnake
  That questioned him in Greek:
He looked again, and found it was
  The Middle of Next Week.
'The one thing I regret', he said,
  'Is that it cannot speak!'

       • • •

He thought he saw a Banker's Clerk
  Descending from the bus:
He looked again, and found it was
  A Hippopotamus:
'If this should stay to dine', he said,
  'There won't be much for us!'

       • • •

He thought he saw a Coach-and-Four
  That stood beside his bed:
He looked again, and found it was
  A Bear without a Head.
'Poor thing', he said, 'poor silly thing!
  It's waiting to be fed!'

       • • •

He thought he saw an Albatross
  That fluttered round the lamp:
He looked again, and found it was
  A Penny-Postage-Stamp.
'You'd best be getting home', he said:
  'The nights are very damp!'

       • • •

He thought he saw an Argument
    That proved he was the Pope:
He looked again, and found it was
    A Bar of Mottled Soap.
'A fact so dread', he faintly said,
    'Extinguishes all hope!'

Lewis Carroll, 'Sylvie and Bruno' and 'Sylvie and Bruno Concluded'

O My agèd Uncle Arly!
Sitting on a heap of Barley
    Thro' the silent hours of night, –
Close beside a leafy thicket: –
On his nose there was a Cricket, –
In his hat a Railway-Ticket; –
    (But his shoes were far too tight.)

Long ago, in youth, he squander'd
All his goods away, and wander'd
    To the Tiniskoop-hills afar.
There on golden sunsets blazing,
Every evening found him gazing, –
Singing, – 'Orb! you're quite amazing!
    'How I wonder what you are!'

Like the ancient Medes and Persians,
Always by his own exertions
    He subsisted on those hills; –
Whiles, – by teaching children spelling, –
Or at time by merely yelling, –
Or at intervals by selling
    Propter's Nicodemus Pills,

Later, in his morning rambles
He perceived the moving brambles –
    Something square and white disclose; –
'Twas a First-class-Railway-Ticket;
But, on stooping down to pick it
Off the ground, – a pea-green Cricket
    Settled on my uncle's Nose.

Never – never more, – oh! never,
Did that Cricket leave him ever, –
  Dawn or evening, day or night; –
Clinging as a constant treasure, –
Chirping with a cheerious measure, –
Wholly to my uncle's pleasure, –
  (Though his shoes were far too tight.)

So for three-and-forty winters,
Till his shoes were worn to splinters,
  All those hills he wander'd o'er, –
Sometimes silent; – sometimes yelling; –
Till he came to Borley-Melling,
Near his old ancestral dwelling; –
  (But his shoes were far too tight.)

On a little heap of Barley
Died my agèd Uncle Arly,
  And they buried him one night; –
Close beside the leafy thicket; –
There, – his hat and Railway-Ticket; –
There, – his ever-faithful Cricket; –
  (But his shoes were far too tight.)

Edward Lear

As music is the quintessential art, so is nonsense humour the
quintessential kind of humour. No more than in the case of music
does quintessential necessarily mean highest. *Alice in Wonderland*
is not a higher achievement than *The Diary of a Nobody*; nor is Lear
a finer humorist than Max Beerbohm – which indeed would be
impossible. But one could read *Zuleika Dobson*, not for its humour,
but for the light it shed on Edwardian Oxford or study *The Diary
of a Nobody* as an informative picture of lower middle-class life
in 19th-century London: whereas to try and read Lear's *Nonsense
Rhymes* or *Alice in Wonderland* in a serious spirit and in order to
acquire information would be clearly futile.

Of course, Lear is a poet as well as a humorist; one of the truest
and most enjoyable of all Victorian poets. But this does not mean
that we can or should read him solemnly. Poetry is not necessarily
solemn any more than life is.

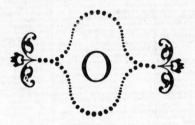

THE OBJECT OF LIFE

The contemplation of truth and beauty is the proper object for
which we are created, which calls forth the most intense desires
of the soul, and of which it never tires.

William Hazlitt

This statement is bold and dogmatic and true.

OBSCURITY

The Maiden caught me in the wild,
Where I was dancing merrily;
She put me into her Cabinet,
And lock'd me up with a golden key.

This Cabinet is form'd of gold
And pearl and crystal shining bright,
And within it opens into a world
And a little lovely moony night.

Another England there I saw,
Another London with its Tower,
Another Thames and other hills,
And another pleasant Surrey bower.

Another Maiden like herself,
Translucent, lovely, shining clear,
Threefold each in the other clos'd –
O, what a pleasant trembling fear!

L.L.G.—G

O, what a smile! a threefold smile
Fill'd me, that like a flame I burn'd;
I bent to kiss the lovely Maid,
And found a threefold kiss return'd.

I strove to seize the inmost form
With ardour fierce and hands of flame,
But burst the Crystal Cabinet,
And like a weeping Babe became –

A weeping Babe upon the wild,
And weeping Woman pale reclin'd,
And in the outward air again
I fill'd with woes the passing wind.

William Blake, 'The Crystal Cabinet'

This poem is obscure in the sense that the reader cannot know
what is meant by it unless he has learned about Blake's symbols
and their significance. However, without doing this, he can enjoy
the poem intensely. For, though its deeper significance may be
hidden from him, the tale it tells is clear; passing before the mental
eye in a series of precise and vivid pictures. Blake's kind of
obscurity can be enjoyed without ceasing to be obscure. In this
it differs from some other kinds which, till they are interpreted,
strike us as a mere unintelligible muddle.

Some 17th-century 'metaphysical' poems, for instance, cannot
be appreciated without a knowledge of medieval philosophy or
the terms of alchemy. Some modern poets too confuse the reader
by confronting him with a series of images, which may or may
not have a symbolic coherence, but which are unconnected by
any logical link. The effect in both cases is that of a conundrum
that conveys nothing to the reader who has not got the key to it.
Blake's poems are more like pictures in the temple of some un-
known religion, whose intended significance is only known to
people who have studied the religion but which are in themselves
and at first sight beautiful and evocative.

I prefer Blake's kind of obscurity.

OLD CHINA

'Tell me now, what should a man want
But to sit alone, sipping his cup of wine?'
I should like to have visitors come and discuss philosophy
And not to have the tax-collector coming to collect taxes:
My three sons married into good families
And my five daughters wedded to steady husbands.
Then I could jog through a happy five-score years
And, at the end, need no Paradise.

Wang Chi (A.D. 584–644) translated by Arthur Waley

Wang Chi's last phrase expresses a vain hope. In this unsatisfying world, man always needs, or thinks he needs, a paradise. Otherwise Wang Chi's wishes, uttered over a thousand years ago, are delightfully sensible; more so than most of those proclaimed by the sages of modern China – or of modern England for that matter.

Chen Tzŭ-ang (A.D. 656–698) also talked good sense.

Business men boast of their skill and cunning
But in philosophy they are like little children.
Bragging to each other of successful depredations
They neglect to consider the ultimate fate of the body.
What should they know of the Master of Dark Truth
Who saw the wide world in a jade cup,
By illumined conception got clear of Heaven and Earth,
On the chariot of Mutation entered the Gate of Immutability?

Translated by Arthur Waley

It is to be noted that both these authors speak warmly of philosophy. Wang Chi desires visitors who would discuss it with him and Chen Tzŭ-ang describes it in terms poetically beautiful.

It cannot have been much like the philosophy expounded in modern English universities.

THE OPERATIVE WORD

I felt as one who had been walking below the sea,
and treading amidst the bones of shipwrecks.

Thackeray

Maurice Baring says that the effect of this sentence depends on the single word 'bones'. Here are some other lines whose effect also depends on one word:

Death's at thy window! Awake, bright Mellida!

John Marston

           . . . as the music of the moon
Sleeps in the plain eggs of the nightingale.

Tennyson

The heavy seas of winter flashing in the cold sunshine.

Conrad

When I am gone, dream me some happiness,
Nor let thy looks our long hid love confess.

Donne

Nor did I wonder at the lily's white
Nor praise the deep vermillion in the rose.

Shakespeare

Omit from these passages the words 'bright', 'plain', 'cold', 'dream', 'vermillion', and their whole effect is lost.

OXFORD

. . . This was a lunch-party at the particular college in which I should find it the highest privilege to reside . . . At the college in question there are no undergraduates . . . This delightful spot exists for the satisfaction of a small society of Fellows who, having no obligation save toward their own culture no care save for learning as learning, and truth as truth, are presumably the happiest and most charming people in the world. The party, invited to lunch, assembled first in the library of the college – a cool, grey hall, of very great length and height, with vast wall-spaces of rich-looking book titles, and statues of noble scholars set in the midst. Had the charming Fellows ever anything more disagreeable to do than to finger these precious volumes and then to stroll about together in the grassy courts in learned comradeship, discussing their precious contents? Nothing, apparently, unless it were to give a lunch at Commemoration in the dining-hall of the college. When lunch was ready there was a very pretty procession to go to it. Learned gentlemen in crimson gowns, ladies in bright finery, paired slowly off and marched in a stately diagonal across the fine, smooth lawn of the quadrangle, in a corner of which they passed through a hospitable door. But here we cross the threshold of privacy; I remained on the further side of it during the rest of the day. But I brought back with me certain memories . . . memories of a *fête champêtre* in the beautiful gardens of one of the other colleges – charming lawns and spreading trees, music of Grenadier Guards, ices in striped marquees, mild flirtation of youthful gownsmen and bemuslined maidens: memories, too, of quiet dinner in common-room, a decorous, excellent repast; old portraits on the walls and great windows open upon the ancient court, where the afternoon light was fading in the stillness; superior talk upon current topics, and over all the peculiar air of Oxford – the air of liberty to care for the things of the mind, assured and secured by machinery which is in itself a satisfaction to the senses.

Henry James, English Hours

This is what Oxford ought to be; and, at its best, what it is. There are times however when it can seem all too much like it seemed to William Hazlitt in 1823.

Rome has been called the 'Sacred City': – might not *our* Oxford be called so too? . . . A dream and a glory hover round its head, as the spirits of former times, a throng of intellectual shapes, are seen retreating or advancing to the eye of memory: its streets are paved with the names of learning that can never wear out: its green quadrangles breathe the silence of thought, conscious of the weight of yearnings innumerable after the past, of loftiest aspirations for the future: Isis babbles of the Muse, its waters are from the springs of Helicon, its Christ-Church meadows, classic, Elysian fields! – We could pass our lives in Oxford without having or wanting any other idea – that of the place is enough. We imbibe the air of thought; we stand in the presence of learning. We are admitted into the Temple of Fame, we feel that we are in the sanctuary, on holy ground, and 'hold high converse with the mighty dead'. . . . Let him then who is fond of indulging in a dream-like existence go to Oxford and stay there; let him study this magnificent spectacle, the same under all aspects, with its mental twilight tempering the glare of noon, or mellowing the silver moonlight; let him wander in her sylvan suburbs, or linger in her cloistered halls; but let him not catch the din of scholars or teachers, or dine or sup with them, or speak a word to any of the privileged in-habitants; for if he does, the spell will be broken, the poetry and the religion gone, and the palace of enchantment will melt from his embrace into thin air!

'Oxford'

Harsh words! but it is comforting for one who has lived and worked there in the twentieth century to learn that he and his generation are not wholly to blame for Oxford's faults and that members of the University could make a bad impression one hundred and fifty years ago. In the same way it is comforting to discover that as early as 1889 the machine age had begun to desecrate Oxford's beauty.

How sad was my coming to the university! Where were those sweet conditions I had pictured in my boyhood? those antique contrasts? Did I ride, one sunset, through fens on a palfrey, watching the gold reflections on Magdalen Tower? Did I ride over Magdalen Bridge and hear the consonance of evening-bells and cries from the river below? Did I rein in to wonder at the raised gates of Queen's, the twisted pillars of St. Mary's, the little shops, lighted with tapers? Did bull-pups snarl at me, or dons, with bent backs, acknowledge my salute? Any one who knows the place as it is, must see that such questions are purely rhetorical. To him I need not explain the disappointment that beset me when, after being whirled in a cab from the station to a big hotel, I wandered out into the streets. *On aurait dit* a bit of Manchester through which Apollo had once passed; for here, among the hideous trams and the brand-new bricks – here, glared at by the electric-lights that hung from poles, screamed at by boys with the *Echo* and the *Star* – here, in a riot of vulgarity, were remnants of beauty, as I discerned. There were only remnants.

Max Beerbohm, 'Diminuendo'

But in spite of scholars and railway trains and traffic Oxford's atmosphere remains unique and seductive. Max himself felt it intensely.

... Over [the meadows] was the usual coverlet of white vapour, trailed from the Isis right up to Merton Wall. The scent of these meadows' moisture is the scent of Oxford. Even in hottest noon, one feels that the sun has not dried *them*. Always there is moisture drifting across them, drifting into the Colleges. It, one suspects, must have had much to do with the evocation of what is called the Oxford spirit – that gentlest spirit, so lingering and searching, so dear to them who as youths were brought into ken of it, so exasperating to them who were not. Yes, certainly, it is this mild, miasmal air, not less than the grey beauty and gravity of the buildings, that has helped Oxford to produce, and foster eternally, her peculiar race of artist-scholars, scholar-artists. The undergraduate, in his brief periods of residence, is too buoyant to be mastered by the spirit of the place. He does but salute it, and catch the manner. It is on him who stays to spend his maturity here that the spirit will in its fulness gradually descend. The buildings and their traditions keep astir in his mind whatsoever is gracious; the climate, enfolding and enfeebling him, lulling him, keep him careless of the sharp, harsh, exigent realities of the outer world. Careless? Not utterly. These realities may be seen by him. He may study them, be amused or touched by them. But they cannot fire him. Oxford is too damp for that. The 'movements' made there have been no more than protests against the mobility of others. They have been without the dynamic quality implied in their name. They have been no more than the sighs of men gazing at what other men had left behind them; faint, impossible appeals to the god of retrogression, uttered for their own sake and ritual, rather than with any intent that they should be heard. Oxford, that lotus-land, saps the willpower, the power of action. But, in doing so, it clarifies the mind, makes larger the vision, gives above all, that playful and caressing suavity of manner which comes of a conviction that nothing matters, except ideas; and that not even ideas are worth dying for, inasmuch as the ghosts of them slain seem worthy of yet more piously elaborate homage than can be given to them in their hey-day. If the Colleges could be transferred to the dry and bracing top of some hill, doubtless they would be more evidently useful to the nation. But let us be glad there is no engineer or enchanter to compass that task. *Egomet*, I would liefer have the rest of England subside into the sea than have Oxford set on a salubrious level. For there is nothing in England to be matched with what lurks in the vapours of these meadows, and in the shadows of these spires – that mysterious, inenubilable spirit, spirit of Oxford. Oxford! The very sight of the word printed, or sound of it spoken, is fraught for me with most actual magic.

Zuleika Dobson

This passage evokes Oxford's characteristic mood, at least in my youth, better than Matthew Arnold's famous purple passage about the University 'spreading its gardens to the moonlight and whispering from its towers the last enchantments of the middle age'. The spirit of 20th-century Oxford never struck me as noticeably mediaeval.

In another district, in residential North Oxford however, we do breathe the lost enchantments of a past age; the Victorian age: or rather that no-man's land between Victorian and Edwardian. Its dignity and its absurdity, its respectability and its romanticism, its enthusiastic sense of natural beauty and its shocking lack of architectural taste – these mirror themselves in its spreading rows of Gothic-style villas with their dark roomy basements, their lancet windows of plate glass, their pinnacled porches all sunk in laburnum and lilac and pyrus japonica. For years an object of disgust to persons of taste, North Oxford has now been made

poetical by one man. Sir John Betjeman has annexed it to form
part of the Kingdom of Poetry.

Belbroughton Road is bonny, and pinkly burst the spray
Of prunus and forsythia across the public way,
For a full spring-tide of blossom seethed and departed hence,
Leaving land-locked pools of jonquils by a sunny garden fence.

And a constant sound of flushing runneth from windows where
The toothbrush too is airing in this North Oxford air.
From Summerfields to Lynam's, the thirsty tarmac dries,
And a Cherwell mist dissolveth on elm-discovering skies.

Oh! well-bound Wells and Bridges! Oh! earnest ethical search
For the wide high-table logos of St. C. S. Lewis's Church.
This diamond-eyed Spring morning my soul soars up the slope
Of the right good rough-cast buttress on the housewall of my
    hope.

And open-necked and freckled, where once there grazed the
    cows,
Emancipated children swing on old apple boughs,
And pastel-shaded book rooms bring New Ideas to birth
As the whitening hawthorn only hears the heart beat of the
    earth.

One must have lived, as I have, within a stone's throw of
Belbroughton Road, fully to realize how accurately evocative are
these lines.

PAST AND PRESENT

(I)

Notre ignorance de l'histoire nous fait calomnier notre temps. On a été toujours comme ça.

Flaubert

History books show this to be a true reflection; a comforting one if we consider the present, but a sobering one, if we consider the future. For if we are no better and no worse than our ancestors, it is likely that our descendants will be no worse but no better than us.

(II)

The past for poets, the present for pigs.

Samuel Palmer

This may seem to contradict Flaubert's statement. But it does not; for Flaubert is talking about history and Palmer is talking about art. To the artist the past is more inspiring than the present, for its records and memories come to him enriched by all manner of imaginative associations which stimulate his creative spirit, as the present cannot do.

The future is even emptier of imaginative stimulant. As Max Beerbohm says 'how on earth is anyone going to draw any inspiration from the Future? let us spell it with a capital letter by all means. But don't let us expect it to give us anything in return. It cannot, poor thing, for the very good reason that it does not yet exist, save as a dry abstract term.'

PERSONIFICATIONS

Since the Day of Creation, two veiled figures, Doubt and
Melancholy are pacing endlessly in the sunshine of the world.

Joseph Conrad, Notes on Life and Letters

She dwells with Beauty – Beauty that must die;
   And Joy, whose hand is ever at his lips
Bidding adieu; . . .

John Keats, 'Ode on Melancholy'

PICTURES

(1)

Pictures are a set of chosen images, a stream of pleasant
thoughts passing through the mind. It is a luxury to have the
walls of our rooms hung round with them, and no less so to
have such a gallery in the mind, to con over the relics of ancient
art bound up 'within the book and volume of the brain, un-
mixed (if it were possible) with baser matter!' A life passed
among pictures, in the study and the love of art, is a happy
noiseless dream: or rather, it is to dream and to be awake at the
same time; for it has all 'the sober certainty of waking bliss,'
with the romantic voluptuousness of a visionary and abstracted
being. They are the bright consummate essences of things, . . .

William Hazlitt, 'On a Landscape of Nicolas Poussin',
Table Talk

This is the best account I have ever read of the particular satisfac-
tion given by the art of painting. It is a satisfaction less immedi-
ately exciting than that given by music which, operating as it does
and painting does not in the dimension of time, can move us by
suspense and surprise and by enabling us to listen to the process
of conflict and discord at last resolving into harmony. But in the
end painting provides a no less powerful satisfaction: the vision

of reality it reveals to us is timeless, changeless, compelling. For a
vision of reality it is. Hazlitt emphasises that the pleasure given
by pictures is no narcotic deceptive dream but rather a sight of
'the bright consummate essences of things'. Like Keats contem-
plating the Grecian Urn, he recognized that the beauty of a work
of art is the earnest and image of its truth.

> When old age shall this generation waste,
> Thou shalt remain, in midst of other woe
> Than ours, a friend to man, to whom thou say'st,
> 'Beauty is truth, truth beauty,' . . .

> *John Keats, 'Ode on a Grecian Urn'*

PICTURES
(II)

There is a curious interest in seeing one art in terms of another,
a work of pictorial art interpreted by a writer who is an artist
in words.

Orion by Poussin:
> Orion, the subject of this landscape, was the classical Nimrod;
> and is called by Homer, 'a hunter of shadows, himself a shade'.
> He was the son of Neptune; and having lost an eye in some
> affray between the Gods and men, was told that if he would go
> to meet the rising sun, he would recover his sight. He is repre-
> sented setting out on his journey, with men on his shoulders to
> guide him, a bow in his hand, and Diana in the clouds greeting
> him. He stalks along, a giant upon earth, and reels and falters
> in his gait, as if just awaked out of sleep, or uncertain of his
> way; – you see his blindness, though his back is turned. Mists
> rise around him, and veil the sides of the green forests; earth is
> dank and fresh with dews, the 'grey dawn and the Pleiades
> before him dance', and in the distance are seen the blue hills
> and sullen ocean. Nothing was ever more finely conceived or
> done. It breathes the spirit of the morning; its moisture, its
> repose, its obscurity, waiting the miracle of light to kindle it

into smiles: the whole is, like the principal figure in it, 'a fore-
runner of the dawn'. The same atmosphere tinges and imbues
every object, the same dull light 'shadowy sets off' the face of
nature: one feeling of vastness, of strangeness, and of primeval
forms pervades the painter's canvas, and we are thrown back
upon the first integrity of things . . .

> *William Hazlitt, 'On a Landscape of Nicolas Poussin'*

The Slave Ship, by Turner:

. . . It is a sunset on the Atlantic, after prolonged storm; but
the storm is partially lulled, and the torn and streaming rain-
clouds are moving in scarlet lines to lose themselves in the
hollow of the night. The whole surface of sea included in the
picture is divided into two ridges of enormous swell, not high,
nor local, but a low broad heaving of the whole ocean, like the
lifting of its bosom by deep-drawn breath after the torture of
the storm. Between these two ridges the fire of the sunset falls
along the trough of the sea, dyeing it with an awful but glorious
light, the intense and lurid splendour which burns like gold,
and bathes like blood. Along this fiery path and valley, the
tossing waves by which the swell of the sea is restlessly divided,
lift themselves in dark, indefinite, fantastic forms, each casting
a faint and ghastly shadow behind it along the illumined foam.
They do not rise everywhere, but three or four together in
wild groups, fitfully and furiously, as the under strength of the
swell compels or permits them; leaving between them treacher-
ous spaces of level and whirling water, now lighted with green
and lamp-like fire, now flashing back the gold of the declining
sun, now fearfully dyed from above with the undistinguishable
images of the burning clouds, which fall upon them in flakes
of crimson and scarlet, and give to the reckless waves the added
motion of their own fiery flying. Purple and blue, the lurid
shadows of the hollow breakers are cast upon the mist of night,
which gathers cold and low, advancing like the shadow of death
upon the guilty ship, as it labours amidst the lightning of the
sea, its thin masts written upon the sky in lines of blood, girded
with condemnation in that fearful hue which signs the sky with
horror, and mixes its flaming flood with the sunlight, and, cast

far along the desolate heave of the sepulchral waves, incarnadines the multitudinous sea.

John Ruskin, Modern Painters

Bacchus and Ariadne by Titian:

. . . Precipitous, with his reeling satyr rout about him, re-peopling and re-illumining suddenly the waste places, drunk with a new fury beyond the grape, Bacchus, born in fire, fire-like flings himself at the Cretan. This is the time present. With this telling of the story, an artist, and no ordinary one, might remain richly proud . . . But from the depths of the imaginative spirit Titian has recalled past time, and laid it contributory with the present to one simultaneous effect. With the desert all ringing with the mad cymbals of his followers, made lucid with the presence and new offers of a god, – as if unconscious of Bacchus, or but idly casting her eyes as upon some unconcerning pageant, her soul undistracted from Theseus – Ariadne is still pacing the solitary shore in as much heart-silence, and in almost the same local solitude, with which she awoke at day-break to catch the forlorn last glances of the sail that bore away the Athenian.

Charles Lamb, Last Essays of Elia

Fête Champêtre by Giorgione:

. . . in the school of Giorgione, the presence of water – the well, or marble-rimmed pool, the drawing or pouring of water, as the woman pours it from a pitcher with her jewelled hand in the *Fête Champêtre*, listening, perhaps, to the cool sound as it falls, blent with the music of the pipes – is as characteristic, and almost as suggestive, as that of the music itself. And the landscape feels, and is glad of it also – a landscape full of clearness, of the effects of water, of fresh rain newly passed through the air, and collected into the grassy channels . . .

Walter Pater, 'The School of Giorgione'

Water, for anguish of the solstice: – nay,
  But dip the vessel slowly, – nay, but lean
  And hark how at its verge the wave sighs in
Reluctant. Hush! beyond all depth away

The heat lies silent at the brink of day:
  Now the hand trails upon the viol-string
  That sobs, and the brown faces cease to sing,
Sad with the whole of pleasure. Whither stray
Her eyes now, from whose mouth the slim pipes creep
  And leave it pouting, while the shadowed grass
  Is cool against her naked side? Let be: —
Say nothing now unto her lest she weep,
  Nor name this ever. Be it as it was, —
Life touching lips with Immortality.

Dante Gabriel Rossetti

PLEASURE

(1)

Sweet cyder is a great thing,
  A great thing to me,
Spinning down to Weymouth town
  By Ridgway thirstily,
And maid and mistress summoning
  Who tend the hostelry:
O cyder is a great thing,
  A great thing to me!

The dance it is a great thing,
  A great thing to me,
With candles lit and partners fit
  For night-long revelry;
And going home when day-dawning
  Peeps pale upon the lea:
O dancing is a great thing
  A great thing to me!

Love is, yea, a great thing,
  A great thing to me,
When, having drawn across the lawn
  In darkness silently,

A figure flits like one a-wing
  Out from the nearest tree:
O love is, yes, a great thing,
  A great thing to me!

Will these be always great things,
  Great things to me? . . .
Let it befall that One will call,
  'Soul, I have need of thee.'
What then? Joy-jaunts, impassioned flings,
  Love, and its ecstasy,
Will always have been great things,
  Great things to me!

                    Thomas Hardy, 'Great Things'

Many poems have been written about joy; but few – at least in these latter days – about pleasure; normal light-hearted pleasure, such as the majority of men and women look for in their moments of relaxation. This poem of Hardy's is one of the few – surprisingly so, considering that his considered view of the human condition was sad, even tragic. But he did know what it was fully to enjoy 'joy-jaunts, impassioned flings, love and its ecstasy' and nothing that happened to darken his days made him doubt the reality of these enjoyments. They always remained great things to him.

PLEASURE

(11)

A life of pleasure requires an aristocratic setting to make it interesting or really conceivable.

                    George Santayana, The Life of Reason

At first reading this seems plausible. How can a man achieve a life that is a succession of exquisitely agreeable moments – the kind of life we see portrayed in the pictures of Watteau or the novels of the court lady Murasaki Shikibu – without the freedom of spirit and the material advantages that come from being a member of an aristocracy – leisure and cultivated taste, self-confidence and servants. But here are Burns's 'Jolly Beggars' saying the opposite to Santayana, and with unhesitating zestful conviction. For them, the freedom that comes from having everything is limited and confining compared with the freedom that comes from having nothing.

What is title, what is treasure,
    What is reputation's care?
If we lead a life of pleasure,
    'Tis no matter how or where!

With the ready trick and fable,
    Round we wander all the day;
And at night, in barn or stable,
    Hug our doxies on the hay.

Does the train-attended carriage
    Thro' the country lighter rove?
Does the sober bed of marriage
    Witness brighter scenes of love?

Life is all a variorum
    We regard not how it goes;
Let them cant about decorum,
    Who have character to lose.

Here's to budgets, bags and wallets!
    Here's to all the wandering train,
Here's our ragged brats and callets,
    One and all cry out, Amen!

This is an exhilarating poem. There is no one like Burns for expressing the particular exhilaration that comes from taking a moral holiday without permission, cheerfully defying the disapproval of society when in pursuit of pleasure.

Yestreen I had a pint o' wine,
    A place where body saw na;
Yestreen lay on this breast o' mine
    The gowden locks of Anna.

The hungry Jew in wilderness,
    Rejoicing o'er his manna,
Was naething to my hiney bliss
    Upon the lips of Anna.

Ye monarchs, take the East and West,
    Frae Indus to Savannah!
Gie me within my straining grasp,
    The melting form of Anna.
There I'll despise Imperial charms,
    An Empress or Sultana,
While dying raptures in her arms
    I give and take wi' Anna!

Awa, thou flaunting god o' day!
    Awa, thou pale Diana!
Ilk Star, gae hide thy twinkling ray!
    When I'm to meet my Anna.
Come, in thy raven plumage, Night;
    Sun, Moon, and Stars, withdrawn a';
And bring an angel pen to write
    My transports wi' my Anna.

The Kirk an' State may join an' tell,
    To do sic things I maunna:
The Kirk an' State may gae to Hell
    And I shall gae to my Anna.
She is the sunshine o' my e'e,
    To live but her I canna;
Had I on earth but wishes three,
    The first should be my Anna.

The reckless impudent gaiety of this poem depends on the fact that Burns lived in puritanical 18th-century Scotland. It is hard to enjoy breaking rules in a world without strict rules: when there is no kirk and state worth bothering about, there is little fun to be got from telling them both to go to hell.

Is this a reason that the 'permissive' literature of our 'permissive' age is in general so dispirited?

POETRY

Our instinctive attitudes towards poetry were very dissimilar, he regarded it from the emotional, and I from the artistic side; and he was thus of a much intenser poetic temperament than I, for when he began to write poetry he would never have written on any subject that did not deeply move him, nor would he attend to poetry unless it expressed his own emotions; and I should say that he liked poetry on account of the power that it had of exciting his valued emotions, and he may perhaps have recognized it as the language of faith. What had led me to poetry was the inexhaustible satisfaction of form, the magic of speech, lying as it seemed to me in the masterly control of the material: it was an art which I hoped to learn. An instinctive rightness was essential, but, given that, I did not suppose that the poet's emotions were in any way better than mine, nor mine than another's . . .

Robert Bridges, Memoir of Digby Mackworth Dolben

His words illustrate an important truth about writers. Two impulses lead people to write poetry; the desire to say something they think worth saying and the desire simply to write a poem, to construct a pleasant object in word and rhythm. Both impulses must be present for the poem to be a work of art. Without the constructive impulse, the result is no more than a statement or an exclamation; without the desire to say something, the result is merely a literary exercise. However, poets vary as to which of the two impulses dominates in them. For Bridges the impulse to write verses came first, for Dolben the desire to say something. Other poets can be grouped under one heading or the other. For example, Pope and Christina Rossetti belong to the Bridges party, Wordsworth and Emily Brontë to that of Dolben.

POLYSYLLABLES

'Self-determination,' one of them insisted. 'Arbitration,' cried another.

'Co-operation?' suggested the mildest of the party.
'Confiscation!' answered an uncompromising female.
I, too, became slightly intoxicated by the sound of these vocables. And were they not the cure for all our ills?
'Inebriation!' I chimed in, 'Inundation, Afforestation, Flagellation,Transubstantiation, Co-education!'

Logan Pearsall Smith, More Trivia

I often recall this passage, when listening to the political pundits of our age disputing with one another on the television screen.

POPLARS

The poplars are felled, farewell to the shade
And the whispering sound of the cool colonnade,
The winds play no longer, and sing in the leaves,
Nor Ouse on his bosom their image receives.

Twelve years have elaps'd since I first took a view
Of my favourite field and the bank where they grew,
And now in the grass behold they are laid,
And the tree is my seat that once lent me a shade.

The blackbird has fled to another retreat
Where the hazels afford him a screen from the heat,
And the scene where his melody charm'd me before,
Resounds with his sweet-flowing ditty no more.

My fugitive years are all hasting away,
And I must ere long lie as lowly as they,
With a turf on my breast, and a stone at my head,
Ere another such grove shall arise in its stead.

'Tis a sight to engage me, if anything can,
To muse on the perishing pleasures of man;
Though his life be a dream, his enjoyments, I see,
Have a being less durable even than he.

William Cowper

My aspens dear, whose airy cages quelled,
Quelled or quenched in leaves the leaping sun,
All felled, felled, are all felled;
   Of a fresh and following folded rank
        Not spared, not one
        That dandled a sandalled
    Shadow that swam or sank
On meadow and river and wind-wandering weed-winding
  bank.

O if we but knew what we do
    When we delve or hew –
  Hack and rack the growing green!
    Since country is so tender
  To touch, her being so slender,
  That, like this sleek and seeing ball
  But a prick will make no eye at all,
  Where we, even where we mean
     To mend her we end her,
    When we hew or delve:
After-comers cannot guess the beauty been.
   Ten or twelve, only ten or twelve
    Strokes of havoc unselve
    The sweet especial scene,
   Rural scene, a rural scene,
   Sweet especial rural scene.

Gerard Manley Hopkins

Cowper's Olney poplars, Hopkins's Binsey poplars – you can take
your choice: one poem is no better than the other. Each teaches
you to see a real poplar through the transfiguring eyes of a poet,
its beauty enriched by a freight of fresh imaginative associations
supplied by him. Dryden said that Milton saw nature 'through the
spectacles of books': so do we see her through Milton's spectacles,
after reading his books. It is a chief function of good writers to
provide us with such spectacles.

PRAYER

When with day's woes night haunts wake-weary eyes,
How deep a blessing from the heart may rise,
  On the happy, the beautiful, the good, the wise!

The poor, the outcast, knave, child, stranger, fool
Need no commending to the merciful;
But, in a world grieved, ugly, wicked or dull,

 Who could the starry influences surmise –
 What praises ardent enough could prayer devise
 For the happy, the beautiful, the good, the wise?

Walter De La Mare

De La Mare would not have needed to say this three hundred
years ago: Elizabethan authors from Shakespeare downwards,
gloried in the happy, the good, the beautiful and the wise. But
since then, from some obscure sense of guilt, writers have grown
so obsessed with 'the poor, the outcast, the knave and the fool'
that many of them have hardly time to spare for anyone else.
Perhaps this is to the credit of their feelings; but it is to the dis-
advantage of their art. An appreciation of beauty and happiness is
needed even for tragedy to make its effect: for, without it, there
is no sense of waste. It is because Romeo and Juliet are radiant
figures capable of the finest happiness that we feel it to be tragic,
and not just pathetic, that they should come to disaster and death.

PROPHECY

In 1922, four years after the First World War and eleven years
before Hitler came to power, Santayana wrote the following
words addressed to the 'liberal' idealists of the day, most of whom
took the hopeful view that the recent war was likely to have been
the last major war:

Let me whisper this counsel in your ears. Reserve a part of

your wrath. You have not seen the worst yet. You suppose that this war has been a criminal blunder and an exceptional horror; you imagine that before long reason will prevail, and all these inferior people that govern the world will be swept aside, and your own party will reform everything and remain always in office. You are mistaken. This war has given you your first glimpse of the ancient, fundamental, normal state of the world, your first taste of reality. It should teach you to dismiss all your philosophies of progress or of a governing reason as the babble of dreamers who walk through one world mentally beholding another. I don't mean that you or they are fools; heaven forbid. You have too much mind. It is easy to behave very much like other people and yet be possessed inwardly by a narcotic dream. I am sure the flowers – and you resemble flowers yourselves, though a bit wilted – if they speculate at all, construct idealisms which, like your own, express their inner sensibility and their experience of the weather, without much resemblance to the world at large. Their thoughts, like yours, are all positings and deductions and asseverations of what ought to be, whilst the calm truth is marching on unheeded outside. No great harm ensues, because the flowers are rooted in their places, and adjusted to the prevailing climate. It doesn't matter what they think. You, too, in your lodgings in Chelsea, quite as in Lhassa or in Mount Athos, may live and die happy in your painted cells. It is the primitive and the ultimate office of the mind to supply such a sanctuary. But if you are ever driven again into the open, if the course of events should be so rapid, that you could catch the drift of it in your short life (since you despise tradition) then you must prepare for a ruder shock. There is eternal war in nature, a war in which every cause is ultimately lost and every nation destroyed. War is but resisted change; and change must needs be resisted so long as the organism it would destroy retains any vitality. Peace itself means discipline at home and invulnerability abroad – two forms of permanent virtual war; peace requires so vigorous an internal regiment that every germ of dissolution or infection shall be repelled before it reaches the public soul. This war has been a short one, and its ravages slight in comparison with what remains standing: a severe war is one in which the entire manhood of a nation is destroyed, its cities razed, and its women and children driven into slavery. In this instance the slaughter has been greater, perhaps, only because modern populations are so enormous; the disturbance has been acute only because the modern industrial system is so dangerously complex and unstable; and the expense seems prodigious because we were so extravagantly rich. Our society was a sleepy glutton who thought himself immortal and squealed inexpressibly, like a stuck pig at the first prick of the sword. An ancient city would have thought this war, or one relatively as costly, only a normal incident; and certainly the Germans will not regard it otherwise.

He was right: the Germans did not. This stylish piece of writing was a remarkable prophecy. Sixteen years later, in the dreadful years of Munich, I remembered and re-read it; and reflected too on the harsh truths about mankind and war which it stated so smoothly.

For, in those days, truths they were. Since then, however, man has invented weapons so powerful as to render Santayana's diagnosis of the human situation obsolete. The war in nature which he postulates as existing eternally may turn out to be near its close – because it will have ended in the destruction of the combatants on both sides. It is to be hoped that this prospect will frighten the human race into making its first serious effort to be peaceful. But, the human race being what it is, this is not certain.

PROSE-POEMS FROM NOVELS

... He had a marvellous power of making trees grow. Although he would seem to shovel in the earth quite carelessly there was a sort of sympathy between himself and the fir, oak or beech that he was operating on; so that the roots took hold of the soil in a few days ...

Hence Winterborne found delight in the work even when, as at present, he contracted to do it on portions of the woodland in which he had no personal interest. Marty, who turned her hand to anything, was usually the one who performed the part of keeping the trees in a perpendicular position whilst he threw in the mould ...

The holes were already dug, and they set to work. Winterborne's fingers were endowed with a gentle conjuror's touch in spreading the roots of each little tree, resulting in a sort of caress under which the delicate fibres all laid themselves out in their proper directions for growth. He put most of these roots towards the south-west; for, he said, in forty years' time, when some great gale is blowing from that quarter, the trees will require the strongest holdfast on that side to stand against it and not fall.

'How they sigh directly we put 'em upright, though while they are lying down they don't sigh at all,' said Marty.

'Do they?' said Giles. 'I've never noticed it.'

She erected one of the young pines into its hole, and held up her finger; the soft musical breathing instantly set in which was not to cease night or day till the grown tree should be felled – probably long after the two planters had been felled themselves.

'It seems to me,' the girl continued, 'as if they sigh because they are very sorry to begin life in earnest – just as we be.'

Thomas Hardy, The Woodlanders

Dew was already on the paths. In the old oak-wood a mist was rising, and he hesitated, wondering whether one whiteness were a strand of fog or only campion-flowers pallid in a cloud.

By the time they came to the pine-trees, Miriam was getting very eager and very tense. Her bush might be gone. She might not be able to find it; and she wanted it so much. Almost passionately she wanted to be with him when he stood before the flowers. They were going to have a communion together – something that thrilled her, something holy. He was walking beside her in silence. They were very near to each other. She trembled, and he listened, vaguely anxious.

Coming to the edge of the wood, they saw the sky in front, like mother-of-pearl, and the earth growing dark. Somewhere on the outermost branches of the pine-wood the honeysuckle was streaming scent.

'Where?' he asked.

'Down the middle path,' she murmured, quivering.

When they turned the corner of the path she stood still. In the wide walk between the pines, gazing rather frightened, she could distinguish nothing for some moments; the greying light robbed things of their colour. Then she saw her bush.

'Ah!' she cried, hastening forward.

It was very still. The tree was tall and straggling. It had thrown its briers over a hawthorn-bush, and its long streamers trailed thick, right down to the grass, splashing the darkness everywhere with great spilt stars, pure white. In bosses of ivory and in large splashed stars the roses gleamed on the darkness of foliage and stems and grass. Paul and Miriam stood close together, silent, and watched. Point after point the steady roses shone out to them, seeming to kindle something in their souls. The dusk came like smoke around, and still did not put out the roses.

D. H. Lawrence, Sons and Lovers

She then moved up the brook until she came to the ruined hamlet, where, pausing with a look of peculiar and softened interest before one of the gables which was still standing, she said in a tone less abrupt, though as solemn as before, 'Do you see that blackit and broken end of a sheeling? there my kettle boiled for forty years; there I bore twelve buirdly sons and daughters. Where are they now? Where are the leaves that were on that auld ash-tree at Martinmas! The west wind has made it bare, – and I'm stripped too. Do you see that saugh-tree? – it's but a blackened rotten stump now – I've sat under it many a bonnie summer afternoon, when it hung its gay garlands ower the poppling water. I've sat there, and,' elevating her voice, 'I've held you on my knee, Henry Bertram, and sung ye sangs of the auld barons and their bloody wars. It will ne'er be green again, and Meg Merrilies will never sing sangs mair, be they blithe or sad. But ye'll forget her, and ye'll gar big up the auld wa's for her sake? and let somebody live there that's ower gude to fear them of another world; for if ever the dead came back amang the living, I'll be seen in this glen mony a night after these crazed banes are in the mould.'

Sir Walter Scott, Guy Mannering

One time however, we were near quarrelling. He said the pleasantest manner of spending a hot July day was lying from morning till evening on a bank of heath in the middle of the moors, with the bees humming dreamily about among the bloom, and the larks singing high up overhead, and the blue sky and bright sun shining steadily and cloudlessly. That was his most perfect idea of heaven's happiness: mine was rocking in a rustling green tree, with a west wind blowing, and bright white clouds flitting rapidly above; and not only larks, but throstles, and blackbirds, and linnets, and cuckoos pouring music on every side, and the moors seen at a distance, broken into cool dusky dells; but close by great swells of long grass undulating in waves to the breeze; and woods and sounding water, and the whole world awake and wild with joy. He wanted all to lie in an ecstasy of peace; I wanted all to sparkle and dance in a glorious jubilee. I said his heaven would be only half alive; and he said mine would be drunk; I said I should fall asleep in his; and he said he could not breathe in mine. . . .

Emily Brontë, Wuthering Heights

There was a great hurry in the streets, of people speeding away to get shelter before the storm broke; the wonderful corner for echoes resounded with the echoes of footsteps coming and going, yet not a footstep was there.

'A multitude of people, and yet a solitude!' said Darnay, when they had listened for a while.

'Is it not impressive, Mr. Darnay?' asked Lucie. 'Sometimes, I have sat here of an evening, until I fancied – but even the shade of a foolish fancy makes me shudder to-night, when all is so black and solemn – '

'Let us shudder too. We may know what it is.'

'It will seem nothing to you. Such whims are only impressive as we originate them, I think; they are not to be communicated. I have sometimes sat alone here of an evening, listening, until I have made the echoes out to be the echoes of all the footsteps that are coming by-and-by into our lives.'

Charles Dickens, A Tale of Two Cities

But what after all is one night? A short space, especially when the darkness dims so soon, and so soon a bird sings, a cock crows, or a faint green quickens, like a turning leaf, in the hollow of the wave. Night, however, succeeds to night. The winter holds a pack of them in store and deals them equally, evenly, with indefatigable fingers. They lengthen; they darken. Some of them hold aloft clear planets, plates of brightness. The autumn trees, ravaged as they are, take on the flash of tattered flags kindling the gloom of cool cathedral caves where gold letters on marble pages describe death in battle and how bones bleach and burn far away in Indian sands. The autumn trees gleam in the yellow moonlight, in the light of harvest moons, the light which mellows the energy of labour, and smooths the stubble, and brings the wave lapping blue to the shore.

Virginia Woolf, To the Lighthouse

These passages are all taken from novels and written in prose. But how close to poetry they are! Lifted from their context and unassisted by them, they make their effect as independent prose-poems. I do not remember any pieces from foreign novels, however poetical in general tone, that can be extracted from their context in this way. Is this because their authors were none of them of the same nation as Shakespeare? Shakespeare has dominated English literature, his influence has soaked itself into its very fibre and basic texture; so that the fact that he was a poet means that many of our novelists are halfway to being poets too and aspire to give their work the concentrated heightened intensity of poetry.

PROSE STYLE

But the iniquity of oblivion blindly scattereth her poppy, and deals with the memory of men without distinction to merit of perpetuity. Who can but pity the founder of the Pyramids? Herostratus lives that burnt the Temple of Diana; he is almost lost that built it. Time hath spared the Epitaph of Adrian's horse, confounded that of himself. In vain we compute our felicities by the advantage of our good names, since bad have equal durations; and Thersites is like to live as long as Agamemnon. Who knows whether the best of men be known or whether there be not more remarkable persons forgot than any that stand remembered in the known account of Time? Without the favour of the everlasting Register, the first man had been as unknown as the last, and Methuselah's long life had been his only chronicle.

Oblivion is not to be hired. The greater part must be content to be as though they had not been, to be found in the register of God, not in the record of man. Twenty-seven names make up the first story before the Flood, and the recorded names ever since contain not one living Century. The number of the dead long exceedeth all that shall live. The night of time far surpasseth the day, and who knows when was the Aequinox? Every houre adds unto that current Arithmetic, which scarce stands one moment. And since death must be the *Lucina* of life, and even Pagans could doubt whether thus to live were to die; since our longest sun sets at right descensions and makes but winter arches, and therefore it cannot be long before we lie down in darkness and have our Light in ashes; since the brother of death daily haunts us with dying mementos, and Time, that grows old in itself, bids us hope no long duration, diuturnity is a dream and folly of expectation.

Sir Thomas Browne, Urn Burial

It happen'd one Day about Noon going towards my Boat, I was exceedingly surprised with the Print of a Man's naked Foot on the Shore, which was very plain to be seen in the Sand. I stood like one Thunder-struck, or as if I had seen an Apparition; I listen'd, I look'd round me, I could hear nothing, nor see any Thing; I went up to a rising Ground to look farther; I went up the Shore and down the Shore, but it was all one, I could see no other Impression but that one; I went to it again to see if there were any more, and to observe if it might not be my Fancy; but there was no Room for that, for there was exactly the very Print of a Foot, Toes, Heel, and every Part of a Foot; how it came thither I knew not, nor could in the least imagine. But after innumerable fluttering Thoughts, like a Man perfectly confus'd and out of my self, I came Home to my Fortification, not feeling, as we say, the Ground I went on, but terrify'd to the last Degree, looking behind me at every two or three Steps, mistaking every Bush and Tree, and fancying every

Stump at a Distance to be a Man; nor is it possible to describe
how many various Shapes affrighted Imagination represented
Things to me in; how many wild Ideas were found every
Moment in my Fancy, and what strange, unaccountable
Whimsies came into my Thoughts by the Way.

Daniel Defoe, Robinson Crusoe

Two examples of prose style at its very best: Defoe plain, Browne
elaborate; but both, in the true sense of the word, 'functional'.
Each word is the exact word to convey the author's meaning; the
movement of the prose exactly echoes the movement of the
author's thought and feeling, and the pervading tone in which
each passage is written, is such as to evoke the appropriate mood
in the reader. People often dispute as to the respective merits of
a plain or an elaborate style, as if style was something that existed
independently of any particular meaning. This is not so. Defoe is
right to employ a plain style because he is writing in the person
of a plain Englishman straightforwardly telling the story of what
purports to be a true adventure. Browne is right to employ a
complex elaborate style because he has a very complex subject, the
meditations of an imaginative, ironical and learned spirit ponder-
ing on the transience of all things human. Each writer has chosen
the right mode for his special purpose. Less obvious but equally
distinct are the differences between two elaborate stylists or be-
tween two plain ones, between Browne and Raleigh or between
Swift and Defoe.

But all these again are vanished; for the inventions of mortal
men are no less mortal than themselves. The fire which the
Chaldeans worshipped for a God, is crept into every man's
chimney, which the lack of fuel starveth, water quencheth and
want of air suffocateth. Jupiter is no more vexed with Juno's
jealousies; death hath persuaded him to chastity, and her to
patience; and that time, which hath devoured itself, hath also
eaten up both the bodies and the images of him and his; yes,
their stately temples of stone and dureful marble. The houses
and sumptuous buildings erected to Baal can no where be found
upon the earth, nor any monument of that glorious temple
consecrated to Diana. There are none now in Phoenicia that

lament the death of Adonis; nor any in Libya, Creta, Thessalia, or elsewhere, that can ask counsel or help from Jupiter. The great god Pan hath broken his pipes; Apollo's priests are become speechless; and the trade of riddles in oracles, with the Devil's telling men's fortunes therein, is taken up by counterfeit Egyptians and cozening astrologers.

Sir Walter Raleigh, A History of the World

My reconcilement to the Yahoo kind in general might not be so difficult, if they would be content with those vices and follies only which nature hath entitled them to. I am not in the least provoked at the sight of a lawyer, a pick-pocket, a colonel, a fool, a lord, a gamester, a politician, a whoremonger, a physician, an evidence, a suborner, an attorney, a traitor, or the like; this is all according to the due course of things: but when I behold a lump of deformity and diseases, both in body and mind, smitten with pride, it immediately breaks all the measures of my patience; neither shall I ever be able to comprehend how such an animal, and such a vice, could tally together.

Jonathan Swift, Gulliver's Travels

These passages, also supremely good in their kind, are subtly different, Raleigh from Browne and Swift from Defoe. Raleigh, though he has his touches of whimsical fancy, speaks swiftly and directly, whereas Brown often pauses on his grand Dead March to turn aside and linger in meditation down some curious byeway of fantasy or thought. Swift's simplicity, unlike Defoe's, is more apparent than real. Defoe's style is clear water; Swift's is like gin which while looking the same as water, tastes very different; for it is saturated with the powerful alcohol of his irony.

Six more examples of prose at its best:

I must not close my letter without giving you one principal event of my history; which was, that – in the course of my late tour – I set out one morning before 5 o'clock, the moon shining through a dark and misty autumnal air, and got to the sea-coast time enough to be at the sun's levee. I saw the clouds and dark vapours open gradually to right and left, rolling over one another in great smoky wreathes, and the tide (as it flowed in gently upon the sands) first whitening, then slightly tinged with gold and blue: and all at once a little line of insufferable brightness that (before I can write these five words) was grown to half an orb, and now to a whole one, too glorious to be distinctly seen. It is very odd it makes no figure upon paper; yet I shall remember it as long as the sun, or at least as long as I endure. I wonder whether anybody ever saw it before; I hardly believe it.

The Letters of Thomas Gray

It was on the day, or rather night, of the 27th of June 1787, between the hours of eleven and twelve, that I wrote the last lines of the last page, in a summer-house in my garden. After laying down my pen, I took several turns in a *berceau*, or covered walk of acacias, which commands a prospect of the country, the lake, and the mountains. The air was temperate, the sky was serene, the silver orb of the moon was reflected from the waters, and all nature was silent. I will not dissemble the first emotions of joy on the recovery of my freedom, and, perhaps, the estab-lishment of my fame. But my pride was soon humbled, and a sober melancholy was spread over my mind, by the idea that I had taken an everlasting leave of an old and agreeable com-panion, and that whatsoever might be the future date of my *History*, the life of the historian must be short and precarious.

Edward Gibbon, Autobiography

I protest Madam, said my uncle Toby, I can see nothing whatever in your eye.

It is not in the white, said Mrs. Wadman: my uncle Toby looked with might and main into the pupil.

Now of all the eyes which ever were created – from your own Madam, up to those of Venus herself, which certainly were as venereal a pair of eyes as ever stood in a head – there never was an eye of them all, so fitted to rob my uncle Toby of his repose, as the very eye, at which he was looking – it was not, Madam, a rolling eye – a romping or a wanton one – nor was it an eye sparkling – petulant or imperious – of high claims and terri-fying exactions, which would have curdled at once that milk of human nature of which my uncle Toby was made up – but 'twas an eye full of gentle salutations – and soft responses – speaking – not like the trumpet stop of some ill-made organ, in which many an eye I talk to, holds coarse converse – but whispering soft – like the last low accents of an expiring saint – 'How can you live comfortless, Captain Shandy, and alone, without a bosom to lean your head on – or trust your cares to?'

It was an eye –

But I shall be in love with it myself, if I say another word about it.

– It did my uncle Toby's business.

Laurence Sterne, Tristram Shandy

. . . He was a stooping, shambling person, rather tall, very pale, with longish and brownish hair. He had a thin vague beard – or rather, he had a chin on which a large number of hairs weakly curled and clustered to cover its retreat. He was an odd-looking person; but in the 'nineties odd apparitions were more frequent, I think, than they are now. The young writers of that era – and I was sure this man was a writer – strove earnestly to be distinct in aspect. This man had striven unsuccessfully. He wore a soft black hat of clerical kind but of Bohemian intention, and a grey waterproof cape which, perhaps because it was waterproof, failed to be romantic. I decided that 'dim' was the *mot juste* for him. I had already essayed to write, and was immensely keen on the *mot juste*, that Holy Grail of the period.

The dim man was now again approaching our table, and this time he made up his mind to pause in front of it. 'You don't remember me,' he said in a toneless voice.

Rothenstein brightly focussed him. 'Yes, I do,' he replied after a moment, with pride rather than effusion – pride in a retentive memory. 'Edwin Soames.'

'Enoch Soames,' said Enoch.

'Enoch Soames,' repeated Rothenstein in a tone implying that it was enough to have hit on the surname.

Max Beerbohm, 'Enoch Soames'

What a place to be in is an old library! It seems as though all

L.L.G.—H

the souls of all the writers, that have bequeathed their labours to these Bodleians, were reposing there, as in some dormitory or middle state. I do not want to handle, to profane the leaves, their winding sheets. I could as soon dislodge a shade. I seem to inhale learning, walking amid their foliage; and the odour of their old moth-scented coverings is fragrant as the first bloom of those sciential apples which grew amid the happy orchard.

Charles Lamb

If I had to choose one sentence as the most beautiful in English prose – beautiful with the specific beauty of prose as distinguished from the specific beauty of verse – it would be this from Sir Thomas Browne's *Urn Burial*.

Time, which antiquates antiquities and hath an art to make dust of all things, hath yet spared these minor monuments.

PUNS

Puns have a bad name. Indeed, when they do not come off, they are distressing. More even than other sorts of joke they need to seem both surprising and spontaneous. The spectacle of a pun perceived some way ahead and then laboriously pursued by the punster freezes the smile on the hearer's lips. Charles Lamb's question to the man he met carrying a hare is a model and pattern pun. 'Is that your own hare?' he asked, 'or do you wear a wig?' My own favourite puns are not humorous but pretty and poetical. One occurs in a poem perhaps by Donne and the other in a poem by Edith Sitwell.

Stay, O sweet, and do not rise
The light that shines comes from thine eyes;
The day breaks not, it is my heart
Because that you and I must part.
    Stay, or else my joys will die
    And perish in their infancy.

Attributed to Donne, 'Break of Day'

The gold-armoured ghost from the Roman road
Sighed over the wheat
'Fear not the sound and the glamour
Of my gold armour
(The sound of the wind and the wheat)
Fear not its clamour. . . .
Fear only the red-gold sun with the fleece of a fox
Who will steal the fluttering bird you hide in your breast.
Fear only the red-gold rain
That will dim your brightness, O my tall tower of the corn,
You, – my blonde girl. . . .'
But the wind sighed 'Rest.' . . .
The wind in his grey knight's armour –
The wind in his grey night armour –
Sighed over the fields of the wheat, 'He is gone . . .
    Forlorn.'

Edith Sitwell, 'The Youth With the Red-Gold Hair'

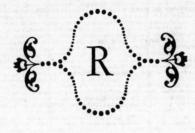

RACHEL

Rachel sings sweet –
 Oh, yes, at night,
Her pale face bent
 In the candle-light
Her slim hands touch
 The answering keys
And she sings of hope
 And of memories:
Sings to the little
 Boy that stands
Watching those slim
 Light, heedful hands.
He looks in her face;
 Her dark eyes seem
Dark with a beautiful
 Distant dream;
And still she plays,
 Sings tenderly
To him of hope
 And of memory.

Walter De La Mare

A pretty poem; but for me something more, so vividly and
strangely does it recall evenings when I myself was a child in the
panelled candle-lit drawing room of my Dorset home and stood
listening to an elder sister playing and singing in the Autumn dusk.
I cannot remember whether the songs she sang – they were mostly
French and English traditional songs – specifically spoke 'of hope
and of memories'. But the phrase sufficiently describes the tender
pensive mood they evoked. Now and again a passage in literature

happens by chance to coincide exactly with something in one's own experience and moves one proportionately more as a result. This makes it hard to judge it impartially. But who cares! In matters of art it is more blessed to respond than to judge.

REALISM

A little boy pickpocket, nick-named Colonel Jack, finds himself in possession of four golden guineas, for him an astronomical sum such as he has never seen before and much more than he can cope with:

> ... I had really more Wealth than I knew what to do with, for Lodging I had none, nor any Box or Drawer to hide my Money in, nor had I any Pocket, but such, *as I say*, was full of Holes; I knew no Body in the World, that I cou'd go and desire them to lay it up for me; for being a poor naked, ragged Boy, they would presently say, I had robb'd some Body, and perhaps lay hold of me, and my Money would be my Crime, *as they say*, it often is in Foreign Countries: And now as I was full of Wealth, behold! I was full of Care, for what to do to secure my Money I could not tell, and this held me so long, and was so vexatious to me the next Day, that I truly sat down and cried.
>
> Nothing cou'd be more perplexing than this Money was to me all that Night, I carried it in my Hand a good while, for it was in Gold all but 14*s*. and that is to say, it was in four Guineas, and that 14*s*. was more difficult to carry than the four Guineas; at last I sat down and pull'd off one of my Shoes, and put the four Guineas into that, but after I had gone a while, my Shoe hurt me so I cou'd not go, so I was fain to sit down again, and take it out of my Shoe, and carry it in my Hand, then I found a dirty linnen Rag in the Street, and I took that up, and wrapt it all together, and carried it in that a good way. I have often since heard People say, when they have been talking of Money that they cou'd not get in, I wish I had it in a foul Clout: in Truth, I had mine in a *foul Clout*, for it was foul according to the Letter of that Saying, but it serv'd me till I came to a convenient Place, and then I sat down and wash'd the Cloth in the Kennel, and so then put my Money in again.

Well, I carried it Home with me to my Lodging in the Glass-House, and when I went to go to Sleep, I knew not what to do with it; if I had let any of the black Crew I was with know of it, I should have been smothered in the Ashes for it, or robb'd of it, or some Trick or other put upon me for it; so I knew not what to do, but lay with it in my Hand, and my Hand in my Bosom, but then Sleep went from Eyes: O! the Weight of human Care! I a poor Beggar Boy cou'd not sleep as soon as I had but a little Money to keep, who before that, cou'd have slept upon a Heap of Brickbats, Stones, or Cinders, or any where, as sound as a rich Man does on his Down Bed, and sounder too.

Every now and then dropping a sleep, I should Dream that my Money was lost, and start like one frighted; then finding it fast in my Hand, try to go to sleep again, but could not for a long while, then drop and start again; at last a Fancy came into my Head, that if I fell a sleep, I should dream of the Money, and talk of it in my Sleep, and tell that I had Money, which if I should do, and one of the Rogues should hear me, they would pick it out of my Bosom, and of my Hand too without waking me, and after that Thought I cou'd not sleep a wink more; so that I pass'd that Night over in Care and Anxiety enough, and this I may safely say, was the first Nights Rest that I lost by the Cares of this Life, and the deceitfulness of Riches.

As soon as it was Day, I got out of the Hole we lay in, and rambled abroad in the Fields towards *Stepney*, and there I mus'd and consider'd what I shou'd do with this Money, and many a Time I wish'd that I had not had it, for after all my ruminating upon it, and what Course I should take with it, or where I should put it, I cou'd not hit upon any one Thing, or any possible Method to secure it, and it perplex'd me so, that at last, as I said just now, I sat down and cried heartily.

When my crying was over, the Case was the same; I had the Money still, and what to do with it I could not tell, at last it came into my Head, that I would look out for some Hole in a Tree, and see to hide it there, till I should have occasion for it: Big with this Discovery, as I then thought it, I began to look about me for a Tree; but there were no Trees in the Fields about *Stepney*, or *Mile-End* that look'd fit for my Purpose, and if there were any, that I began to look narrowly at, the Fields were so

full of People, that they wou'd see if I went to hide any Thing
there, and I thought the people eyed me as it were, and that
two Men in particular follow'd me, to see what I intended to
do.

This drove me farther off, and I cross'd the Road at *Mile-End*,
and in the middle of the Town went down a Lane that goes away
to the *Blind Beggars* at *Bednal-Green*; when I came a little way in
the Lane, I found a Foot Path over the Fields, and in those
Fields several Trees for my Turn, as I thought; at last one Tree
had a little Hole in it, pretty high out of my Reach, and I
climb'd up the Tree to get to it, and when I came there, I put
my Hand in, and found, (as I thought) a Place very fit, so I
placed my Treasure there and was mighty well satisfied with it,
but behold, putting my Hand in again to lay it more commodi-
ously as I thought, of a sudden it slipp'd away from me, and I
found the Tree was hollow, and my little Parcel was fallen in
quite out of my Reach, and how far it might go in, I knew not;
so, that in a Word, my Money was quite gone, irrecoverably
lost, there could be no Room, so much as to hope ever to see it
again, for it was a vast great Tree.

As young as I was, I was now sensible what a Fool I was
before, that I could not think of Ways to keep my Money, but
I must come thus far to throw it into a Hole where I could not
reach it; well, I thrust my Hand quite up to my Elbow, but no
Bottom was to be found, or any end of the Hole or Cavity; I
got a Stick off the Tree, and thrust it in a great Way, but all was
one; then I cry'd, nay, roar'd out, I was in such a Passion, then
I got down the Tree again, then up again, and thrust in my
Hand again till I scratch'd my Arm and made it bleed, and cry'd
all the while most violently: Then I began to think I had not so
much as a Halfpenny of it left for a Halfpenny Roll, and I was
hungry, and then I cry'd again: Then I came away in Despair,
crying and roaring like a little Boy that had been whipp'd, then
I went back again to the Tree, and up the Tree again, and thus
I did several Times.

The last Time I had gotten up the Tree, I happen'd to come
down not on the same Side that I went up and came down be-
fore, but on the other Side of the Tree, and on the other side
of the Bank also; and behold the Tree had a great open Place
in the Side of it close to the Ground, as old hollow Trees often

have; and looking into the open Place, to my inexpressible Joy, there lay my Money, and my linnen Rag, all wrapp'd up just as I had put it into the Hole: For the Tree being hollow all the Way up, there had been some Moss or light Stuff, (which I had not Judgment enough to know) was not firm, and had given way when it came to drop out of my Hand, and so it had slipp'd quite down at once.

I was but a Child, and I rejoic'd like a Child, for I hollow'd quite out aloud when I saw it; then I run to it and snatch'd it up, hug'd and kiss'd the dirty Rag a hundred Times; then danc'd and jump'd about, run from one End of the Field to the other, and in short, I knew not what, much less do I know now, what I did, tho' I shall never forget the Thing, either what a sinking Grief it was to my Heart when I thought I had lost it, or what a Flood of Joy o'erwhelm'd me when I had got it again.

Daniel Defoe, The Life of Colonel Jack

If the best novelist were he who gave the most convincing illusion of reality, Defoe would be the best novelist that ever lived. It is almost impossible not to believe that this passage is not a true record of a real incident. Defoe makes use of no fictional convention: we seem to be reading a simple autobiographical narrative told in his own words by a plain man recollecting his experience as an uneducated child. The narrator never comes between the reader and the subject, Defoe has identified wholly with Jack.

The passage is also interesting as evidence that human nature has changed little since the eighteenth century. A boy thief today would feel just as Jack did, given that he had stolen a sum equivalent to the value of four guineas in Queen Anne's day. This point is worth making because other action might lead us to believe otherwise. Dickens's boy thieves for instance – Charley Bates and the Artful Dodger in *Oliver Twist* – strike us as very different from their modern counterparts. But this is because Dickens draws his figures less from the world around him than from the world of his imaginative vision; and also because his picture is strongly coloured by his moral views, which were very much those of his age.

Now, however much we may enjoy Dickens's vision, we cannot share it: the world seen by the average person is very unlike the world imagined by Dickens. Moreover, the moral views of Dickens's day have dated. Defoe, on the other hand, has concentrated on drawing from life and pays no more than a perfunctory lip service to the moral views of his age. The result is that Colonel Jack presents a picture of life as recognizably real as anything written today.

RELIGIOUS

We were entrusted to one another, in the days that mattered, she thought. Entrusted to one another by chance, not choice. Chance, and its agents, time and place. Chance is better than choice; it is more lordly . . . Chance is God, choice is man . . .

Elizabeth Bowen, The Little Girls

Elizabeth Bowen was a religious woman and here she states a religious view of the human situation. She sees man as a creature frail, helpless, ignorant, bewildered, never the master of his fate, always and inevitably the sport of chance and circumstance. But, to her, fate and chance and circumstance are not blind purposeless forces. Behind them and directing them is a conscious mysterious purpose. 'Chance is lordly' she says, 'chance is God.'

'Issues from the hand of God, the simple soul'
To a flat world of changing lights and noise,
To light, dark, dry or damp, chilly or warm;
Moving between the legs of tables and of chairs,
Rising or falling, grasping at kisses and toys,
Advancing boldly, sudden to take alarm,
Retreating to the corner of arm and knee,
Eager to be reassured, taking pleasure
In the fragrant brilliance of the Christmas tree,
Pleasure in the wind, the sunlight and the sea;
Studies the sunlit pattern on the floor
And running stags around a silver tray;
Confounds the actual and the fanciful,
Content with playing-cards and kings and queens,

What the fairies do and what the servants say.
The heavy burden of the growing soul
Perplexes and offends more, day by day;
Week by week, offends and perplexes more
With the imperatives of 'is and seems'
And may and may not, desire and control.
The pain of living and the drug of dreams
Curl up the small soul in the window seat
Behind the *Encyclopaedia Britannica*.
Issues from the hand of time the simple soul
Irresolute and selfish, misshapen, lame,
Unable to fare forward or retreat,
Feeling the warm reality, the offered good,
Denying the importunity of the blood,
Shadow of its own shadows, spectre in its own gloom,
Leaving disordered papers in a dusty room;
Living first in the silence after the viaticum.

Pray for Guiterriez, avid of speed and power,
For Boudin, blown to pieces,
For this one who made a great fortune,
And that one who went his own way.
Pray for Floret, by the boarhound slain between the yew trees,
Pray for us now and at the hour of our birth.

T. S. Eliot, 'Animula'

Eliot also presents the religious view of the human situation, this time interpreted in a specifically Christian sense. For him too, man is the frail and helpless creature of a mysterious power actuated by a mysterious purpose. But this power is benignant and active, a Divine Being to whom he can relate himself by prayer and sacrament and with Whose help he may, after death, attain a truer, fuller life, so that he will live first 'in the silence after the viaticum'.

> Fears and scruples shake us:
> In the great hand of God I stand.

Here Shakespeare, through the lips of Banquo, states the religious view of the human predicament with an incomparable terse grandeur. It is often said that Shakespeare was not a religious poet; and it is true that he tells us nothing about his private personal religion. This does not prevent Macbeth from being the most impressive expression in English literature of the Christian doctrine of Damnation as King Lear is the most impressive expression of the Christian doctrine of Redemption.

THE RIGHT PLACE FOR READING

It is interesting – or at least amusing – to consider what are the most appropriate places in which different authors should be read. Pope is doubtless at his best in the midst of a formal garden, Herrick in an orchard, and Shelley in a boat at sea. Sir Thomas Browne demands, perhaps, a more exotic atmosphere. One could read him floating down the Euphrates, or past the shores of Arabia; and it would be pleasant to open the *Vulgar Errors* in Constantinople, or to get by heart a chapter of the *Christian Morals* between the paws of a Sphinx. In England, the most fitting background for his strange ornament must surely be some habitation consecrated to learning, some University which still smells of antiquity, and has learnt the habit of repose . . .

Lytton Strachey, Essay on Sir Thomas Browne

Lytton Strachey's advice is not very practical. Few of us, alas, ever get the chance to read Sir Thomas Browne's works when floating down the river Euphrates; or can wait till we are at sea before opening a volume of Shelley's poems. All the same, Strachey has something to say to us: the art of reading does include choosing the right place to read in. It is impossible to lay down a general rule about this, it depends on the individual temperament of the reader, also on his or her age. I remember, when I was eighteen, reading Turgenev's *House of Gentlefolk* in the front hall of a Munich hotel with people coming and going all round me and the place full of the noise of doors swinging open and shut and visitors giving orders about their luggage, but with myself deaf to all this and my eyes becoming blurred with tears when I got to the passage where Lisa the heroine renounces the hero Lavretsky. I doubt if this could happen to me now, even if I had the luck to come upon a new novel by Turgenev. It is harder to lose oneself in a book at the age of seventy-three than it was at the age of eighteen.

Yet, looking back, I see that in spite of the noise and bustle, a Munich hotel was not the worst place for me to read that particular book. It was the first time that I was travelling abroad on my own and my new and foreign situation made my imagination receptive to what was to me a new and foreign book. Similarly I have found Henry James an appropriate writer to read in Paris or Venice or any other town with historic and artistic associations; was he not a traveller peculiarly sensitive to such associations? It is a pleasure to read *The Aspern Papers* anywhere. It is an especial pleasure to read it in Venice, its home town. Hazlitt and Lamb have something to say on the same topic; naturally enough, since they are the English authors who seem to have enjoyed reading the most. Here is Hazlitt remembering an occasion when book and time and place all chanced to compose together to produce a fuller, more delightful harmony.

> The last time I tasted this luxury in its full perfection was one day after a sultry day's walk in summer between Farnham and Alton. I was fairly tired out; I walked into an inn-yard (I think at the latter place); I was shewn by the waiter to what looked at first like common out-houses at the other end of it, but they turned out to be a suite of rooms, probably a hundred years old – the one I entered opened into an old-fashioned garden, embellished with beds of larkspur and a leaden Mercury; it was wainscoted, and there was a grave-looking, dark-coloured portrait of Charles II hanging over the tiled chimney-piece. I had Love for Love in my pocket and began to read; coffee was brought in in a silver coffee-pot; the cream, the bread and butter, everything was excellent, and the flavour of Congreve's style prevailed over all.
>
> *The Plain Speaker*

Hazlitt is concerned with the right time to read a book, as well as with the right place. So also – but more ironically and fancifully – is Lamb.

> Much depends upon *when* and *where* you read a book. In the five or six impatient minutes, before dinner is quite ready, who

would think of taking up the Faerie Queene for a stop-gap, or a volume of Bishop Andrewe's sermons?

Milton almost requires a solemn service of music to be played before you enter upon him. But he brings his music, to which, who listens, had need bring docile thoughts and purged ears.

Winter evenings – the world shut out – with less of ceremony the gentle Shakespeare enters. At such a season The Tempest, or his own Winter's Tale –

These two poets you cannot avoid reading aloud – to yourself, or (as it chances) to some single person listening. More than one – and it degenerates into an audience . . .

I should not care to be caught in the serious avenues of some cathedral alone, and reading *Candide*.

'Detached Thoughts on Books and Reading'; Last Essays of Elia

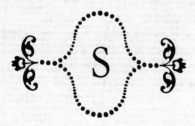

SCENTS

... It grew late. Through the open door, stealthily, came the scent of madonna lilies, almost as if it were prowling abroad. Suddenly he got up and went out of doors.

The beauty of the night made him want to shout. A half-moon, dusky gold, was sinking behind the black sycamore at the end of the garden, making the sky dull purple with its glow. Nearer, a dim white fence of lilies went across the garden, and the air all round seemed to stir with scent, as if it were alive. He went across the bed of pinks, whose keen perfume came sharply across the rocking, heavy scent of the lilies, and stood alongside the white barrier of flowers. They flagged all loose, as if they were panting. The scent made him drunk. He went down to the field to watch the moon sink under.

A corncrake in the hay-close called insistently. The moon slid quite quickly downwards, growing more flushed. Behind him the great flowers leaned as if they were calling. And then, like a shock, he caught another perfume, something raw and coarse. Hunting round, he found the purple iris, touched their fleshy throats and their dark, grasping hands. At any rate, he had found something. They stood stiff in the darkness. Their scent was brutal. The moon was melting down upon the crest of the hill. It was gone; all was dark ...

D. H. Lawrence, Sons and Lovers

Scents and smells are not quite so hard to describe in words as the taste of food is: their appeal is not so purely physical, they do stir imaginative associations. But it is far from easy to find the right words with which to convey them. Lawrence finds them here. He takes risks; to describe the scent of lilies and irises, he employs words like 'raw' and 'brutal' which might have been expected to spoil his effect by making it ugly or comic. But the intensity with which he communicates the sentiment of the scene is such as to make this impossible and the harsh words help him to do this by bringing the actual physical presence of the flowers more forcefully and vividly home to us.

Bacon's achievement is even more remarkable. He manages to suggest a flower's scent without describing it at all and simply by mentioning its name. Of course we may not interpret his intentions correctly, we may imagine individual scents differently from what he intended: but there is no mistake about the strong fresh garden sweetness that seems to breathe from his words.

And because the Breath of Flowers is farre Sweeter in the Aire (where it comes and Goes, like the Warbling of Musick) than in the hand, therefore nothing is more fit for that delight, than to know, what be the Flowers, and Plants, that doe best perfume the Aire. Roses, Damask & Red, are fast Flowers of their Smels; So that you may walke by a whole row of them, and finde Nothing of their Sweetnesse; yea though it be in a Mornings Dew. Bayes likewise yield no Smell, as they grow. Rosemary little; Nor Sweet Marjoram. That, which aboue all Others, yeelds the Sweetest Smell in the Aire, is the Violet; Specially the White-double-Violet, which comes twice a Yeare; About the middle of Aprill, and about Bartholomew-tide. Next to that is the Muske-Rose. Then the Strawberry-Leaues dying, with a most Excellent Cordiall Smell. Then the Flower of the Vines; It is a little dust, like the dust of a Bent, which growes vpon the Cluster, in the First comming forth. Then Sweet Briar. Then Wall-Flowers, which are very Delightfull, to be set vnder a Parler, or Lower Chamber Window. Then Pinks, and Gilly-Flowers specially the Matted Pinck, and Clove Gilly-Flower. Then the Flowers of the Lime Tree. Then the Honny-Suckles, so they be somewhat a farre off. Of Beane Flowers I speake not, because they are Field Flowers. But those which Perfume the Aire most delightfully, not passed by as the rest, but being Troden vpon and Crushed, are Three: That is

Burnet, Wilde-Time, and Water-Mints. Therefore, you are to set whole Alleys of them, to haue the Pleasure, when you walke or tread.

Francis Bacon, Essay on Gardens

THE SENSE OF THE PAST

The Past is the only dead thing that smells sweet.

Edward Thomas, 'Early one Morning'

(1)

PERSONAL

But whether he meditated the Muses or the philosophers, the loneliness of Hintock life was beginning to tell upon his impressionable nature. Winter in a solitary house in the country, without society, is tolerable, nay, even enjoyable and delightful, given certain conditions; but these are not the conditions which attach to the life of a professional man who drops down into such a place by mere accident. They were present to the lives of Winterborne, Melbury and Grace; but not to the doctor's. They are old association – an almost exhaustive biographical or historical acquaintance with every object, animate and inanimate, within the observer's horizon. He must know all about those invisible ones of the days gone by, whose feet have traversed the fields which look so grey from his windows; recall whose creaking plough has turned those sods from time to time; whose hands planted the trees that form a crest to the opposite hill; whose horses and hounds have torn through that underwood; what birds affect that particular brake; what bygone domestic dramas of love, jealousy, revenge, or disappointment have been enacted in the cottages, the mansions, the street or on the green. The spot may have beauty, grandeur, salubrity, convenience; but if it lack memories it will ultimately pall upon him who settles there without opportunity of intercourse with his kind.

Thomas Hardy, The Woodlanders

I know not how it may be with others
   Who sit amid relics of householdry
That date from the days of their mothers' mothers,
    But well I know how it is with me
      Continually.

I see the hands of the generations
   That owned each shiny familiar thing
In play on its knobs and indentations,
    And with its ancient fashioning
      Still dallying:

Hands behind hands, growing paler and paler,
   As in a mirror a candle-flame
Shows images of itself, each frailer
    As it recedes, though the eye may frame
      Its shape the same.

On the clock's dull dial a foggy finger,
   Moving to set the minutes right
With tentative touches that lift and linger
    In the wont of a moth on a summer night,
      Creeps to my sight.

On this old viol, too, fingers are dancing –
   As whilom – just over the strings by the nut,
The tip of a bow receding, advancing
    In airy quivers, as if it would cut
      The plaintive gut.

And I see a face by that box for tinder,
   Glowing forth in fits from the dark,
And fading again, as the linten cinder
    Kindles to red at the flinty spark,
      Or goes out stark.

Well, well. It is best to be up and doing,
   The world has no use for one to-day
Who eyes things thus – no aim pursuing!
    He should not continue in this stay,
      But sink away.

               Thomas Hardy, 'Old Furniture'

. . . although there is a trace of the bagman, something a trifle
smug and mainchancy in travelling chiefly to acquire memories
– and the best will come and stay unsought – Memory itself is
of capital importance. Its aid alone can bring full recognition
of all that is encountered, and of the slight novelty which that
encountering may secure. And this is no less true – physical
activity for the moment entirely in abeyance – of travelling
into the Past; a venture which, like the astronomer's cipher-
infested sallies into the black and icy voids of space, is almost
wholly of the mind. For memory, even when childhood is left
behind, may retain the grace to keep for its owner's use and
pleasure the best and brightest, however wantonly meagre
that best may be; and with a sovereign irony or humour or
absence of self-conceit, may even gild what once was lead. That
hapless little picnic when the rain dripped minute-drops from
the rusty railway bridge over the river into the salad; the tryst
she failed to keep; the comfortless inn; the wrong and vacant
train; tedious company; the flies; the mob – all such little
distresses may at length give a pleasing edge to recollection;
and what was once the mind's fast may, in retrospect, resemble
a feast.

Walter De La Mare, Private View

(II)

HISTORICAL

On this kindly yellow day of mild low-travelling winter sun
    The stirless depths of the yews
    Are vague with misty blues:
Across the spacious pathways stretching spires of shadow run,
And the wind-gnawed walls of ancient brick are fired vermillion.

Two or three early sanguine finches tune
Some tentative strains, to be enlarged by May or June:
    From a thrush or blackbird
    Comes now and then a word,
While an enfeebled fountain somewhere within is heard.

Our footsteps wait awhile,
Then draw beneath the pile,
When an inner court outspreads
As 'twere History's own aisle,
Where the now-visioned fountain its attenuate crystal sheds
In passive lapse that seems to ignore the yon world's clamorous
    clutch,
And lays an insistent numbness on the place, like a cold hand's
    touch.

And there swaggers the Shade of a straddling King, plumed,
    sworded, with sensual face,
And lo, too, that of his Minister, at a bold self-centred pace:
Sheer in the sun they pass; and thereupon all is still,
Save the mindless fountain tinkling on with thin enfeebled will.

Thomas Hardy, 'A Spellbound Palace (Hampton Court)'

So I proceed to tell you that my health is much improved by
the sea, not that I drank it, or bathed in it, as the common
people do: no! I only walked by it and looked upon it. The
climate is remarkably mild, even in October and November;
no snow has been seen to lie there for these thirty years past;
the myrtles grow in the ground against the houses, and
Guernsey lilies bloom in every window: the town, clean and
well-built, surrounded by its old stone walls, with their towers
and gateways, stands at the point of a peninsula, and opens full
south to an arm of the sea, which, having formed two beautiful
bays on each hand of it, stretches away in direct view, till it
joins the Bristol Channel; it is skirted on either side with gently-
rising grounds, clothed with thick wood, and directly cross its
mouth rise the high lands of the Isle of Wight at distance, but
distinctly seen. In the bosom of the woods (concealed from
profane eyes) lie hid the ruins of Netley Abbey; there may be
richer and greater houses of religion, but the abbot is content
with his situation. See there, at the top of that hanging meadow,
under the shade of those old trees that bend into a half circle
about it, he is walking slowly (good man!) and bidding his
beads for the souls of his benefactors, interred in that venerable
pile that lies beneath him. Beyond it, (the meadow still descend-

ing) nods a thicket of oaks that mask the building, and have excluded a view too garish and luxuriant for a holy eye; only on either hand they leave an opening to the blue glittering sea. Did you not observe how, as that white sail shot by and was lost, he turned and crossed himself to drive the tempter from him that had thrown that distraction in his way? I should tell you that the ferryman who rowed me, a lusty young fellow, told me that he would not for all the world pass a night at the Abbey (there were such things near it) though there was a power of money hid there.

The Letters of Thomas Gray

. . . The light in her beautiful, formal room was dim, though it would do, as everything would always do; the hot night had kept out lamps, but there was a pair of clusters of candles that glimmered over the chimney-piece like the tall tapers of an altar. The windows were all open, their redundant hangings swaying a little, and he heard once more, from the empty court, the small plash of the fountain. From beyond this, and as from a great distance – beyond the court, beyond the *corps de logis* forming the front – came, as if excited and exciting, the vague voice of Paris. Strether had all along been subject to sudden gusts of fancy in connexion with such matters as these – odd starts of the historic sense, suppositions and divinations with no warrant but their intensity. Thus and so, on the eve of the great recorded dates, the days and nights of revolution, the sounds had come in, the omens, the beginnings broken out. They were the smell of revolution, the smell of the public temper – or perhaps simply the smell of blood.

Henry James, The Ambassadors

. . . The age was the Elizabethan; their morals were not ours; nor their poets; nor their climate; nor their vegetables even. Everything was different. The weather itself, the heat and cold of summer and winter, was, we may believe, of another temper altogether. The brilliant amorous day was divided as sheerly from the night as land from water. Sunsets were redder and more intense; dawns were whiter and more auroral. Of our

crepuscular half-lights and lingering twilights they knew no-
thing. The rain fell vehemently, or not at all. The sun blazed
or there was darkness. Translating this to the spiritual regions
as their wont is, the poets sang beautifully how roses fade and
petals fall. The moment is brief they sang; the moment is over;
one long night is then to be slept by all. As for using the artifices
of the greenhouse or conservatory to prolong or preserve these
fresh pinks and roses, that was not their way. The withered
intricacies and ambiguities of our more gradual and doubtful
age were unknown to them. Violence was all. The flower
bloomed and faded. The sun rose and sank. The lover loved and
went.

Virginia Woolf, Orlando

She waited for a moment in the hall. Her eyes were dimmed
after the glare of the road. Everything seemed pale and frail
and friendly. The rugs were faded; the pictures were faded.
Even the Admiral in his cocked hat over the fireplace wore a
curious look of faded urbanity. In Greece one was always
going back two thousand years. Here it was always the eight-
eenth century. Like everything English, she thought, laying
down her umbrella on the refectory table beside the china bowl,
with dried rose leaves in it, the past seemed near, domestic,
friendly.

Virginia Woolf, The Years

Henry James, though he had a sense of the past as acute as
Virginia Woolf's – the passage from *The Ambassadors* shows this –
did not so easily find the past friendly. He preferred it to be close
enough for him to identify with it and, perhaps because he was a
child of the New World, he could not do this, if it was at any
great distance from him.

I delight in a palpable imaginable visitable past – in the nearer
distances and the clearer mysteries, the marks and signs of a
world we may reach over to as by making a long arm we grasp
an object at the end of our own table. The table is the one, the
common expanse, and where we lean, so stretching, we find it
firm and continuous. That, to my imagination, is the past frag-
rant of all, or of almost all, the poetry of the thing outlived and

lost and gone, and yet in which the precious element of close-
ness, telling so of connexions but tasting so of differences,
remains appreciable.

Henry James, Preface to the Aspern Papers

SHAKESPEARE ON THE STAGE

The Forbes Robertson Hamlet at the Lyceum is, very unexpec-
tedly at that address, really not at all unlike Shakespeare's play
of the same name. I am quite certain I saw Reynaldo in it for a
moment; and possibly I may have seen Voltimand and Cor-
nelius; but just as the time for their scene arrived, my eye fell
on the word 'Fortinbras' in the program, which so amazed me
that I hardly know what I saw for the next ten minutes. Ophelia,
instead of being a strenuously earnest and self-possessed young
lady giving a concert and recitation for all she was worth, was
mad – actually mad. The story of the play was perfectly intelli-
gible, and quite took the attention of the audience off the
principal actor at moments. What is the Lyceum coming to?
Is it for this that Sir Henry Irving has invented a whole series
of original romantic dramas, and given the credit of them with-
out a murmur to the immortal bard . . . whose works have been
no more to him than the word-quarry from which he has hewn
and blasted the lines and titles of masterpieces which are really
all his own? And now, when he has created by these means a
reputation for Shakespeare, he no sooner turns his back for a
moment on London that Mr. Forbes Robertson competes with
him on the boards of his own theatre by actually playing off
against him the authentic Swan of Avon . . .

. . . Mr. Forbes Robertson takes the part quite easily and
spontaneously. There is none of that strange Lyceum intensity
which comes from the perpetual struggle between Sir Henry
Irving and Shakespeare. The lines help Mr. Forbes Robertson
instead of getting in his way at every turn, because he wants to
play Hamlet, and not to slip into his inky cloak a changeling of
quite another race. We may miss the craft, the skill double-
distilled by constant peril, the sublety, the dark rays of heat
generated by intense friction, the relentless parental tenacity
and cunning with which Sir Henry nurses his own pet creations

on Shakespearean food like a fox rearing its litter in the den of a lioness; but we get light, freedom, naturalness, credibility, and Shakespeare . . .

Bernard Shaw, Our Theatres in the Nineties

The above is a comment from Shaw's review of Forbes Robertson's production of *Hamlet*, comparing it with that of Irving, at that time King of the Lyceum Theatre and of the English stage. All he says should be read by every would-be producer and actor of *Hamlet* nowadays. Some of the latest productions of Shakespeare's plays that I have seen have offended against Shakespeare's intentions as much as ever Irving's can have done. Strenuously and deliberately they have disregarded the text, either by omission or by misinterpretation. I have seen the triumphant end of *King Henry IV Part I* twisted into a feeble attempt at a Grand Guignol horror: I have seen Ophelia in her madness, not 'turning all to favour and to prettiness' but rolling and howling hideously on the floor in the manner of the mad Mrs Rochester in *Jane Eyre*. I am told that, in a much praised production of *King Lear*, Edmund's dying repentance was omitted on the grounds that the producer took the view that nowadays no one could be expected to believe anything so incredible. This explanation is significant. It implies that in the producer's view Shakespeare is an irretrievably dead author, whose plays may have literary and dramatic merits which make them still worth performing, but whose beliefs are those of an age so remote from our own as to make them unintelligible. This is of course untrue: Shakespeare's beliefs may not be the same as those current in the producer's circle of acquaintances – he believed in such unmodish things as chastity and a sense of sin – but they are still intelligible and even tenable. Played straight and with conviction, Shakespeare's dramas easily delight audiences today. It is the up-to-date productions that confuse them – as much as would a Mozart opera rescored for a jazz band and sung by pop singers. No doubt this too might be defended on the ground that, performed in its original form, it would be unintelligible to a modern audience.

This is not to say that a new-style production of Shakespeare, if well executed, cannot generate its own excitement. But this is not a Shakespearian kind of excitement. To adapt Shaw's words to our own day; a straightforward production of a Shakespeare play 'may miss the craft, the skill – distilled by constant peril, the dark rays of heat, generated by intense friction, the relentless parental tenacity and cunning with which Mr "X" of the National Theatre or Mr "Y" of the Royal Shakespeare Company, nurses his own pet creations on Shakespearean food like a fox rearing its litter in the den of a lioness; but we get light, freedom, naturalness, credibility, and Shakespeare.'

SHEPHERDS

Now as they were going along and talking, they espied a boy feeding his father's sheep. The boy was in very mean clothes, but of a very fresh and well-favoured countenance; and as he sat by himself, he sung. Hark, said Mr. Great-heart, to what the shepherd's boy saith. So they hearkened, and he said,

He that is down needs fear no fall,
He that is low, no pride;
He that is humble, ever shall
Have God to be his guide.
    I am content with what I have,
Little be it or much:
And, Lord, contentment still I crave,
Because thou savest such.
    Fulness to such a burden is
That go on pilgrimage;
Here little, and hereafter bliss,
Is best from age to age.

Then said the guide, Do you hear him? I will dare to say, that this boy lives a merrier life, and wears more of that herb called heart's-ease in his bosom, than he that is clad in silk and velvet . . .

John Bunyan, The Pilgrim's Progress

How sweet is the Shepherd's sweet lot!
From the morn to the evening he strays;

He shall follow his sheep all the day,
And his tongue shall be filled with praise.

For he hears the lamb's innocent call,
And he hears the ewe's tender reply;
He is watchful while they are in peace;
For they know when their Shepherd is nigh.

William Blake, 'Songs of Innocence'

For we were nursed upon the self-same hill,
Fed the same flock, by fountain, shade and rill:
Together both, ere the high lawns appeared
Under the opening eyelids of the Morn,
We drove a-field, and both together heard
What time the grey-fly winds her sultry horn
Battening our flocks with the fresh dews of night,
Oft till the star that rose at evening bright
Toward heaven's descent had sloped his westering wheel.

John Milton, 'Lycidas'

Go, for they call you, Shepherd, from the hill;
    Go, Shepherd, and untie the wattled cotes:
        No longer leave thy wistful flock unfed,
    Nor let thy bawling fellows rack their throats,
        Nor the cropp'd grasses shoot another head.
            But when the fields are still,
        And the tired men and dogs all gone to rest,
        And only the white sheep are sometimes seen
            Cross and recross the strips of moon-blanch'd green;
    Come, Shepherd, and again renew the quest.

Matthew Arnold, 'The Scholar Gypsy'

As these passages show, shepherds have been in the highest
degree inspiring to English authors. I suppose the reason is that
they are symbolic figures in the two traditions from which English
culture derives; the classical and the Biblical. In classical literature

they stand for a simple and innocent existence lived close to Nature and her beauties. For a Christian, the shepherd stands for Christ himself, the Good Shepherd ready to lay down his life for his sheep. Milton's and Arnold's shepherds are classical; Blake's and Bunyan's are Christian.

> . . . Upon the forest-side in Grasmere Vale
> There dwelt a Shepherd, Michael was his name;
> An old man, stout of heart, and strong of limb.
> His bodily frame had been from youth to age
> Of an unusual strength: his mind was keen,
> Intense, and frugal, apt for all affairs,
> And in his shepherd's calling he was prompt
> And watchful more than ordinary men.
> Hence had he learned the meaning of all winds,
> Of blasts of every tone; and oftentimes,
> When others heeded not, He heard the South
> Make subterraneous music, like the noise
> Of bagpipers on distant Highland hills.
> The Shepherd, at such warning, of his flock
> Bethought him, and he to himself would say,
> 'The winds are now devising work for me!'
> And, truly, at all times, the storm, that drives
> The traveller to a shelter, summoned him
> Up to the mountains: he had been alone
> Amid the heart of many thousand mists,
> That came to him, and left him, on the heights.
> So lived he till his eightieth year was past.
> And grossly that man errs, who should suppose
> That the green valleys, and the streams and rocks
> Were things indifferent to the Shepherd's thoughts.
> Fields, where with cheerful spirits he had breathed
> The common air; hills, which with vigorous step
> He had so often climbed; which had impressed
> So many incidents upon his mind
> Of hardship, skill or courage, joy or fear;
> Which, like a book, preserved the memory
> Of the dumb animals, whom he had saved,
> Had fed or sheltered, linking to such acts
> The certainty of honourable gain;

Those fields, those hills – what could they less? had laid
Strong hold on his affections, were to him
A pleasurable feeling of blind love,
The pleasure which there is in life itself.

William Wordsworth, 'Michael'

Wordsworth's Michael is not a symbol but a realistically des-
cribed individual man. Yet – deliberately or not – Wordsworth
does describe him as fulfilling both the shepherd's symbolic
functions. Michael cares for his flock and he owes much of his
strength and nobility to the fact that he lives a life close to nature.

What did Shakespeare think of shepherds? They make an
agreeable appearance both in *A Winter's Tale* and *As You Like It*:
but in neither are they designed to represent any ideal. Perdita,
though bred a shepherdess is, as her creator is careful to empha-
size, born a princess. A princess, he suggests, is a superior being
to a shepherdess. Rosalind and Celia, two other high-born ladies,
enjoy themselves playing at rustic life and helping to run a sheep-
fold in the Forest of Arden; but they are happy enough to go
back to Court when the time comes: while Touchstone, their
follower, asked by Corin the shepherd if he likes a shepherd's
life, replies very unenthusiastically: 'Truly Shepherd, in respect
of itself, it is a good life; but, in respect that it is a shepherd's life,
it is naught.' Corin will not agree: he defends his way of life with
dignity and conviction. But he does so on down-to-earth and sens-
ible grounds with no romantic mysticism about them.

Sir, I am a true labourer; I earn that I eat, get that I wear; owe
no man hate, envy no man's happiness; glad of other men's
good, content with my harm; and the greatest of my pride is
to see my ewes graze and my lambs suck.

I suspect that Shakespeare understood the average shepherd
better than Wordsworth did.

SOLITUDE

Is not this great globe itself a celestial solitary?

Hope, fear, false joy and trouble –
These the four winds which daily toss this Bubble.
His breath's a vapour and his life a span,
'Tis glorious misery to be born a man.

That bubble floats on in the severing ether, voyaging, as I have read somewhere, towards a remote (and somewhat inscrutable) goal in the void of space called *Mu* in Leo. And as with the world, so with the conscious beings that inhabit it – possibly the only beings of their specific nature, as our modern astronomers surmise, in the complete stellar and physical universe. Almost impassably cut off as we now are from the natural trust and fellowship of unhumanized beast and bird, so too in some degree we are severed even from our nearest and dearest. By means of those frail tentacles, our senses, we explore the outward semblance of our fellow-creatures; but flesh is flesh and bone is bone, and only by insight and by divination can we pierce inward to the citadel of the mind and soul. We can only translate their touch, their gestures, the words they use, the changing looks on their faces into terms of our own consciousness and spirit. We believe them to be in all essential things like ourselves – whatever their arresting and delightful differences. We trust them not to be mere deceiving automata. Nevertheless, the inmost self of each one of us is a livelong recluse.

[As Matthew Arnold writes:]

Yes; in the sea of life enisled,
    With echoing straits between us thrown,
Dotting the shoreless watery wild,
    We mortal millions live *alone*.
The islands feel the enclasping flow,
And then their endless bounds they know.

But when the moon their hollows lights,
   And they are swept by balms of spring,
And in their glens, on starry nights,
   The nightingales divinely sing,
And lovely notes, from shore to shore,
Across the sounds and channels pour;

O then a longing like despair
   Is to their farthest caverns sent;
For surely once, they feel, we were
   Parts of a single continent . . .

The vivid and positive realization of this may come seldom, but, when it does, it is sharp and appalling. The moment falls, unforeseen, inexplicable and, as if at the insidious wave of an enchanter's wand, the faces, the voices of the believed-in and beloved seem to be nothing but the creation of our own fantasy, and we are 'enisled'. Even the 'echoes' then, like the language-less scream of sea-bird and the drumming of wave on rock, are nothing but a mockery. We may work or play away most of our lives in evading this realization, but in the end we shall become our own Showman's boy and know that as mortals we are alone.

                     Walter De La Mare, Desert Islands

True? not wholly. Certain relationships, above all a long-lived and happy marriage, do diminish and even obliterate man's sense of solitude. Other blood relationships, like those of brother and sister or parent and child do so too – that is if they are rooted in that strongest of communal units, a united and affectionate family. Friendship, also at its intensest can communicate a subtle and intimate feeling of affinity that triumphs over the sense of solitude. But this triumph is seldom long-lived: this intense feeling of affinity tends to fade with the years. When it is faded, man feels more solitary than ever; and then, as Arnold says, he is filled with 'a longing like despair'.

Moreover ultimately De La Mare is right. Dying is always a solitary experience. In the end we know that 'as mortals we are alone'.

SPRING

Spring, the sweet Spring, is the year's pleasant king;
Then blooms each thing, then maids dance in a ring,
Cold doth not sting, the pretty birds do sing:
Cuckoo, jug-jug, pu-we, to-witta-woo!

The palm and may make country houses gay,
Lambs frisk and play, the shepherds pipe all day;
And we hear aye birds tune this merry lay:
Cuckoo, jug-jug, pu-we, to-witta-woo!

The fields breathe sweet, the daisies kiss our feet,
Young lovers meet, old wives a-sunning sit,
In every street these tunes our ear do greet:
Cuckoo, jug-jug, pu-we, to-witta-woo!
   Spring, the sweet Spring!

Thomas Nashe

Frost-locked all the winter,
Seeds, and roots, and stones of fruits,
What shall make their sap ascend
That they may put forth shoots?
Tips of tender green,
Leaf, or blade, or sheath;
Telling of the hidden life
That breaks forth underneath,
Life nursed in its grave by Death.

Blows the thaw-wind pleasantly,
Drips the soaking rain,
By fits looks down the waking sun:
Young grass springs on the plain;
Young leaves clothe early hedgerow trees;
Seeds, and roots, and stones of fruits,
Swollen with sap put forth their shoots;
Curled-head ferns sprout in the lane;
Birds sing and pair again.

There is no time like Spring,
When life's alive in everything,
Before new nestlings sing,
Before cleft swallows speed their journey back
Along the trackless track –
God guides their wing,
He spreads their table that they nothing lack, –
Before the daisy grows a common flower,
Before the sun has power
To scorch the world up in his noontide hour.

There is no time like Spring
Like Spring that passes by;
There is no life like spring-life born to die, –
Piercing the sod,
Clothing the uncouth clod,
Hatched in the nest,
Fledged on the windy bough,
Strong on the wing:
There is no time like Spring that passes by,
Now newly born, and now
Hastening to die.

Christina Rossetti

Spring like Autumn arouses mixed feelings in poets; or, rather, it has come to do so in the course of time. Elizabethans, such as Nashe, rejoice simply and wholeheartedly in it as the season of re-birth and renewal, of buds and bird-song and young love. But, in the last one hundred and fifty years or so, many poets have found themselves unable to sing about Spring with such an un-qualified cheerfulness. They look ahead and see only too clearly that if summer comes, winter is not all that far behind. Of course earlier poets realized this too: they frequently pointed out that the daffodil hastes away all too soon. But they did not allow this to spoil their pleasure in it, while it was still blooming. They were able to yield themselves to the mood of the moment completely and uninhibitedly. Latter-day poets seldom do this. Spring sad-ness, as voiced by Christina Rossetti and others, was an especially poignant sadness because it arose from a sharp sense of the con trast between the budding present and the fading future. Even the anticipation of Spring stirred in these writers' conflicting feelings, blending hope and anxiety, foreboding and joyous expectation.

I wonder if the sap is stirring yet,
If wintry birds are dreaming of a mate,
If frozen snowdrops feel as yet the sun
And crocus fires are kindling one by one:
    Sing robin, sing;
I still am sore in doubt concerning Spring.

            Christina Rossetti, 'The First Spring Day'

So also, with a little more confidence, Edward Thomas:

Now I know that Spring will come again,
Perhaps tomorrow: however late I've patience
After this night following on such a day.

While still my temples ached from the cold burning
Of hail and wind, and still the primroses
Torn by the hail were covered up in it,
The sun filled earth and heaven with a great light
And a tenderness, almost warmth, where the hail dripped.
As if the mighty sun wept tears of joy.
But 'twas too late for warmth. The sunset piled
Mountains on mountains of snow and ice in the west:
Somewhere among their folds the wind was lost,
And yet 'twas cold, and though I knew that Spring
Would come again, I knew it had not come
That it was lost too in those mountains chill.
What did the thrushes know? Rain, snow, sleet, hail,
Had kept them quiet as the primroses.
They had but an hour to sing. On boughs they sang,
On gates, on ground; they sang while they changed perches
And while they fought, if they remembered to fight:
So earnest were they to pack into that hour
Their unwilling hoard of song before the moon
Grew brighter than the clouds. Then 'twas no time
For singing merely. So they could keep off silence
And night, they cared not what they sang or screamed;
Whether it was hoarse or sweet or fierce or soft;

And to me all was sweet: they could do no wrong.
Something they knew – I also, while they sang
And after. Not till night had half its stars
And never a cloud, was I aware of silence
Stained with all that hour's songs, a silence
Saying that Spring returns, perhaps tomorrow.

Edward Thomas, 'March'

For T. S. Eliot, writing a few years later during the disillusioned
nineteen-twenties, joy has been wholly eclipsed by sadness: spring
he sees only as an image of life's power to delude wretched man-
kind with hopes certain to be disappointed.

April is the cruellest month, breeding
Lilacs out of the dead land, mixing
Memory and desire, stirring
Dull roots with spring rain.
Winter kept us warm, covering
Earth in forgetful snow . . .

T. S. Eliot, 'The Waste Land'

This is a long way from Nashe and 'Spring, the sweet Spring':
yet a faint breath of vernal sweetness lingers round Eliot's des-
pondent lines, stirring in reader as well as writer mingled poignant
feelings of memory and desire.

SUPERSTITION

The intelligible forms of ancient poets,
The fair humanities of old religion,
The Power, the Beauty, and the Majesty,
That had their haunts in dale, or piny mountain
Or forest by slow stream, or pebbly spring,
Or chasms and wat'ry depths; all these have vanished.
They live no longer in the faith of reason.
But still the heart doth need a language, still
Doth the old instinct bring back the old names . . .

From Schiller's 'The Piccolomini'; or the First Part of Wallenstein
Translated by S. T. Coleridge

It comes hard on poets – and not on poets only – that we no longer find ourselves able to people the world with nymphs and fauns as did the ancients or with elves and witches as did our mediaeval forefathers. It may save us from some irrational and superstitious fears, but it also makes us feel ourselves aliens in a universe composed of elements, physical and mental, with which we can feel no relationship and in which our most intimate and precious feelings have no counterpart.

But perhaps it is unnecessary to take so depressed a view of the matter. Man's power to breathe imaginative life into his surroundings is incorrigible. Children are born with it; and, even if they have the bad luck never to be told any fairy tales or to hear of elves and fauns, they manage to create similar beings from the human material they find around them. Charles Lamb's childish imagination was fired by the figures of the old Pensioners of the Inner Temple whom he saw walking in their gowns around the gardens where he played as a little boy. He recalls them and what they once meant to him in one of the most exquisite passages of prose that even he ever wrote.

Fantastic forms, whither are ye fled? Or, if the like of you exist, why exist they no more for me? Ye inexplicable, half-understood appearances, why comes in reason to tear away the preternatural mist, bright or gloomy, that enshrouded you? Why make ye so sorry a figure in my relation, who made up to me – to my childish eyes – the mythology of the Temple? In those days I saw Gods, as 'old men covered with a mantle', walking upon the earth. Let the dreams of classic idolatry perish, – extinct be the fairies and fairy trumpery of legendary fabling, – in the heart of childhood, there will, for ever, spring up a well of innocent or wholesome superstition – the seeds of exaggeration will be busy there, and vital – from every-day forms educing the unknown and the uncommon. In that little Goshen there will be light when the grown world flounders about in the darkness of sense and materiality. While childhood, and while dreams, reducing childhood, shall be left, imagination shall not have spread her holy wings totally to fly the earth.'

Charles Lamb, Essays of Elia

SWANS

Fair is the Swan, whose majesty, prevailing
O'er breezeless water, on Locarno's lake,
Bears him on while proudly sailing
He leaves behind a moon-illumined wake:
Behold! the mantling spirit of reserve
Fashions his neck into a goodly curve;
An arch thrown back between luxuriant wings
Of whitest garniture, like fir-tree boughs
To which, on some unruffled morning, clings
A flaky weight of winter's purest snows!
– Behold! – as with a gushing impulse heaves
That downy prow, and softly cleaves
The mirror of the crystal flood,
Vanish inverted hill, and shadowy wood,
And pendent rocks, where'er, in gliding state,
Winds the mute Creature without visible Mate
Or Rival, save the Queen of night
Showering down a silver light,
From heaven, upon her chosen Favourite!

Wordsworth, 'Dion'

Now to be clean he must abandon himself
To that fair yielding element whose lord he is.
There in the mid-current, where she is strongest:
Facing the stream, he half sinks, who knows how?
His armed head, his prow wave-worthy, he dips under:
The meeting streams glide rearward, fill the hollow
Of the proud wings: then as if fainting he falls sidelong,
Prone, without shame, reveals the shiplike belly
Tumbling reversed, with limp black paddles waving,
And down, gliding abandoned, helplessly wallows,
The head and neck, wrecked mast and pennon, trailing.

It is enough: satisfied he rears himself,
Sorts with swift movement his disordered tackle,
Rises, again the master; and so seated
Riding, with spreading wings he flogs the water

Lest she should triumph: in a storm of weeping
And a great rainbow of her tears transfigured,
With spreading circles of his force he smites her
Till remote tremblings heave her rushy verges
And all her lesser lives are rocked with rumour.

Now they are reconciled: with half-raised pinion
And backward-leaning head pensively sailing,
With silver furrow the reflected evening
Parting, he softly goes: and one cold feather
Drifts, and is taken gently by the rushes;
By him forgotten, and by her remembered.

Ruth Pitter, 'The Swan Bathing'

Swans are almost as inspiring to poets as the moon is and for
similar reasons; because they are white and beautiful and, com-
pared with most birds, solitary; though the most beautiful of all
swan poems does describe a whole flight of them.

The trees are in their autumn beauty,
The woodland paths are dry,
Under the October twilight the water
Mirrors a still sky;
Upon the brimming water among the stones
Are nine-and-fifty swans.

The nineteenth autumn has come upon me
Since I first made my count;
I saw, before I had well finished,
All suddenly mount
And scatter wheeling in great broken rings
Upon their clamorous wings.

I have looked upon those brilliant creatures,
And now my heart is sore,
All's changed since I, hearing at twilight,
The first time on this shore,
The bell-beat of their wings above my head,
Trod with a lighter tread.

Unwearied still, lover by lover,
They paddle in the cold
Companionable streams or climb the air;
Their hearts have not grown old;
Passion or conquest, wander where they will,
Attend upon them still.

But now they drift on the still water,
Mysterious, beautiful;
Among what rushes will they build,
By what lake's edge or pool
Delight men's eyes when I awake some day
To find they have flown away?

W. B. Yeats, 'The Wild Swans at Coole'

SYDNEY SMITH

I do not think that we have made nearly enough of Sydney Smith. For me he is along with Halifax the wisest of Englishmen so far as life in this world is concerned. Listen to him advising Lady Georgiana Morpeth on how to combat low spirits:

Dear Lady Georgiana,
 . . . Nobody has suffered more from low spirits than I have done – so I feel for you. 1st. Live as well as you dare. 2nd. Go into the shower-bath with a small quantity of water at a temperature low enough to give you a slight sensation of cold, 75° or 80°. 3rd. Amusing books. 4th. Short views of human life – not further than dinner or tea. 5th. Be as busy as you can. 6th. See as much as you can of those friends who respect and like you. 7th. And of those acquaintances who amuse you. 8th. Make no secret of low spirits to your friends, but talk of them freely – they are always worse for dignified concealment. 9th. Attend to the effects tea and coffee produce upon you. 10th. Compare your lot with that of other people. 11th. Don't expect too much from human life – a sorry business at the best. 12th. Avoid poetry, dramatic representations (except comedy), music, serious novels, melancholy sentimental people, and everything

likely to excite feeling or emotion not ending in active benevolence. 13th. *Do good*, and endeavour to please everybody of every degree. 14th. Be as much as you can in the open air without fatigue. 15th. Make the room where you commonly sit, gay and pleasant. 16th. Struggle by little and little against idleness. 17th. Don't be too severe upon yourself, or underrate yourself, but do yourself justice. 18th. Keep good blazing fires. 19th. Be firm and constant in the exercise of rational religion. 20th. Believe me, dear Lady Georgiana,

Very truly yours,

Sidney Smith

Every English child should be made to learn this by heart. Its precepts put into practice would do more to increase the well-being of mankind than all the noisy advice proffered by self-appointed prophets that have flourished since Sydney's time, from Carlyle and Ruskin down to D. H. Lawrence – with Nietzsche and Sartre and the rest of the intellectual Foreign Legion thrown in. How precisely Sydney keeps the balance between man's physical and spiritual needs, alternating recommendations about the one with recommendations about the other! It will be noted he ends with a spiritual recommendation. 'Be firm and constant in the exercise of a rational religion.'

Here is some more of Sydney Smith's wisdom; from a letter to Lady Holland, who had commiserated with him on the dullness of his life in a country vicarage:

. . . I hear you laugh at me for being happy in the country, and upon this I have a few words to say. In the first place whether one lives or dies I hold and always have held to be of infinitely less moment than is generally supposed; but if life is the choice then it is commonsense to amuse yourself with the best you can find where you happen to be placed. I am not leading precisely the life I should choose, but that which (all things considered, as well as I could consider them) appeared to be the most eligible. I am resolved therefore to like it and to reconcile myself to it . . . In short, if my lot be to crawl, I will crawl contentedly; if to fly, I will fly with alacrity; but as long as I can possibly avoid it, I will never be unhappy.

Once again he keeps the balance. Life is too imperfect for a sensible man to expect happiness, still less to look on happiness as a duty. He indulges in no Stevensonian clap-trap about 'not faltering in his great task of happiness', none of Browning's boisterous fuss about 'greeting the unseen with a cheer'. Indeed he does not believe in making much fuss about anything; 'Whether one lives or dies I hold to be of infinitely less moment than is generally supposed' he says.

In all this he reminds us of Jane Austen. Like her, he is cheerful without shallowness, robust without cynicism, pious yet not priggish. I hope Mr John Sparrow's guess is true and that the two did meet at Bath in the 1790's and that Sydney Smith was the model for Henry Tilney.

Catherine Morland, we remember, was bewildered and delighted by Tilney's 'nonsense'. So also are we by Sydney Smith's. Wisdom was not his only good quality: he would be less unique if it were. His peculiar individuality comes from the mixture in him of good sense and fantasy. His jokes are amongst the best ever made and, at their most characteristic they are extravagantly fanciful as well as witty – more like Charles Lamb's jokes than Bernard Shaw's. Here are a few of my favourites:

He once saw a child stroking the shell of a turtle. 'Why are you doing that?' he asked. 'To please the turtle,' the child replied. 'Why,' said Sydney, 'you might as well stroke the dome of St Paul's to please the Dean and Chapter.'

Someone mentioned that a young Scot was about to marry an Irish widow, twice his age and more than twice his size. 'Going to marry her!' cried Sydney Smith, 'going to marry her! Impossible! You mean a part of her; he could not marry her all himself. It would be a case, not of bigamy, but trigamy; the neighbourhood or the magistrates should interfere. There is enough of her to furnish wives for a whole parish. One man marry her! it is monstrous! You might people a colony with her; or give an assembly with her; or perhaps take your morning's walk round her, always provided there were frequent resting-places, and you were in rude health. I once was rash enough to try walking round her before breakfast, but only got half-way and gave it up exhausted. Or you might read the Riot Act and disperse her; in short, you might do anything with her but marry her.'

I must believe in the Apostolic Succession, there being no other way of accounting for the descent of the Bishop of Exeter from Judas Iscariot.

My idea of heaven is, eating *pâté de foie gras* to the sound of trumpets.

Here are some other remarks of his, less fanciful but equally amusing:

Your critique on Mrs. Apreece is just; but she seems a friendly, goodhearted, rational woman, and as much under the uterine dominion as is graceful and pleasing. I hate a woman who seems to be hermetically sealed in the lower regions.

Death must be distinguished from dying, with which it is often confused.

To Macaulay who was a compulsive talker: 'When I am dead, Macaulay, you will be sorry that you never heard me speak.' A description of Lord John Russell, 'There is no better man in England that Lord John Russell; but his worst failure is that he is utterly ignorant of all moral fear; there is nothing he would not undertake. I believe he would perform the operation for the stone – build St. Peter's – or assume (with or without ten minutes notice) the command of the Channel Fleet; and no one would discover by his manner that the patient had died – the Church tumbled down – and the Channel Fleet been knocked to atoms.' Sometimes he combines sense and fantasy as in this letter to Miss Lucy Austen, aged eight years old:

Lucy, Lucy, my dear child, don't tear your frock: tearing frocks is not of itself a proof of genius; but write as your mother writes, act as your mother acts; be frank, loyal, affectionate, simple, honest; and then integrity or laceration of frock is of little import.

And Lucy, dear child, mind your arithmetic. You know, in the first sum of yours I ever saw, there was a mistake. You had carried two (as a cab is licensed to do) and you ought, dear Lucy, to have carried but one. Is this a trifle? What would life be without arithmetic, but a scene of horrors?

You are going to Boulogne, the city of debts, peopled by men who never understood arithmetic; by the time you return, I shall probably have received my first paralytic stroke, and shall have lost all recollection of you; therefore I now give you my parting advice. Don't marry anybody who has not a tolerable understanding and a thousand a year; and God bless you, dear child.

Every parent of a daughter will echo this last sentence.

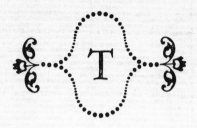

TASTE

As some fond virgin, whom her mother's care
Drags from the town to wholesome country air,
Just when she learns to roll a melting eye,
And hear a spark, yet think no danger nigh;
From the dear man unwilling she must sever,
Yet takes one kiss before she parts for ever:
Thus from the world fair Zephalinda flew,
Saw others happy, and with sighs withdrew;
Not that their pleasures caus'd her discontent,
She sigh'd not that they stay'd, but that she went.

She went to plain-work, and to purling brooks,
Old-fashioned halls, dull aunts, and croaking rooks;
She went from Op'ra, Park, Assembly, Play,
To morning-walks, and prayers three hours a-day;
To part her time 'twixt reading and bohea,
To muse, and spill her solitary tea,
Or o'er cold coffee trifle with the spoon,
Count the slow clock, and dine exact at noon:
Divert her eyes with pictures in the fire,
Hum half a tune, tell stories to the squire;
Up to her godly garret after sev'n,
There starve and pray, for that's the way to Heav'n.

Some squire, perhaps, you take delight to rack;
Whose game is whisk, whose treat a toast in sack;
Who visits with a gun, presents you birds,
Then gives a smacking buss, and cries – No words!

Or with his hounds comes hallooing from the stable,
Makes love with nods, and knees beneath a table;
Whose laughs are hearty, though his jests are coarse,
And loves you best of all things – but his horse.

In some fair ev'ning, on your elbow laid,
You dream of triumphs in the rural shade;
In pensive thought recall the fancied scene,
See coronations rise on every green;
Before you pass th' imaginary sights
Of lords, and earls, and dukes, and garter'd knights,
While the spread fan o'ershades your closing eyes;
Then give one flirt, and all the vision flies.
Thus vanish sceptres, coronets, and balls,
And leave you in lone woods, or empty walls.

So when your slave, at some dear idle time,
(Not plagu'd with head-aches, or the want of rhyme)
Stands in the streets, abstracted from the crew,
And while he seems to study, thinks of you;
Just when his fancy paints your sprightly eyes,
Or sees the blush of soft Parthenia rise,
Gay pats my shoulder, and you vanish quite,
Street, chairs, and coxcombs rush upon my sight;
Vex'd to be still in town, I knit my brow,
Look sour, and hum a tune, as you do now.

Alexander Pope, 'Epistle to Mrs. Teresa Blount'

This poem throws an interesting light on the vagaries of taste.
Pope was one of the great English poets and it shows him at his
best; yet it is not included in either of the leading 19th-century
anthologies of short poems, *The Golden Treasury* and Q's *Oxford
Book of English Verse*. Why? Because by 19th-century standards of
taste – which were Romantic standards – it is not a true poem at
all. Romantic taste equated poetry with certain qualities of feeling;
it thought it had to be passionate or imaginative or aspiring or all
three. But prose can exhibit these qualities as much as verse. The
difference between it and poetry is a matter of form not feeling.
The nearest we can get to defining poetry is to say that it is some-

thing that would lose its essential quality and value, if it was translated into prose.

I cannot imagine any piece of writing that would lose more by translation into prose than this poem would.

THEATRE

I believe that the purpose of the theatre is to show mankind to himself, and thereby to show to man God's image.

I believe that this purpose is ill served by *consciously* using the theatre as a moral, social or political platform . . . Its ministers must not be so arrogant as to suppose that their work is to do good to their fellow men. Their work is to glorify their Creator by expressing themselves. They will choose the material to express themselves which they feel, rather than think will suit what they believe they have it in them from time to time to express. In this choice they will feel 'guided' or 'inspired', as all God's prophets have been, from Elijah down to the humblest, dottiest, squalidest persons who have believed themselves to be guided and inspired. If this is not so, then for me the term artist is entirely meaningless.

I believe that the theatre makes its effect not by means of illusion, but by ritual.

People do not believe that what they see or hear on the stage is 'really' happening. Action on the stage is a stylized re-enactment of real action, which is then imagined by the audience. The re-enactment is not merely an imitation but a symbol of the real thing. If I may quote this instance without irreverence, it expresses the point clearly: the priest in Holy Communion re-enacts, with imitative but symbolic gestures and in a verbal ritual, the breaking of bread and the pouring of wine. He is at this moment an actor impersonating Christ in a very solemn drama. The congregation, or audience, is under no illusion that at that moment he really is Christ. It should, however, participate in the ritual with sufficient fervour to be rapt, literally 'taken out of itself', to the extent that it shares the emotion which the priest or actor is suggesting. It completes the circle of action and reaction; its function is not passive but active. This, I think, is exactly what happens to an audience at a successful theatrical performance.

Just as the sacred drama of Holy Communion is non-illusionary, so is the sacred drama of *Oedipus Rex*, where the actor, also originally a priest, impersonates a symbol of sacrifice. Equally non-illusionary, though more secular, is *Macbeth,* for instance, where the protagonist performs actions symbolic of regicide, usurpation, remorse, and so on. The same principle can be applied to all drama; and in all drama, even the most frivolous, I think that there is some attempt, rarely conscious, to relate the participants to God, or at least to some aspect of God, albeit such aspects are often those represented in Greece by such figures as Dionysus or Aphrodite, where God is seen not in his capacity of all-wise, all-powerful Father but as the personification of Sex, or Mirth, or as the glorification of youth.

The theatre is the direct descendant of fertility rites, war dances and all the corporate ritual expressions by means of which our primitive ancestors, often wiser than we, sought to relate themselves to God, or the gods, the great abstract forces which cannot be apprehended by reason, but in whose existence reason compels us to have faith.

Tyrone Guthrie, A Life in the Theatre

Tyrone Guthrie's true words are even more clearly true of opera and ballet, which do not pretend to give an illusion of every day actuality. Though even the most 'realistic' drama of contemporary life does not, in fact, make such a pretence. If we thought somebody on the stage was actually being murdered, we should call for the police instead of waiting till the curtain had come down and then applauding the performance.

TIME TRANSCENDING

. . . The Tilney's were soon engaged in another [subject] on which she had nothing to say. They were viewing the country with the eyes of persons accustomed to drawing; and decided on its capability of being formed into pictures, with all the eagerness of real taste. Here Catherine was quite lost. She knew nothing of drawing, nothing of taste; and she listened to them with an attention which brought her little profit, for they talked in phrases which conveyed scarcely any idea to her. The little which she could understand however appeared to contradict the very few notions she had entertained on the matter before. It seemed as if a good view were no longer to be taken from the top of a high hill, and that a clear blue sky was no longer a proof of a fine day. She was heartily ashamed of her ignorance – a misplaced shame. Where people wish to attach, they should always be ignorant. To come with a well-informed mind is to come with an inability of administering to the vanity of others, which a sensible person would always wish to avoid. A woman, especially, if she have the misfortune of knowing anything, should conceal it as well as she can.

The advantages of natural folly in a beautiful girl have been already set forth by the capital pen of a sister author; and to her treatment of the subject, I will only add, in justice to men, that though to the larger and more trifling part of the sex, imbecility in females is a great enhancement of their personal charms, there is a portion of them too reasonable and too well-informed themselves, to desire anything more in woman than ignorance. But Catherine did not know her own advantages – did not know that a good-looking girl, with an affectionate heart and a very ignorant mind, cannot fail of attracting a clever young man, unless circumstances are particularly untoward. In the present instance, she confessed and lamented her want of knowledge, declared that she would give anything in the world to be able to draw; and a lecture on the picturesque immediately followed, in which his instructions were so clear that she soon began to see beauty in every thing admired by him; and her attention was so earnest that he became perfectly satisfied of her having a great deal of natural taste. He talked of foregrounds, distances, and second distances; side-screens and perspectives; lights and shades; and Catherine was so hopeful a scholar, that when they gained the top of Beechen Cliff she voluntarily rejected the whole city of Bath as unworthy to take part of a landscape. Delighted with her progress, and fearful of wearying her with too much wisdom at once, Henry suffered the subject to decline, and by an easy transition from a piece of rocky fragment and the withered oak which he had placed near its summit, to oaks in general – to forests, the enclosure of them, waste lands, crown lands and government – he shortly found himself arrived at politics; and from politics it was an easy step to silence.

Jane Austen, Northanger Abbey

Every word of this might have been written about a similar conversation today. How often have I felt like Catherine, when listening to people talking on a subject of which I was ignorant – for me, it could be monetary policy or the workings of the internal combustion engine – that I understood nothing of what was being said beyond the fact that any ideas I had previously entertained on the subject were wrong.

Jane Austen writing one hundred and fifty years ago, again and again transcends the limitations of time. When Mr Woodhouse says that his grandchildren are all remarkably clever – '. . . they will come and stand by my chair and say "Grandpapa, can you give me a bit of string",' – he speaks for all fond foolish grandparents in every age: when Mr Darcy tells Elizabeth Bennett 'I have been selfish all my life in practice not in principle', he is confessing the characteristic weakness of conscientious but dominating males in any period of the world's history: and what Jane Austen herself says of a discontented young wife of her acquaintance applies at least as pointedly to young wives in these unsettled and feminist days as it did when she wrote it in 1807. 'As to pitying a young woman merely because she cannot live in two places at the same time and at once enjoy the comforts of being married and being single, I would not attempt it.'

TOUCHSTONES

Matthew Arnold invented the touchstone plan for judging poems. It worked like this. He chose some brief passages by poets recognized as supremely great to be used as touchstones of merit. After reading a poem for the first time, he said, one should then read one of the touchstones to oneself and then estimate the newly-read poem by how well it stood up to the comparison. It

is not a good plan for its purpose; for one thing, one cannot com-
pare a whole with a part: no one would judge a whole picture by
Mr Graham Sutherland let us say, by setting it beside five square
inches cut out of a canvas by Rembrandt. Moreover different
poems are good in different ways and each should be judged on its
own terms. Repeating a passage of *Paradise Lost* to oneself will
not help one to judge a poem by Sir John Betjeman. He and Milton
are trying to do different things. All the same it is a pleasant pas-
time to make up one's own list of touchstone lines; to pick out
what to one's own taste represents the concentrated essence of
poetry. Here is a list of my own!

Wrapt in eternal silence, far from enemies.

Spenser

Flowers of all hue, and without thorn the rose.

Milton

By our first strange and fatal interview.

Donne

Ah, woe is me winter is come and gone,
But grief returns with the revolving year;

Shelley

You have 'oft for these two lips
Neglected Cassia or the natural sweets
Of the Spring violet:
They are not yet much withered.

Webster

My eyes are dim with childish tears,
My heart is idly stirred,
For that same sound is in my ears,
Which in those days I heard.

Wordsworth

Parthenophil is lost and I would see him;
For he is like to something I remember,
A great while since, a long, long time ago.

John Ford

. . . for to bear all naked truths
And to envisage circumstance, all calm
That is the top of sovereignty . . .

Keats

Ye flowery banks o' bonnie Doon
How can ye blume sae fair;
How can ye chant, ye little birds,
And I sae fu' o' care!

Robert Burns

These lines are not all by supreme poets: but you do not need
to be a supreme poet to write a supreme line. Supreme poets are
those whose inspiration showed itself in the power to conceive on
a grand scale and to execute their conceptions on a sustainedly
high level. It has been said that if only a handful of Donne's best
lines were all that had survived of him, we should think him the
greatest poet that ever lived: the same thing might be said of
Webster or Ford. The whole of *Hamlet* on the other hand is even
greater than the sum of its parts. Mention of *Hamlet* reminds me
that I have omitted Shakespeare from my list. I did this on
purpose; I thought that he had written so many more touchstone
lines than anyone else and most of them so well known that I
would try and do without him. But I cannot; the pleasure of
quoting from Shakespeare is irrestistible. Here are some passages,
not among his very best-known, that are yet touchstones by any
standard.

O, but they say the tongues of dying men
Enforce attention like deep harmony.

Richard II

. . . the burning crest
Of the old, feeble and day-wearied sun.

King John

Come not to me again; but say to Athens,
Timon hath made his everlasting mansion
Upon the beachèd verge of the salt flood;
Who once a day with his embossèd froth
The turbulent surge shall cover . . .

Timon of Athens

TRUTH

Here, in this little Bay,
Full of tumultuous life and great repose,
Where, twice a day,
The purposeless, glad ocean comes and goes,
Under high cliffs, and far from the huge town,
I sit me down.
For want of me the world's course will not fail:
When all its work is done, the lie shall rot,
The truth is great, and shall prevail,
When none cares whether it prevail or not.

Coventry Patmore

This is a reassuring little poem. It is odd that it should be so; for the truth, which it informs us will ultimately prevail, may well be an unpleasant truth. This thought, if it ever crossed his mind, does not appear to have disturbed Patmore: and his mood of tranquil acceptant detachment, enhanced as it was by the vast unceasing murmur of the ocean waves which he was contemplating, communicates itself to the reader.

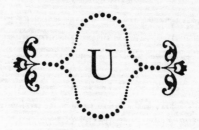

UNCONCEALED ART

It is or used to be a commonplace of criticism that the best art conceals itself. All the same it is untrue. No doubt if a writer wants convincingly to express spontaneous emotion he must do it in such a way that we do not notice his skill: King Lear's lamentation over the dead Cordelia would fail of its effect were our attention to be drawn to the art with which Shakespeare had written it. But if an author's concern with his subject is more detached, much of our pleasure in his achievement is often pleasure in his skill. Listen to Pope commenting on the old age of fashionable beauties:

> . . . Pleasures the sex, as children Birds, pursue,
> Still out of reach, yet never out of view;
> Sure, if they catch, to spoil the Toy at most,
> To covet flying, and regret when lost:
> At last, to follies Youth could scarce defend,
> It grows their Age's prudence to pretend;
> Asham'd to own they gave delight before,
> Reduc'd to feign it, when they give no more:
> As Hags hold Sabbaths, less for joy than spite,
> So these their merry, miserable Night;
> Still round and round the Ghosts of Beauty glide,
> And haunt the places where their Honour died.
>   See how the World its Veterans rewards!
> A Youth of Frolics, an old Age of Cards;
> Fair to no purpose, artful to no end,
> Young without Lovers, old without a Friend;
> A Fop their Passion, but their Prize a Sot;
> Alive, ridiculous; and dead, forgot!

'Of the Character of Women'

Herrick's compliments to the various ladies of his heart owe much of their charm to the ostentatious and glittering virtuosity with which he expresses them:

> So smooth, so sweet, so silv'ry is thy voice,
> As, could they hear, the Damn'd would make no noise;
> But listen to thee, (walking in thy chamber)
> Melting melodious words to Lutes of Amber.

> *'Upon Julia's Voice'*

> More white then whitest Lillies far,
> Or Snow, or whitest Swans you are:
> More white then are the whitest Creames,
> Or Moone-light tinselling the streames:
> More white then Pearls, or Juno's thigh;
> Or Pelop's Arme of Yvorie.
> True, I confesse; such Whites as these
> May me delight, not fully please:
> Till, like Ixion's cloud you be
> White, warme, and soft to lye with me.

> *Herrick, 'To Electra'*

In these passages, Pope is ironical, and Herrick light-hearted. This might suggest that the art of the poet is rightly made noticeable, only when the poet is detached enough to smile. This also turns out to be untrue, when tested by examples:

> Marvel of marvels, if I myself shall behold
> With mine own eyes my King in His city of gold;
> Where the least of lambs is spotless white in the fold,
> Where the least and last of saints in spotless white is stoled,
> Where the dimmest head beyond a moon is aureoled.
> O saints, my beloved, now mouldering to mould in the mould,
> Shall I see you lift your heads, see your cerements unrolled,
> See with these very eyes? who now in darkness and cold
> Tremble for the midnight cry, the rapture, the tale untold,
> 'The Bridegroom cometh, cometh, His Bride to enfold.'

Cold it is, my beloved, since your funeral bell was tolled:
Cold it is, O my King, how cold alone on the wold.

Christina Rossetti

Christina Rossetti is here writing solemnly about the most solemn of subjects, death and religion. Yet it is written with an unconcealed virtuosity. She has set herself an extraordinarily difficult technical task; fourteen lines all ending in the same rhyme. The reader watches her as he might watch a tight-rope walker, who at any moment could fall off into an abyss; in her case, the abyss of the ridiculous. But confidently, effortlessly, gracefully she walks the tight-rope, even taking the risk in the sixth line of repeating the same rhyme twice inside the line:

O saints, my beloved, now mouldering to mould in the mould.

The effect of this virtuosity is to make the poem formal and ritualistic, rather as an anthem of Purcell, say, is formal and ritualistic. But, as with an anthem of Purcell, this adds to the moving solemnity of the effect.

UNIVERSITIES

The universities are a sort of lunatic asylum for keeping young men out of mischief.

Bishop Creighton

Undergraduates owe their happiness chiefly to the consciousness that they are no longer at school. The nonsense which was knocked out of them at school is all put gently back at Oxford or Cambridge.

Max Beerbohm

UNWORLDLY WISDOM

Much on earth is hidden from us, but there is given us in recompense the secret conviction of our living bond with another world, a celestial and loftier world; and the very roots of our thoughts and sensations are not here but there, in other worlds. And that is why philosophers say that in earth it is impossible to know the essence of things.

Dostoievsky, The Brothers Karamazov

Dostoievsky states the crucial fundamental truth about the human situation; namely that man is a divided being, born into the material world and subject to its limitations but in part also the native of a spiritual region which has implanted in him longings and aspirations not to be satisfied here, except in fleeting moments of vision.

Worldly wisdom, such as we find in the works of Johnson and Sidney Smith, may recognize this division but is itself concerned with life in the material world and how man should conduct himself there. Unworldly wisdom is concerned with the spiritual world and our relation to it. Its masters include Sir Thomas Browne and Samuel Palmer and a number of poets; Blake, Keats, Wordsworth. Wordsworth works on so spacious a scale that he has a section to himself later in this volume. But here are examples of the others.

Now for my life, it is a miracle of thirty years, which to relate, were not a History, but a piece of Poetry, and would sound to common ears like a Fable; for the World, I count it not an Inn, but an Hospital; and a place not to live, but to die in. The world that I regard is myself; it is the Microcosm of my own frame that I cast mine eye on; for the other, I use it but like my Globe, and turn it round sometimes for my recreation. Men that look upon my outside, perusing only my condition and Fortunes, do err in my Altitude, for I am above Atlas's shoulders. The earth is a point not only in respect of the Heavens above us, but of that heavenly and celestial part within us: that mass of Flesh that circumscribes me limits not my mind: that surface that tells the Heavens it hath an end, cannot persuade me I have any: I take my circle to be above three hundred and sixty; though the number of the Ark do measure my body, it comprehendeth not my mind: whilst I study to find how I am a Microcosm, or little World, I find

myself something more than the great. There is surely a piece
of Divinity in us, something that was before the Elements, and
owes no homage unto the Sun. Nature tells me I am the Image
of God, as well as Scripture.

... It is my temper, and I like it the better, to affect all harmony;
and sure there is musick even in the beauty, and the silent note
which Cupid strikes, far sweeter than the sound of an instru-
ment. For there is a musick where ever there is a harmony,
order, or proportion; and thus far we may maintain the musick
of the Sphears; for those well-ordered motions, and regular
paces, though they give no sound unto the ear, yet to the under-
standing they strike a note most full of harmony. Whosoever
is harmonically composed delights in harmony, which makes
me much distrust the symmetry of those heads which declaim
against all Church-Musick. For myself, not only from my
obedience, but my particular Genius, I do embrace it: for even
that vulgar and Tavern-Musick, which makes one man merry,
another mad, strikes in me a deep fit of devotion, and a pro-
found contemplation of the First Composer. There is something
in it of Divinity more than the ear discovers: it is an Hiero-
glyphical and shadowed lesson of the whole World, and crea-
tures of God; such a melody to the ear, as the whole World,
well understood, would afford the understanding. In brief, it
is a sensible fit of that harmony, which intellectually sounds in
the ears of God ...

Sir Thomas Browne, Religio Medici

How does all animate and inanimate creation, all the range of
high arts and exquisite sciences proclaim the immortality of the
soul, by exciting, as they were intended to excite, large longings
after wisdom and blessedness, which three-score or three hun-
dred years would be too short to realise. We are like the
chrysalis, asleep and dreaming of its wings!

Samuel Palmer, Letters

... I am certain of nothing but of the holiness of the Heart's
affections and the truth of Imagination – What the imagination
seizes as Beauty must be truth – whether it existed before or
not – for I have the same Idea of all our Passions as of Love

they are all in their sublime, creative or essential Beauty . . .

The Imagination may be compared to Adam's dream – he awoke and found it truth. I am the more zealous in this affair, because I have never yet been able to perceive how anything can be known for truth by consequitive reasoning – and yet it must be. Can it be that even the greatest Philosopher ever arrived at his goal without putting aside numerous objections. However it may be, O for a Life of Sensations rather than of Thoughts! It is 'a Vision in the form of Youth' a Shadow of reality to come – and this consideration has further convinced me for it has come as auxiliary to another favourite Speculation of mine, that we shall enjoy ourselves hereafter, by having what we call happiness on Earth repeated in a finer tone and so repeated. And yet such a fate can only befall those who delight in Sensation rather than hunger as you do after Truth. Adam's dream will do here and seems to be a conviction that Imagination and its empyreal reflection is the same as human Life and its Spiritual repetition . . .

John Keats, Letters

The Eternal Body of Man is The Imagination, that is, God himself.

Babel mocks, saying there is no God or Son of God, that thou, O Human imagination, O Divine Body are all a delusion. But I know thee, O Lord, when thou lightest upon my weary eyes, even in this Dungeon.

Man has no Body distinct from his Soul; for that call'd Body is a portion of Soul discern'd by the five Senses, the chief inlets of Soul in this age.

William Blake

Blake and Keats do not oppose the spiritual to the physical but rather to the activities of the intellect unillumined by the light of imagination. Though Blake was not an orthodox Christian and Keats not a Christian at all, both take the Christian view that body and soul are alike manifestations of Divinity. As Blake puts it, 'that call'd Body is a portion of Soul discern'd by the five Senses.'

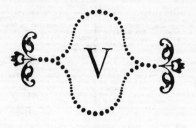

VENICE

. . . The salt breeze, the white moaning sea-birds, the masses of black weed separating and disappearing gradually, in knots of heaving shoal, under the advance of the steady tide, all proclaimed it to be indeed the ocean on whose bosom the great city rested so calmly; not such blue, soft, lake-like ocean as bathes the Neapolitan promontories, or sleeps beneath the marble rocks of Genoa, but a sea with the bleak power of our own northern waves, yet subdued into a strange spacious rest, and changed from its angry pallor into a field of burnished gold, as the sun declined behind the belfry tower of the lonely island church, fitly named 'St. George of the Seaweed.' As the boat drew nearer to the city, the coast which the traveller had just left sank behind him into one long, low, sad-coloured line, tufted irregularly with brushwood and willows: but at what seemed its northern extremity, the hills of Arqua rose in a dark cluster of purple pyramids, balanced on the bright mirage of the lagoon; two or three smooth surges of inferior hill extended themselves about their roots, and beyond these, beginning with the craggy peaks above Vicenza, the chain of the Alps girded the whole horizon to the north – a wall of jagged blue, here and there showing through its clefts a wilderness of misty precipices, fading far back into the recesses of Cadore, and itself rising and breaking away eastward, where the sun struck opposite upon its snow, into mighty fragments of peaked light, standing up behind the barred clouds of evening, one after another, countless, the crown of the Adrian Sea, until the eye turned back from pursuing them to rest upon the nearer burning of the campaniles of Murano, and on the great city, where

it magnified itself along the waves, as the quick silent pacing
of the gondola drew nearer and nearer. And at last, when its
walls were reached, and the outmost of its untrodden streets
was entered, not through towered gate of guarded rampart, but
as a deep inlet between two rocks of coral in the Indian Sea,
when first upon the traveller's sight opened the long ranges of
columned palaces, – each with its black boat moored at the
portal, – each with its image cast down, beneath its feet, upon
that green pavement which every breeze broke into new fan-
tasies of rich tessellation; when first, at the extremity of the
bright vista, the shadowy Rialto threw its colossal curve slowly
from behind the palace of the Camerlenghi; that strange curve,
so delicate, so adamantine, strong as a mountain cavern, grace-
ful as a bow just bent; when first, before its moonlike circum-
ference was all risen, the gondolier's cry 'Ah! Stali,' struck
sharp upon the ear, and the prow turned aside under the mighty
cornices that half met over the narrow canal, where the plash
of the water followed close and loud, ringing along the marble
by the boat's side; and when at last that boat darted forth upon
the breadth of silver sea across which the front of the Ducal
palace, flushed with its sanguine veins, looks to the snowy
dome of Our Lady of Salvation, it was no marvel that the mind
should be so deeply entranced by the visionary charm of a
scene so beautiful and so strange, as to forget the darker truths
of its history and its being . . .

Ruskin, The Stones of Venice

No writer describes Venice so eloquently as Ruskin does. But I
do not find his descriptions the most accurate. Like Turner's
pictures of it, they are altogether too golden and dreamlike;
rhapsodies of genius inspired by Venice, rather than pictures of it
drawn with the eye on the object portrayed. In particular they do
not bring out Venice's unique, distinctive blend of the exquisite
and the shabby. Henry James does this best:

. . . If we were asked what is the leading colour at Venice we
should say pink, and yet, after all, we cannot remember that this
elegant tint occurs very often. It is a faint, shimmering, airy,
watery pink; the bright sea-light seems to flush with it, and the

pale whitish-green of lagoon and canal to drink it in. There is, indeed, in Venice a great deal of very evident brickwork, which is never fresh or loud in colour, but always burnt out, as it were, always exquisitely mild. There are certain little mental pictures that rise before the sentimental tourist at the simple mention, written or spoken, of the places he has loved. When I hear, when I see, the magical name I have written above these pages, it is not of the great Square that I think, with its strange basilica and its high arcades, nor of the wide mouth of the Grand Canal, with the stately steps and the well-poised dome of the Salute; it is not of the low lagoon, nor the sweet Piazzetta, nor the dark chambers of St. Mark's. I simply see a narrow canal in the heart of the city – a patch of green water and a surface of pink wall. The gondola moves slowly; it gives a great, smooth swerve, passes under a bridge, and the gondolier's cry, carried over the quiet water, makes a kind of splash in the stillness. A girl is passing over the little bridge, which has an arch like a camel's back, with an old shawl over her head, which makes her look charming; you see her against the sky as you float beneath. The pink of the old wall seems to fill the whole place; it sinks even into the opaque water. Behind the wall is a garden, out of which the long arm of a white June rose – the roses of Venice are splendid – has flung itself by way of spontaneous ornament. On the other side of this small waterway is a great shabby façade of Gothic windows and balconies – balconies on which dirty clothes are hung and under which a cavernous-looking doorway opens from a low flight of slimy water-steps. It is very hot and still, the canal has a queer smell, and the whole place is enchanting . . .

Portraits of Places

Now for a 20th-century response to the Venetian scene more ironical than the others, but not less discriminating:

Careful not to entangle himself in the furled wings of the snowy mosquito net, Eustace got out of bed and walked to the window. There were three windows in the room: two facing the bed, widely spaced like far-apart eyes, and one in the far right-hand corner, a cross-light.

Eustace visited them each in turn, but it was the third he liked best, for it had a long view down the Grand Canal, terminating in a level iron bridge, a concession to utility without which Venice to his ascetic northern eye seemed almost overdressed. His thoughts were at home with the bridge; elsewhere they were still uneasily resisting the seduction of the undisciplined, unashamed opulence around him.
. . .

Everything Eustace saw clamoured for attention. The scene was like an orchestra without a conductor; and to add to the confusion the sights, unlike the sounds, did not come from any one place; they attacked him from all sides, and even the back of his head felt bombarded by impressions. There was no refuge from the criss-cross flights of the Venetian visual missiles, no calculating the pace at which they came. That huge square palace opposite, with its deep windows like eye-sockets in a skull, was on you in a moment with its frontal attack. The building next to it, red, shabby and almost unadorned, was withholding its fire, but the onslaught would come – Eustace could see it collecting its charm, marshalling its simplicity, winging its pensive arrow. Nor, looking at the water, did the eye get any rest. Always broken, it was for ever busy with the light, taking it on one side of a ripple, sending it back from the other; and the boats, instead of going straight up and down, crossed each other's path at innumerable angles that were like a geometrician's nightmare, and at varying degrees of slowness that were like a challenge to a quadratic equation. The rhythm within him which, in Eustace's case, was to some extent determined by the rhythm outside him, kept starting and stopping like a defective motor-engine, while the variations in the quality of the light made him feel that he was taking messages from a hundred heliographs. Even the angle of the walls between the two windows was not, he suddenly noticed, a true right angle – it was slightly acute; he felt it compressing him like a pair of scissors. Upon examination, every angle in the room seemed out of true; he was living in a trapezium, and would never be able to feel a mathematical relationship with his surroundings . . .

How did Venetians ever achieve stability of mind, Eustace wondered, turning away from the window. Rope ladders of

light chased each other across the ceiling. He felt extraordin-
arily stimulated and renewed. Watching, taking in, was an
arduous exercise, but it loosened the spirit and discovered
delicious new sensations.

L. P. Hartley, Eustace and Hilda

JOHN WEBSTER

Little Prince Giovanni speaks of his dead mother:

Giovanni: What do the dead do, uncle? do they eat,
Hear music, go a hunting, and be merry,
As we that live?

Francisco: No, coz; they sleep.

Giovanni: Lord, Lord, that I were dead!
I have not slept these six nights. – When
do they wake?

Francisco: When God shall please.

Giovanni: Good God, let her sleep ever!
For I have known her wake an hundred nights,
When all the pillow where she laid her head
Was brine-wet with her tears. I am to complain
to you, sir;
I'll tell you how they have used her now she's dead;
They wrapped her in a cruel fold of lead,
And would not let me kiss her.

The White Devil

No passage in all English literature is more beautiful than this.
Webster is one of our few very great writers. But, for all that he
has been praised by Charles Lamb and Swinburne and T. S. Eliot,
he has never been rated as high as he deserves. Even those who

profess themselves his admirers have, most of them, spoken of him as a morbid freak genius, the author of a couple of confused horror melodramas lit up from time to time by flashes of lurid oratory. As this quotation shows, some of his most characteristic poetry is not lurid but subtle, tender and restrained: and his plays are high and religious tragedies whose subject is the working out of sin in a fallen world. The impression they make is certainly terrible; for Webster's was a stern Calvinist religion which saw the world as profoundly corrupt. But the lesson he draws from the spectacle is one to strengthen the spirit. His good characters heroically resist evil; even though they come to a tragic end, it is with their virtue unshaken, whereas the wicked are punished for their misdeeds and die despairing. As Catherine in *The Duchess of Malfi* says, 'Sorrow is held the eldest child of sin.'

Some more passages from Webster marked in my copy of his works; five from *The Duchess of Malfi* and three from *The White Devil*.

What would it pleasure me to have my throat cut
With diamonds? or to be smothered
With cassia? or to be shot to death with pearls?
I know death hath ten thousand several doors
For men to take their exits; and 'tis found
They go on such strange geometrical hinges,
You may open them both ways . . .

I stand like one
That long hath ta'en a sweet and golden dream:
I am angry with myself, now that I wake . . .

You may discern the shape of loveliness
More perfect in her tears than in her smiles:

And on the sudden, a clear light
Presented me a face folded in sorrow.

You're passionately met in this sad world.

Thou has a wife, our sister: would I had given
Both her white hands to death bound, locked fast
In her last winding sheet, when I gave thee
But one.

O men that lie upon your death-beds are haunted
With howling wives, ne'er trust them! They'll re-marry
Ere the worm pierce your winding sheet, ere the spider
Make a thin curtain for your epitaphs.

WINTER

Snow is comparatively infrequent in England at any time of the
year: but the poets who write about an English winter generally
concentrate on its snowy moments – because, I suppose, these are
more arresting and pictorial.

The keener tempests come: and, fuming dun
From all the livid east or piercing north,
Thick clouds ascend, in whose capacious womb
A vapoury deluge lies, to show congealed.
Heavy they roll their fleecy world along,
And the sky saddens with the gathered storm.
Through the hushed air the whitening shower descends,
At first thin-wavering; till at last the flakes
Fall broad and wide and fast, dimming the day
With a continual flow. The cherished fields
Put on their winter-robe of purest white.
'Tis brightness all; save where the new snow melts
Along the mazy current. Low the woods
Bow their hoar head; and, ere the languid sun
Faint from the west emits his evening ray,
Earth's universal face, deep-hid and chill,
Is one wild dazzling waste, that buries wide
The works of man . . .

James Thomson, 'The Seasons'

'Tis morning; and the sun, with ruddy orb
Ascending, fires th' horizon: while the clouds,
That crowd away before the driving wind,
More ardent as the disk emerges more,
Resemble most some city in a blaze,
Seen through the leafless wood. His slanting ray
Slides ineffectual down the snowy vale,

And, tinging all with his own rosy hue,
From ev'ry herb and ev'ry spiry blade
Stretches a length of shadow o'er the field.
Mine, spindling into longitude immense,
In spite of gravity, and sage remark
That I myself am but a fleeting shade,
Provokes me to a smile. With eye askance
I view the muscular proportion'd limb
Transform'd to a lean shank. The shapeless pair,
As they design'd to mock me, at my side
Take step for step; and, as I near approach
The cottage, walk along the plaster'd wall,
Prepost'rous sight! the legs without the man.
The verdure of the plain lies buried deep
Beneath the dazzling deluge; and the bents,
And coarser grass, upspearing o'er the rest,
Of late unsightly and unseen, now shine
Conspicuous, and, in bright apparel clad
And fledg'd with icy feathers, nod superb.
The cattle mourn in corners where the fence
Screens them, and seem half petrified to sleep
In unrecumbent sadness. There they wait
Their wonted fodder; not like hung'ring man,
Fretful if unsupply'd; but silent, meek,
And patient of the slow-pac'd swain's delay.
He from the stack carves out th' accustom'd load,
Deep-plunging, and again deep-plunging oft,
His broad keen knife into the solid mass:
Smooth as a wall the upright remnant stands,
With such undeviating and even force
He severs it away: no needless care,
Lest storms should overset the leaning pile
Deciduous, or its own unbalanc'd weight.
Forth goes the woodman, leaving unconcern'd
The cheerful haunts of man; to wield the axe
And drive the wedge, in yonder forest drear
From morn to eve his solitary task.
Shaggy, and lean, and shrewd, with pointed ears
And tail cropp'd short, half lurcher and half cur –
His dog attends him. Close behind his heel

L.I.G.—K

Now creeps he slow; and now, with many a frisk
Wide-scamp'ring, snatches up the drifted snow
With iv'ry teeth, or ploughs it with his snout;
Then shakes his powder'd coat, and barks for joy.
Heedless of all his pranks, the sturdy churl
Moves right toward the mark; nor stops for aught,
But now and then with pressure of his thumb
T' adjust the fragrant charge of a short tube
That fumes beneath his nose: the trailing cloud
Streams far behind him, scenting all the air . . .

Cowper, from 'The Task'

When men were all asleep the snow came flying,
In large white flakes falling on the city brown,
Stealthily and perpetually settling and loosely lying,
    Hushing the latest traffic of the drowsy town;
Deadening, muffling, stifling its murmurs failing;
Lazily and incessantly floating down and down:
    Silently sifting and veiling road, roof and railing;
Hiding difference, making unevenness even,
Into angles and crevices softly drifting and sailing.
    All night it fell, and when full inches seven
It lay in the depth of its uncompacted lightness,
The clouds blew off from a high and frosty heaven;
    And all woke earlier for the unaccustomed brightness
Of the winter dawning, the strange unheavenly glare:
The eye marvelled – marvelled at the dazzling whiteness;
    The ear hearkened to the stillness of the solemn air;
No sound of wheel rumbling nor of foot falling,
And the busy morning cries came thin and spare . . .

Robert Bridges, 'London Snow'

How well these poems communicate a sense of cold! Shakespeare, as if to show that he can always do things better than anyone else, has written two stanzas that make this reader for one feel colder than do the descriptions of any other poet:

When icicles hang by the wall,
   And Dick the shepherd blows his nail;
And Tom bears logs into the hall,
   And milk comes frozen home in pail;
When blood is nipped and ways be foul,
   Then nightly sings the staring owl,
         Tu-whit;
Tu-who, a merry note,
While greasy Joan doth keel the pot.

When all aloud the wind doth blow,
   And coughing drowns the parson's saw,
And birds sit brooding in the snow,
   And Marian's nose looks red and raw,
When roasted crabs hiss in the bowl,
   Then nightly sings the staring owl,
         Tu-whit;
Tu-who, a merry note,
While greasy Joan doth keel the pot.

There are other winter days not snowy; fine days in which we
are made subtly aware of the Spring to come but which yet by
their strange mixture of winter landscape with a Spring softness
in the air remain paradoxically in the memory as noticeably
winter days. These also have inspired poets. Coleridge has written
four unforgettable lines about them:

All Nature seems at work. Slugs leave their lair –
The bees are stirring – birds are on the wing –
And Winter slumbering in the open air,
Wears on his smiling face a dream of spring!

Coleridge, 'Work without Hope'

Coventry Patmore has written at greater length on this theme,
in one of the few wholly satisfactory poems by that distinguished
and quirky genius:

  I, singularly moved
To love the lovely that are not beloved,

Of all the Seasons, most
Love Winter, and to trace
The sense of the Trophonian pallor on her face.
It is not death, but plenitude of peace;
And the dim cloud that does the world enfold
Hath less the characters of dark and cold
Than warmth and light asleep;
And correspondent breathing seems to keep
With the infant harvest, breathing soft below
Its eider coverlet of snow.
Nor is in field or garden anything
But, duly look'd into, contains serene
The substance of things hoped for, in the Spring,
And evidence of Summer not yet seen.
On every chance-mild day
That visits the moist shaw,
The honeysuckle, 'sdaining to be crost
In urgence of sweet life by sleet or frost,
'Voids the time's law
With still increase
Of leaflet new, and little, wandering spray;
Often, in sheltering brakes,
As one from rest disturb'd in the first hour,
Primrose or violet bewilder'd wakes,
And deems 'tis time to flower;
Though not a whisper of her voice he hear,
The buried bulb does know
The signals of the year,
And hails far Summer with his lifted spear;
The gorse-field dark, by sudden, gold caprice,
Turns, here and there, into a Jason's fleece;
Lilies, that soon in Autumn slipp'd their gowns of green
And vanish'd into earth,
And came again, ere Autumn died, to birth,
Stand full-array'd, amist the wavering shower,
And perfect for the Summer, less the flower;
In nook of pale or crevice of crude bark,
Thou canst not miss,
If close thou spy, to mark
The ghostly chrysalis,

That, if thou touch it, stirs in its dream dark;
And the flush'd Robin, in the evening's hoar,
Does of Love's Day, as if he saw it, sing;
But sweeter yet than dream or song of Summer or Spring
Are Winter's sometime smiles, that seem to well
From infancy ineffable;
Her wandering, languorous gaze,
So unfamiliar, so without amaze,
On the elemental, chill adversity,
The uncomprehended rudeness; and her sigh
And solemn, gathering tear,
And look of exile from some great repose, the sphere
Of ether, moved by ether only, or
By something still more tranquil.

Coventry Patmore, 'Winter'

The last lines of this poem are mysterious and magical, but this does not weaken its reality. On the contrary it is an example of Art's peculiar power to reveal the heart of its subject by exposing this to the X-ray of the artist's imaginative vision. 'My art,' said Thomas Hardy, 'is to intensify the expression of things so that their heart and innermost meaning is vividly made visible.' This is what Patmore does in this poem.

WIT

References to wit figure almost as much in my end-papers as do references to humour. It has often been pointed out that, though they both are designed to make us smile, they are not the same thing. The word humour describes an attitude of mind, the word wit describes a mode of expression. A man can be said to have a humorous outlook; he cannot be said to have a witty outlook. In books however the two things very often go together: for writing is itself a mode of expression, so that humorists often use wit in order to make a humorous point. Many writers, for instance Wilde and Shaw and Max Beerbohm, are equally distinguished as wits and as humorists. But some of their most famous words are remembered primarily for their wit, that is to say they amuse us less for what they say than for the way they say it.

LADY BRACKNELL: I feel bound to tell you that you are not down on my list of eligible young men, although I have the same list as the dear Duchess of Bolton has. We work together, in fact. However, I am quite ready to enter your name, should your answers be what a really affectionate mother requires. Do you smoke?

JACK: Well, yes, I must admit I smoke.

LADY BRACKNELL: I am glad to hear it. A man should always have an occupation of some kind. There are far too many idle men in London as it is. How old are you?

JACK: Twenty-nine.

LADY BRACKNELL: A very good age to be married at. I have always been of opinion that a man who desires to get married should know either everything or nothing. Which do you know?

JACK: I know nothing, Lady Bracknell.

LADY BRACKNELL: I am pleased to hear it. I do not approve of anything that tampers with natural ignorance. Ignorance is like a delicate exotic fruit; touch it and the bloom is gone. The whole theory of modern education is radically unsound. Fortunately in England, at any rate, education produces no effect whatsoever. If it did, it would prove a serious danger to the upper classes, and probably lead to acts of violence in Grosvenor Square. What is your income?

JACK: Between seven and eight thousand a year.

LADY BRACKNELL: In land, or in investments?

JACK: In investments, chiefly.

LADY BRACKNELL: That is satisfactory. What between the duties expected of one during one's lifetime, and the duties exacted from one after one's death, land has ceased to be either a profit or a pleasure. It gives one position, and prevents one from keeping it up. That's all that can be said about land.

Oscar Wilde, The Importance of Being Earnest

BARBARA: Oh, there you are, Mr. Shirley! This is my father: I told you he was a Secularist, didn't I? Perhaps you'll be able to comfort one another.

UNDERSHAFT: A Secularist! Not the least in the world; on the contrary, a confirmed mystic.

BARBARA: Sorry, I'm sure. By the way, papa, what is your religion? In case I have to introduce you again.

UNDERSHAFT: My religion? Well, my dear, I am a Millionaire. That is my religion.

BARBARA: Then I'm afraid you and Mr. Shirley wont be able to comfort one another after all. You're not a Millionaire, are you Peter?

SHIRLEY: No; and proud of it.

UNDERSHAFT: Poverty, my friend, is not a thing to be proud of.

SHIRLEY: Who made your millions for you? Me and my like. What's kep us poor? Keepin you rich. I wouldn't have your conscience, not for all your income.

UNDERSHAFT: I wouldn't have your income, not for all your conscience, Mr. Shirley.

Bernard Shaw, Major Barbara

Max Beerbohm on the acting of Eleanor Duse:

Age cannot wither her nor custom stale
Her endless uniformity.

and on modern thinkers:

It distresses me, this failure to keep pace with the leaders of thought, as they pass into oblivion.

Sydney Smith on Macaulay's conversation:

. . . he has occasional flashes of silence, that make his conversation perfectly delightful.

Hilaire Belloc:

'The Pacifist'

Pale Ebenezer thought it wrong to fight,
But Roaring Bill (who killed him) thought it right.

On a General Election:

The accursed power which stands on privilege
(And goes with Women and Champagne and Bridge)
Broke and Democracy resumed her reign
(Which goes with Bridge and Women and Champagne).

Here is a witty line of Pope describing the activities of dull poets:

Sleepless themselves, to give their readers sleep.

The Dunciad

Here is an even wittier one, in which he comments on the fact that the same dull poets often sought to brighten their works with a touch of humour.

And gentle Dullness ever loves a joke.

The Dunciad

Alas, this last remark is true of other persons besides dull poets!

WORDS

Words, however, may die on us not because we cannot pronounce them but because they have fallen into bad company, have become defaced and ostracised – 'genteel,' 'couch,' 'frantic,' 'limbs,' 'sedate,' 'demure,' 'dignified,' even 'pious'. They are of service only as ghosts, as it were, of their own misusage; for purposes of irony or of unashamed jocosity. As for that ass-of-all-work, 'psychology', what now should we do without it? 'Amiable' again, once a word of price is now no more 'likeable' than it is 'lovable', and must be retained on sufferance; while as for 'naïve' – if only we might once and for all de-diærisize and de-alienize it and add it to our homonyms by calling it 'nave'! It is not a mere substitute for artless or ingenuous.

There are rows and rows of other words shivering on the brink – superior, respectful, elegant, the adjectives choice and fancy, modish, ascertain, inebriated, felicitous and felicitations, marriageable (husbandable and wifeable?), objurgation, hymeeneal, conjoogal, those old horrors, fiancé and parti, those fetiches, transpire and strenuous . . . And what about stipend, remuneration, emolument, honorarium, salary, even fee? Why not the plain, calm equalizing, honest old M.E. 'wages'? The wages of sin is death – in spite of its emoluments . . .

Walter de la Mare, Pleasures and Speculations

Written in 1923, this passage is now a little dated. Since then, 'sedate', 'demure', 'dignified', have recovered the good reputation they may have lost by keeping bad verbal company and are now used in their true sense by the most fastidious of authors: so are 'elegant', and 'felicitous'. On the other hand the noble word 'compassion' has declined into a journalistic sentimental cliché, while 'glamorous', which de la Mare himself has employed in full confidence that it retained its meaning of 'romantic' and 'magical' has, by its association with fashion models and pop stars, become degraded to a point where no prudent poet would dare use it except in a tone of mockery.

However most of what de la Mare says remains very true, especially about the tendency to use long and colourless words and phrases instead of plain brief ones; for instance 'remuneration' and 'emoluments' instead of 'wages'. Other examples are 'escalate' for 'grow', 'industrial action' for 'strike' and 'mentally ill' for 'mad'.

'Oh Fool, I shall go mad!' cried King Lear in his agony. I suppose a modern poet, if he wanted to be truly of his time, would make him say, 'Oh Fool, I shall become mentally ill!'

One reason for all this is man's incurable addiction to euphemism, his uncontrollable shrinking from telling the brutal truth. He thinks that to call a madman mad may hurt the feelings of any other madmen who heard him do so. Advertisers are particularly given to euphemism. I once saw a preparation advertised as 'able to assist you in solving your skin problem'. This meant that it helped you to cure your spots.

A second reason for using these long elaborate terms and phrases is to make statements sound more impressive: 'emolument' sounds more dignified than 'wages': to go 'on strike' sounds less dignified than to 'take industrial action'. I note that public figures addressing their fellow countrymen on television are given to using the phrases 'in this day and age' and 'at this moment of time'. All that the speaker means by them is expressed by the monosyllable 'now'. But 'now' is brief and plain and therefor regarded as unworthy to pass the lips of an important public figure.

This is not to say that plain words are always the best words to use. Some of the greatest writers – Lamb and Gibbon for example – often prefer to use long or esoteric words. But this is because they wish to create an effect on the mind and imagination of their readers that requires such words. Gibbon's baroque grandeur of language is the appropriate expression of the baroque grandeur of his historical vision: Lamb's mixture of homely colloquialism and far-fetched archaic phrases is the only true mirror of his spirit with its odd blend of homely intimacy with a delight in the antique and the fantastic. As Doctor Johnson said of Sir Thomas Browne: 'In defence of his uncommon words and expressions we must consider that he had uncommon sentiments.'

The trouble about the elaborate words used by public men to-day is that they generally clothe very common sentiments indeed.

WORDSWORTH

I

There is a Yew-tree, pride of Lorton Vale,
Which to this day stands single, in the midst
Of its own darkness, as it stood of yore:
Not loth to furnish weapons for the bands
Of Umfravile or Percy ere they marched
To Scotland's heaths; or those that crossed the sea
And drew their sounding bows at Azincour,
Perhaps at earlier Crécy, or Poictiers.
Of vast circumference and gloom profound
This solitary Tree! a living thing
Produced too slowly ever to decay;
Of form and aspect too magnificent
To be destroyed. But worthier still of note
Are those fraternal Four of Borrowdale,
Joined in one solemn and capacious grove;
Huge trunks! and each particular trunk a growth
Of intertwisted fibres serpentine
Up-coiling, and inveterately convolved;
Nor uninformed with Phantasy, and looks
That threaten the profane; a pillared shade,
Upon whose grassless floor of red-brown hue,
By sheddings from the pining umbrage tinged
Perennially – beneath whose sable roof

Of boughs, as if for festal purpose decked
With unrejoicing berries – ghostly Shapes
May meet at noontide; Fear and trembling Hope,
Silence and Foresight; Death the Skeleton
And time the Shadow; – there to celebrate,
As in a natural temple scattered o'er
With altars undisturbed of mossy stone,
United worship; or in mute repose
To lie, and listen to the mountain flood
Murmuring from Glaramara's inmost caves.

'*Yew-Trees*'

(11)

Brook and road
Where fellow-travellers in this gloomy Pass,
And with them did we journey several hours
At a slow step. The immeasurable height
Of woods decaying, never to be decayed,
The stationary blasts of waterfalls,
And in the narrow rent, at every turn,
Winds thwarting winds bewildered and forlorn,
The torrents shooting from the clear blue sky,
The rocks that muttered close upon our ears,
Black drizzling crags that spake by the wayside
As if a voice were in them, the sick sight
And giddy prospect of the raving stream,
The unfettered clouds, and region of the heavens,
Tumult and peace, the darkness and the light –
Were all like workings of one mind, the features
Of the same face, blossoms upon one tree,
Characters of the great Apocalypse,
The types and symbols of Eternity,
Of first, and last, and midst, and without end.

'*The Simplon Pass*'

(III)

                            I remember well,
That once, while yet my inexperienced hand
Could scarcely hold a bridle, with proud hopes
I mounted, and we journeyed towards the hills:
An ancient servant of my father's house
Was with me, my encourager and guide:
We had not travelled long, ere some mischance
Disjoined me from my comrade; and, through fear
Dismounting, down the rough and stony moor
I led my horse, and, stumbling on, at length
Came to a bottom, where in former times
A murderer had been hung in iron chains.
The gibbet-mast had mouldered down, the bones
And iron case were gone; but on the turf,
Hard by, soon after that fell deed was wrought,
Some unknown hand had carved the murderer's name.
The monumental letters were inscribed
In times long past; but still, from year to year,
By superstition of the neighbourhood,
The grass is cleared away, and to this hour
The characters are fresh and visible:
A casual glance had shown them, and I fled,
Faltering and faint, and ignorant of the road:
Then, reascending the bare common, saw
A naked pool that lay beneath the hills,
The beacon on the summit, and, more near,
A girl, who bore a pitcher on her head,
And seemed with difficult steps to force her way
Against the blowing wind. It was, in truth,
An ordinary sight; but I should need
Colours and words that are unknown to man,
To paint the visionary dreariness
Which, while I looked all round for my lost guide,
Invested moorland waste, and naked pool,
The beacon crowning the lone eminence,
The female and her garments vexed and tossed
By the strong wind. When, in the blessèd hours

Of early love, the loved one at my side,
I roamed, in daily presence of this scene,
Upon the naked pool and dreary crags,
And on the melancholy beacon, fell
A spirit of pleasure and youth's golden gleam;
And think ye not with radiance more sublime
For these remembrances, and for the power
They had left behind? . . .

From 'The Prelude'

(IV)

O Joy! that in our embers
Is something that doth live,
That nature yet remembers
What was so fugitive!
The thought of our past years in me doth breed
Perpetual benediction: not indeed
For that which is most worthy to be blest;
Delight and liberty, the simple creed
Of Childhood, whether busy or at rest,
With new-fledged hope still fluttering in his breast: –
Not for these I raise
The songs of thanks and praise;
But for those obstinate questionings
Of sense and outward things,
Fallings from us, vanishings;
Blank misgivings of a Creature
Moving about in worlds not realised,
High instincts before which our mortal Nature
Did tremble like a guilty Thing surprised:
But for those first affections,
Those shadowy recollections,
Which, be they what they may,
Are yet the fountain-light of all our day,
Are yet a master-light of all our seeing;
Uphold us, cherish, and have power to make
Our noisy years seem moments in the being
Of the external Silence: truths that wake,
To perish never:

Which neither listlessness, nor mad endeavour,
  Nor Man nor Boy,
Nor all that is at enmity with joy,
Can utterly abolish or destroy!
  Hence in a season of calm weather
  Though inland far we be,
Our Souls have sight of that immortal sea
  Which brought us hither,
  Can in a moment travel thither,
And see the Children sport upon the shore
And hear the mighty waters rolling evermore.

     From 'Ode on Intimations of Immortality'

(v)

    I have seen
A curious child, who dwelt upon a tract
Of inland ground, applying to his ear
The convolutions of a smooth-lipped shell;
To which, in silence hushed, his very soul
Listened intensely; and his countenance soon
Brightened with joy; for from within were heard
Murmurings, whereby the monitor expressed
Mysterious union with its native sea.
Even such a shell the universe itself
Is to the ear of Faith; and there are times
I doubt not, when to you it doth impart
Authentic tidings of invisible things;
Of ebb and flow, and ever-during power;
And central peace, subsisting at the heart
Of endless agitation.

       From 'The Excursion'

Wordsworth is the great spiritual autobiographer of our literature;
and these passages recall his intimations of 'unknown modes of
being', of a spiritual region existing behind the show of things.
Other authors – such as Blake and Traherne – have written of this
region. Wordsworth differs from them in that he relates it, as they

do not, to man's day-to-day life in the visible material world. He tells us how he experienced his moments of vision, in definite localized times and places; crossing the Simplon Pass or contemplating the yew trees in Borrowdale.

It is a mysterious vision and not, on the face of it, a reassuring one. The spirits under the yew trees were those of Fear and Death and Time the Shadow; the scene of Wordsworth's boyish recollections on the moor was one of 'visionary dreariness' perceived beneath a gibbet; the memories he thanked Heaven for in later life are of 'blank misgivings of a creature moving about in worlds not realised'. Yet though Wordsworth's intimations appear disturbing, in fact they communicate a strange feeling of serenity. This is not so paradoxical as it might seem. Most records of spiritual vision seem untrue to the nature of reality because they are so exclusively blissful and ecstatic. Not so Wordsworth's vision. Not only does he face the fact that life in the visible world is an insoluble and often a tragic riddle, he recognizes that the spiritual world too is a place of mystery and awe, even sometimes of terror. Yet in spite of this, he mysteriously retains his sense of a Divine and benignant spirit inspiring the universe. To use his own phrase, he finds himself in the end aware of a 'central peace, subsisting at the heart of endless agitation'.

Acknowledgements

Acknowledgement to the following publishers and authors or their representatives is made for the use of copyright material:

Geoffrey Bles Ltd, *They Asked for a Paper* by C. S. Lewis.

The Bodley Head, and Dodd Mead & Company, *Diminuendo* by Max Beerbohm.

Jonathan Cape Ltd, *The Little Girls* by Elizabeth Bowen, and works by A. E. Housman and W. H. Davies.

Chatto & Windus Ltd, *La Prisonnière* by Proust, translated by Scott Moncrieff, and extracts from works by Aldous Huxley.

Constable & Co. Ltd, *More Trivia* by Logan Pearsall Smith, *Reason in Religion* and *Soliloquies in England* by George Santayana, and extracts from other works by him, and extracts from works by Beachcomber (J. B. Morton), George Bernard Shaw and Arthur Waley.

The Cresset Press, extracts from works by Ruth Pitter and Frances Cornford.

Faber & Faber Ltd, and Harcourt Brace Jovanovich Inc., extracts from works by T. S. Eliot, and Faber & Faber Ltd, extracts from works by W. H. Auden.

Hamish Hamilton Ltd, *Sixth Heaven* and *Eustace and Hilda* by L. P. Hartley.

Harper & Row Inc., *The Owl in the Attic* by James Thurber.

William Heinemann Ltd and the Estate of the late Max Beerbohm, *Around Theatres*, *Hosts and Guests*, *Going for a Walk*, *Zuleika Dobson*, and *Enoch Soames* by Max Beerbohm, and *Sons and Lovers* by D. H. Lawrence.

Hogarth Press Ltd, *Essay on Sir Thomas Browne* by Lytton Strachey, and Hogarth Press Ltd and the Author's Literary Estate and Harcourt Brace Jovanovich Inc., *To the Lighthouse*, *The Common Reader*, *Mrs Dalloway*, *A Room of One's Own*, *Jacob's Room*, *The Years* and *Orlando* by Virginia Woolf.

Longman Ltd, *The Foundations of Belief* by A. J. Balfour.

Macmillan London & Basingstoke and the Trustees of the Hardy Estate, *The Woodlanders*, *Far from the Madding Crowd*, *The Return of the Native*, *The Mayor of Casterbridge*, *The Trumpet Major*, *Old Furniture*, and *A Spellbound Palace* (*Hampton Court*) by Thomas Hardy, and extracts from works by W. B. Yeats, and Macmillan London & Basingstoke and Vanguard Press Inc., *The Collected Poems of Edith Sitwell*.

John Murray Ltd, *Perseus in the Wind* by Freya Stark, and *My Day Song for North Oxford* by Sir John Betjeman.

Oxford University Press, Oxford, *Digby Dolben* and *The Testament of Beauty* by Robert Bridges, and extracts from poems by him, and extracts from poems by John Meade Faulkner.

A. D. Peters & Co. Ltd, *Sonnets and Verse* by Hilaire Belloc.

G. P. Putnam's Sons, extracts from works by Desmond McCarthy.

The Literary Trustees of Walter de la Mare and The Society of Authors as their representative, extracts from *Private View*, *Desert Islands*, *Pleasures and Speculations*, and other poems by Walter de la Mare.

University of Minnesota Press, extracts from the work of Tyrone Guthrie.

Index